Teaching Literature

Nine to Fourteen

Michael Benton
Geoff Fox

Oxford University Press

Oxford University Press, Walton Street, Oxford OX2 6DP

Oxford New York Toronto
Delhi Bombay Calcutta Madras Karachi
Petaling Jaya Singapore Hong Kong Tokyo
Nairobi Dar es Salaam Cape Town
Melbourne Auckland

and associated companies in
Berlin Ibadan

Oxford is a trade mark of Oxford University Press

© Geoff Fox & Michael Benton 1985

First published 1985
Reprinted with corrections 1985, 1987, 1988, 1990, 1992

ISBN 0 19 919066 6

Typeset in Linotron 202 by
Graphicraft Typesetters Limited, Hong Kong
Printed in Hong Kong

For
Jane, Alison, Jonathan, Mark and Paul

Contents

Foreword

In handling any of the creative arts in school, where the syllabus is less prescriptive than elsewhere, teachers are properly thrown back upon their personal resources; consequently, it is easier to lose nerve, to feel uncertain about why, what and how to teach. Yet the arts thrive on risk; on sharing the uncertainty of exploration and the satisfactions of discovery with our pupils.

Given the nature and broad appeal of literature coupled with the demands of the crowded school day, it is all too easy for the teacher to move from one story to another, prompted by whim or what is left in the book cupboard; or to teach the same poems as last year because they seemed to go pretty well then. We may become repetitive in our teaching methods. The enemy within is habit.

The enemy without is retrenchment. At a time when literature teachers could reap the harvest of twenty five years of unprecedentedly good publishing of children's fiction and poetry, increasingly utilitarian attitudes and financial cuts have often forced a narrowness of vision on those who control policy and resources in schools. The battle against the apathetic, the unsympathetic or the unconvinced can be fought effectively only by individual teachers who defeat the enemy within. We hope this book will help such teachers.

Our book is made of three interlocking pieces which fit together to make up a whole. The pieces could be termed theory, knowledge and practice. They arose out of three questions we kept in constant view in writing the book:

What happens inside our heads when we read stories and poems?
What experiences do different types of literature offer children?
What are the best ways of handling literature in the classroom?

Direct answers to these questions are given in Chapters 1 and 2, 3 and 4, 6 and 7 respectively; but such is the relationship between theory and knowledge and practice, that answers appear in oblique ways throughout. Theory, knowledge and practice illuminate each other; if the pieces are not fitted together, a teacher cannot base classroom practice upon a secure personal methodology of literature teaching.

Our purposes have been to explore the nature of the reader's response in so far as it illuminates children's reading; to be aware of the variety of texts as well as the variety of readers; and to work through the practical implications of both of these for young readers in and out of school. From such a mix, the methodology we urge in Chapter 5 developed. Our approach reflects a dominant emphasis in modern literary theory that the reader's response is fundamental to the meaning of text; it reflects our knowledge of the literature appropriate and available to the 9–14 age range; and, in particular, it reflects our sense of how children respond as readers, whether as individuals lost in a book or as classes sharing stories and poems in school.

Michael Benton and Geoff Fox
1984

Chapter 1

What happens when we read stories?

'The reader does quite half the labour'

The short answer is that we can never fully know what happens when we read stories. Perhaps the most fruitful fictional answer to our chapter title dates from the period in which the modern novel emerged from the chrysalis of story into the form we know today. Between 1759 and 1767 Laurence Sterne was writing the nine volumes that make up one of the zaniest stories ever published, *Tristram Shandy*. It is a much-loved work amongst critics and theorists of fiction but regarded with a certain ambivalence by many readers. The reasons are not hard to find. E.M. Forster has noted that

> There is a charmed stagnation about the whole epic — the more the
> characters do, the less gets done, the less they have to say the more
> they talk, the harder they think the softer they get, facts have an
> unholy tendency to unwind and trip up the past instead of begetting
> the future, as in well-conducted books.... Obviously a god is
> hidden in *Tristram Shandy* and his name is Muddle, and some readers
> cannot accept him. (*1*)

Tristram Shandy certainly does not fulfil the reader's customary expectations about the experience of fiction. It is a book full of oddities, some trivial and some with profound implications for an understanding of what happens inside our heads when we read stories. There is a solemn, black page when Parson Yorick dies and 'a marbled page' which the author offers us as 'a motley emblem of my work!' Two eccentricities which may provoke our thoughtful laughter are, first, Sterne's omission of Volume 4, Chapter 24 and his suggestion that the reader can fill in this 'chasm of ten pages' from his own imagination; and, secondly, the episode when Uncle Toby falls in love with the delectable Widow Wadman. With his tongue firmly in his cheek, Sterne writes:

> Let love therefore be what it will, — my Uncle Toby fell into it. —
> And possibly, gentle reader, with such a temptation — so wouldst
> thou. For never did thy eyes behold, or thy concupiscence covet
> anything in the world, more concupiscible than Widow Wadman.

Chapter 38

To conceive this right, — call for pen and ink — here's paper ready
to your hand. — Sit down, Sir, paint her to your mind — as like
your mistress as you can — as unlike your wife as your conscience
will let you — 'tis all one to me — please put your own fancy in it. (2)

And there follow two blank pages on which the reader is invited to draw his
imagined portrait of the lady!

Literature abounds, albeit less dramatically, with writers who testify to
the need for participatory readers. Ten years before *Tristram Shandy*, Fielding
had invited the reader of *Tom Jones* to fill up 'the vacant spaces of time with
his own conjectures' (3); Henry James claimed that the author makes 'his
reader very much as he makes his characters.... When he makes him well,
that is makes him interested, then the reader does quite half the labour' (4);
and Virginia Woolf, writing about the experience of reading Jane Austen,
says 'She stimulates us to supply what is not there.' (5) The same is true of
children's authors. Alan Garner's explanation of why he left out Alison's
mother in *The Owl Service* is that ' ... it was powerful to have this fulcrum
which was not there, this terrible woman.... ' (6). When asked why Max's
mother does not appear in *Where The Wild Things Are*, Maurice Sendak
commented:

Because you should only *imagine* what she looks like. It would be
very wrong to show her. Because for some children she would look
more scaring than the wild things. And for some children she is fine.
I leave the mother to the imagination. But you feel her there. By her
absence she is more available. (7)

These instances all point towards the special relationship that exists
between author and reader (at least as authors conceive of it). Clearly, reading
is seen as a collaborative act but what form does this collaboration take? The
commonest idea among authors and readers is that they share in the creation
of an imagined world.

The secondary world

Writing and reading are indivisible. The writer's sense of audience and the
reader's sense of textual voice complement each other and form a social bond.
The invented worlds that lie between author and reader form an imaginative
bond. The worlds that the author and reader imagine in connection with the
same text will be different but related. Tolkien implies as much in his well-
known essay *On Fairy-Stories* when he says:

Children are capable, of course, of *literary belief*, when the story-
maker's art is good enough to produce it. That state of mind has

been called 'willing suspension of disbelief'. But this does not seem to me a good description of what happens. What really happens is that the story-maker proves a successful 'sub-creator'. He makes a Secondary World which your mind can enter. Inside it, what he relates is 'true': it accords with the laws of that world. You therefore believe it, while you are, as it were, inside. The moment disbelief arises, the spell is broken; the magic, or rather art has failed. You are then out in the Primary World again, looking at the little abortive Secondary World from outside. (8)

That children do enter the secondary world of story is apparent if you ask them how they visualize events and characters in their reading. Here is what eleven year old Lesley Anne said about part of Chapter 5 of *The Growing Summer* by Noel Streatfield: (9)

> ... two girls called Penny and Naomi came into the bedroom and they started putting sheets onto the chairs. I felt very close to the girls but not so close to the boys. That night Steven was found in an empty bedroom. Penny and Robin started talking to him. I was saying aloud 'Please don't talk to him. Stay away, you don't know what he will do to you'. As they went into the room I crossed my fingers and toes. I was reading this bit of the book in bed and I was getting scared and pulling the sheets over my face. Naomi was downstairs, I felt sorry for her because she was in a big house and her brothers were scaring her. Back upstairs when Penny and Robin came out of the bedroom, I felt very relieved and I then closed the book and went to sleep.

Here is Colin, also eleven, talking about the Prologue to Alistair Maclean's *River of Death:*

> The sun is setting over a monastery in Greece. I am next to the officers; they are talking about gold together. The two officers stop the men carrying the wooden boxes holding gold. The box is opened and the two men look into the box, I look in ... I am in the control tower watching all that's going on as I read the book. Then the planes take off, making a noise like rusty old Thunder.

The secondary world of the book, as children experience it during reading, is the fundamental phenomenon with which literature teachers have to deal, yet we know so little about it. We need to ask:

> *Where does this world exist?*
> *What is it made of?*
> *How is it sustained?*

For the more we know about the secondary world, the more sensitive teachers of literature we are likely to become.

3

a) Where does the secondary world exist? When we write or read we enter, as Tolkien suggests, an imaginative limbo, an in-between state of mind which draws upon both the unique psychic make-up of an individual and the actual world that is everyone's possession. This 'third area', as D.W. Winnicott has called it (10), is best thought of as a sort of mental playground in which makers and readers of stories can operate in relative freedom and security. The time and place of the primary world fade and are replaced by the time and place that the story decrees. We become 'lost' in a book; or, more precisely, in an imaginative game that entails writer or reader constructing an alternative world to replace the one that the book has temporarily obliterated. The world we make is not literal: it has presence and power to engage and move us but no substance with which to threaten. Indeed, for the adult reader, the 'security' of a novel may well be reflected by a relished routine: the comfortable chair, the familiar lamp, a drink to sip. Children who read regularly talk of specific areas of their homes where they prefer to read: their beds, the bath or, oblivious to domestic tension, the lavatory, are places where young readers report that they lose themselves in their books. The trick is to shut out one world to enter another.

> It seems my ears switch off, and my mum's just standing there
> yelling her head off, and I just sit there reading.

The reader's physical contentment releases, and reinforces, a frame of mind:

> I read mostly on the side by my bed, on the floor where it is nice and
> quiet and if my sister comes up I can duck my head down;

and even,

> I like reading standing on my head on the sofa because I like to
> practise upside down.

Whatever physical contortions we get up to we can play the game in our own imaginative style, take our pleasure from it in the way we want and stop playing when we choose. Yet, this game, like any other, has rules and conventions which must be observed. Even infants (perhaps they most of all) know this.

Children learn early that words are powerful makers of stories. Whatever their individual difficulties in coming to terms with print, all children seem responsive to oral story-telling. The two conventions that sustain their responses are the willingness to believe in an acknowledged illusion and the need to know the end. The insubstantial fabric of story is created and supported by these twin pressures. Belief in the illusion gives a sense of place to the world of story and grows out of the child's easy exploration of the relationship between the actual and the fantasized in his play. The sense of an ending gives it a temporal dimension and reflects the need to know what happens next, a need which quickly develops into a sense of structure — of beginnings, middles and endings — and comprises a fundamental part of the child's imaginative investment in fiction.

Words are toys, playthings with which to make up a game in the head.

The ease with which a two or three year old inhabits both the world that is and the world that might be and shifts effortlessly between the two, is a facility that dims with age, however hard we fight to retain our sense of play. Where teachers and parents can help is in nourishing and preserving the childlike sense of story as a play activity.

As a child gets older, whatever his ability as a reader, one principle remains constant: reading is idiosyncratic. How a child reads reflects his whole person so that to read at all inevitably involves the stored experiences of the reader and his characteristic ways of being and acting. In the act of creating, what the reader brings to a story is as important as what the text offers in the sense that we fit the reading of a new story into the blend of our literary and life experiences to date, drawing upon our knowledge of other fictions as well as upon analogies in the primary world, in order to make our own, unique meaning.

The answer, then, to our first question, 'Where does the secondary world exist?' is that it lies in an area of play activity between the reader's inner reality and the outer reality of the words on the page. The world of the book draws its idiosyncratic nature from the former and is shaped by the latter. Different readers' responses to a story thus have enough in common to be shared while remaining highly individual. The literature classroom becomes a place where pupils may gain from others' responses while preserving their sense of uniqueness as readers.

b) What is the secondary world made of? If the reading experience is an amalgam of individual associations and memories mingling with more precisely traceable reactions provoked by the text, how does the infinite variety of this world manifest itself? The commonest answer, but not the only one, is by way of mental imagery — pictures which form in the reader's head. Writers and readers frequently testify to their visual sense of the world they imagine. Less frequently they refer to auditory images and only relatively rarely to those drawn from the other senses. If we accept that mental imagery is the prime coinage of the brain during the creative activity of writers and readers, several caveats must be entered immediately. First, that the use made of images varies greatly from one person to the next. Secondly, that an important aspect of this variability is in the degree of mental control that any individual exercises. The images that the mind constructs to fill the 'third area' may arrive unbidden like those of night-dreams or, like those of day-dreams, be indulged or banished at will. Writers and readers need both bidden and unbidden images to make their secondary worlds. The writer shapes his images, via the use of words, into a text; the reader shapes the text, via the use of images, into a meaning. The role of images, thus delimited, leads us to the third point: images are a means to an end, not the end itself. It is the *manner* in which the secondary world is made by each reader that endows it with personally significant meaning. Indeed, there are some who appear to experience little picturing during reading, claiming to have merely the sense of being *in the presence* of a world. Also, most habitual readers have

5

had the sensation of thinking in pure meanings when, in periods of profound engrossment in a story, the mind may by-pass imaging as a means to comprehending.

A particularly interesting example (11) of the use of picturing is eleven year old Elizabeth's responses to C.S. Lewis's science fiction story, *Forms of Things Unknown*. In the story two men, recent graduates from a space school, go to the moon to find out why some of their colleagues had disappeared whilst doing routine investigation of the moon's surface. Their anxieties turn to terror as they realize that three objects which they had taken at a distance to be misshapen stones are in fact the petrified corpses of lost spacemen. The story is a futuristic odyssey with the Gorgon as the instigator of the petrifaction. Elizabeth was asked to pause in her reading at ten pre-determined points and to jot down what she saw in her mind's eye, where she stood in relation to what was going on, any sounds, other sense impressions or feelings that she noticed. Her introspective recall produced the following responses, which are reported exactly as she wrote them:

1   I wonder what is going to happen very strongly. I see two men going into a country pub.
2   I have a feeling of curiosity of what happened. I see the moon as though I was standing on it and looking forward.
3   I wonder what happened to them and who or what took them. I see someone looking over their shoulder.
4   I feel lonely. I am looking over someone's shoulder into a black space with the moon in front of us.
5   I feel shut in and cramped. I see the same thing as in 4.
6   I feel scared because I do not know what will happen next.
7   I feel sick. I wonder what will happen next.
8   I feel that Jenkin is very silly because I myself would have just stood still (not of fear). But I would be scared of course.
9   I feel puzzled at what happened. I have begun to understand a few things that I cannot explain.
10 I just don't know what happened. I see the shape of a head swaying and waving without the wind.

Elizabeth's changing feelings and viewpoints indicate her growing involvement with the story. At the first three response points her images are distinct and definite, recording mental pictures of the men, the pub and the moon as things 'outside herself'. Then, at point 4, a change begins: she draws closer to the 'someone' who had appeared at point 3 and, together, they look 'into a black space'. This image persists and feelings of being 'shut in and cramped' gather around it. Elizabeth's association with this 'someone' and the sense of her being lost in the story are powerfully conveyed. A measure of her engrossment is the absence of recorded images in points 5 to 9, as she becomes fully absorbed emotionally and intellectually with the implications of the events and is left with the vague 'shape of a head swaying and waving without the wind' at point 10. Elizabeth said that she thoroughly enjoyed the story. The gradual disappearance of stated images in this sequence is not a sign of any loss of interest but an indication of her progress in 'getting into' the story. As this example suggests, there are many variations in and uncertainties about the role of imaging. However, it remains a reasonable generalization that the secondary world is conveyed to us primarily through the medium of mental picturing. It is this facility that gives form and movement and often colour and sound to the literary experience, frequently with such immediacy and power that the writer may describe himself as 'inspired' or the reader as 'lost in a book'.

How are such images experienced? Our mental pictures may dissolve or be discarded; in James Britton's terms (12), they may emerge slowly like the shadowy outlines of a photographic negative forming in a developing-dish, or flash upon the inward eye with sudden and unpredictable vividness. During their emergence, existence and dissolution, processes of super-imposition, collision and modification take place, ensuring that each image is unique. These changing images of the secondary world give us the illusion of fictional time passing at a different rate from the actual time-flow of the primary world in which we sit reading. The substance of the secondary world, then, is not composed of a sequence of complete, discrete images of similar status and definition. It is made up of a series of more or less formed images of unequal importance and clarity which occur during writing and reading in a rich variety of manifestations. This variety is determined by which senses the images draw upon, the relative precision or vagueness of the images and whether they appear alone or in a context. For example, some writers share with their readers a single, controlling image whose characteristics pervade every aspect of a story and whose essence may be mirrored in its title. A woman at the end of a quay, a stone book, a rainbow, a mechanical toy of two mice, a place on a map like Watership Down, all become symbolic images with which the reader has to come to terms if he is to make satisfying meaning. Similarly, we must be prepared for the varying durability of mental images, from the stereotyped memory images that writers and readers construct to serve as stage sets or backdrops for the story's events to the vivid but momentary image of a particular idiosyncratic memory triggered by a few words in the text or the partially-glimpsed fragment of a room or landscape.

The substance of the secondary world is thus elusive, constantly changing and highly individualized. By the same token, it is the most productive area to share if we want to know about a reader's process of responding to a story. To ask children regularly, 'What pictures do you have in your mind's eye?' is to honour the validity and importance of the individual's response while simultaneously generating discussion in which the sharing of likenesses and differences can take place. It is one of the fundamental questions which will inform later chapters in this book concerned with the classroom teaching of literature.

c) How is the secondary world sustained? We saw how Elizabeth's viewpoint shifted as she made her way through C.S. Lewis's story. There is an ambiguity in the very word 'viewpoint' which indicates the difference between teaching concerned primarily with response and teaching concerned primarily with value judgements. Our present business is with the viewpoint the reader adopts *during reading* rather than the viewpoint he takes *upon what he reads*.

Consider this famous passage from *The Wind in the Willows* when Toad, having heard the seductive 'poop-poop' of a motor car in the yard of The Red Lion, slips out to investigate:

> 'There cannot be any harm,' he said to himself, 'in my only just *looking* at it!'
> The car stood in the middle of the yard, quite unattended, the stable-helps and other hangers-on being all at their dinner. Toad walked slowly round it, inspecting, criticizing, musing deeply.
> 'I wonder,' he said to himself presently, 'I wonder if this sort of car *starts* easily?'
> Next moment, hardly knowing how it came about, he found he had hold of the handle and was turning it. As the familiar sound broke forth, the old passion seized on Toad and completely mastered him, body and soul. As if in a dream he found himself, somehow, seated in the driver's seat; as if in a dream, he pulled the lever and swung the car round the yard and out through the archway; and, as if in a dream, all sense of right and wrong, all fear of obvious consequences, seemed temporarily suspended. He increased his pace, and as the car devoured the street and leapt forth on the high road through the open country, he was only conscious that he was Toad once more, Toad at his best and highest, Toad the terror, the traffic-queller, the Lord of the lone trail, before whom all must give way or be smitten into nothingness and everlasting night. He chanted as he flew, and the car responded with sonorous drone; the miles were eaten up under him as he sped he knew not whither, fulfilling his instincts, living his hour, reckless of what might come to him.
>
> *   *   *   *
>
> 'To my mind,' observed the Chairman of the Bench of Magistrates cheerfully, 'the *only* difficulty that presents itself in this otherwise very clear case is, how we can possibly make it sufficiently hot for the incorrigible rogue and hardened ruffian whom we see cowering in the dock before us'. (*13*)

A question which opens out this passage is, 'Where were you as you were reading?' For the reader to reflect (perhaps through jotting down some brief notes) upon where he stands — or moves — as the narrative advances is not only a useful means of exploring the act of reading but it is also a way of illuminating the subtlety with which an author like Kenneth Grahame involves the reader in telling his tale. In the first few lines of the passage we may be outside Toad, watching him looking at the car; inside Toad, experiencing some of his feelings of fascination; and ahead of Toad, guessing all too accurately that he will give in to his 'old passion'. The shift from Toad's wondering 'if this sort of car *starts* easily' to his driving away is made like a cinematic 'cut' from thoughts to actions. Its effect is to draw the reader deeper into the narrative and the repetition of 'as if in a dream' carries the reader as well as Toad farther along the road. Once he becomes the reckless, self-dramatizing 'Toad the terror', other resonances begin to sound, our view of events changes and we start anticipating the consequences of Toad's actions both with the law and with his friends. The break in the text provides a gap for such speculations. We are not seriously worried about Toad's fate: he will not kill himself, not in this kind of book. As the magistrate begins to speak, we must engage in some rapid 'footwork'; filling in what has evidently happened, finding our expectations confirmed, and taking our place in the courtroom, looking across, with conflicting feelings of sympathy and amusement perhaps, at the cowering figure of the deflated Toad. This type of exploration of where we are imaginatively during reading demonstrates that our viewpoint moves constantly. It is one of the growth points in helping children to become sensitive readers.

Narrative viewpoint is a complex issue about which literary criticism has much to say. The two essential qualities of this viewpoint are its 'inside' position and its continuous mobility. That the reader is an 'insider' is indicated in Harding's portrayal of him as 'a ghostly watcher' (*14*), or in fourteen year old Claire's description of her reading experience:

> It's as if I'm a sort of dark watcher, who is there at the scene, but
> none of the characters pays any attention to me. I'm like a power, as
> if everything is happening because I'm there. (*15*)

Claire's account suggests a static spectator role; descriptions of a moving viewpoint are rare. Norman Holland quotes his eight year old daughter as saying: 'When I read a book, I sort of feel like I'm invisible and walking around unseen with the things or people in the book . . . ' (*16*). Catherine, aged eleven, is also on the move in her involvement with Agatha Christie's *Murder on the Orient Express*.

> Hercule Poirot does not know the English people, but he sits with
> them on the other side of the table. It is cold outside but we are warm
> and quiet inside on the train. I just watch them, they cannot see me.
> . . . When they arrive at Konya they get out to stretch their legs. I get
> out too. Poirot watches them as if he were spying on them! I sort of
> feel the cold they feel. (*17*)

The shifting viewpoint that we adopt during reading then, is located inside the secondary world amidst movements and uncertainties; yet nothing is required of it in the way of judgements and reasons save that of being an alert observer and recorder.

The practice of exploring this aspect of literary experience is rare in classroom teaching. Yet the question of viewpoint and the changing sense of distance from the imagined events that follows from it are fundamental to every act of reading. They allow us to describe the varying degrees of involvement we experience during the reading of a story. The reader undergoes phases of relative absorption with and detachment from the fictional events. His spectatorship will vary in the intensity of its commitment and attention at different phases of a novel. The shifting viewpoint we adopt as we read expresses our sense of relationship with the fictional world, acknowledges that it is in a state of continuous change, and indicates the horizons beyond which that world ceases to exist. For, if involvement becomes obsessive and takes on psychotic characteristics, it leads to belief in the literal existence of fictional characters and events. Conversely, if the sense of detachment from the secondary world is taken to the limit, it is but a short distance before a reader becomes disengaged from the fiction and the story is deemed unreadable.

The unasked questions in lessons which purport to be concerned with children's responses to literature are the simple ones that we asked earlier: 'Where are you and what are you doing when you read?' They invite children to come to see themselves as active readers, to realize the worth and uniqueness of their responses and to begin to understand their role in the implied dialogue that exists in any story among 'the author, narrator, the other characters and the reader'. (*18*)

'The attractions of the journey'

If, as we have argued, the engrossment of the reader in the fictional world varies in the course of reading a story, does this imply a number of phases to the reading process? Writers and critics are prone to use metaphor to describe the experience of moving from the beginning, through the middle to the end of a story. The idea of a journey is popular. Coleridge says that 'the reader should be carried forward ... by the pleasurable activity of mind excited by the attractions of the journey ... ' (*19*). Fielding invites his readers to think of themselves as his 'fellow-travellers in a stage-coach' (*20*), Thomas Hughes exhorts his intended schoolboy readers into some energetic foot-slogging through *Tom Brown's Schooldays* (*21*), whereas Gabriel Josipovici says that 'Reading an intricately plotted nineteenth-century novel is very much like travelling by train' (*22*). To update the metaphor, reading much twentieth-century fiction is like travelling by plane. The tendency of writers to work by juxtaposition and association rather than by painstaking explanation, the shift from 'novelist historian' to the assumption of impersonality, from 'telling' to 'showing', in the writer's craft, mean that the speed with which the reader's journey unfolds has greatly increased. Far from the relaxed state of being able to 'settle down in comfort and forget all everyday worries until one reaches one's destination ... ' that Josipovici describes, the reader of John Fowles or John le Carré or Alan Garner or Gene Kemp finds that the pace and nature of life in the secondary world are such that he must keep his wits about him or he will lose his way.

What the reader cannot have is a total view of the journey. However unified and coherent the text may be, its *effect* is going to be fragmented; the reader's view will reflect the text in piecemeal fashion. Any unified meaning the reader achieves comes from the patterns the reader projects. If we can understand how good readers make such evidently satisfying and coherent patterns from such fragmented experiences as they read, we may have a surer foundation on which to build our classroom practice.

Clichés about reading give useful clues as to the nature of this mental travelling. We speak of 'getting into a story', 'reading between the lines', 'being really into a book' or 'lost in a book', all expressions that indicate that there are different phases to our willing, collaborative reading. A young reader picks up *The Machine-Gunners* or a 'Grange Hill' book for the first time, finds it interesting enough to read, gets involved with the story, reads so that he is partly taken over by the book, sometimes oblivious of time and surroundings, and reaches the end with that satisfying mixture of pleasure at seeing how it all works out and regret at the vanished story. We might characterize the phases as

> feeling like reading;
> getting into the story;
> being lost in the book; and
> having an increasing sense of an ending.

What do these phases — which have strong implications, we shall suggest, for the classroom — imply about the nature of the reading state?

1 Children at home *feeling like reading* might pick up a book a brother or sister has left lying around. Children in bookshops or public libraries or at school flit along the shelves, sampling as they go. The cover, the publisher's blurb, the illustrations, a couple of sentences randomly tested, come into play with the previous literary experiences and the present mood of the potential reader. Will this new book be as funny or as exciting as previous successes? Will it come close to current interests or carry him away into the realm of fantasy?

This phase has clear implications for the ways in which children meet books in school. However the first phase of the journey into a book is described, the reader's anticipation of pleasure is a crucial prerequisite to a book's being read; without it, stories and novels have little hope in the classroom.

2 *Getting into the story* is the most familiar phase, and phrase, describing the reading experience. It may signal a time of some doubt: 'Shall I go on, or not?'

When embarking upon a novel the reader has to make continuous adjustments. Most of these adjustments relate to the voices within the text, implied or direct; once he has 'tuned in' to these, the reader's mind is ready

11

for the next phase. He is invited to play a game devised by the author. The rules are given in the first few pages which may indicate the setting, the narrative voice and mode of address. (The opening of *The Otterbury Incident* where C. Day Lewis uses George, his child narrator, to entice the reader into the story is a particularly clear example.) Once he has agreed to play, the reader is rapidly drawn farther into the story world and his preoccupations change from trying to resolve his uncertainties about the game and its rules to apprehending as fully as possible the world opening around him.

3 When the reader is **lost in the book**, collaboration has become engrossment. Metaphorically, a reader steps into the mental picture his mind creates and is 'lost'. The word reminds us of both the temporal and spatial images that combine in the idea of the journey through the world of a novel. Yet 'lost' is not pejorative: the reader knows there is a predetermined end. His fascination is with how he is going to get there and what he will see on the way.

4 As the journey unfolds, the reader has an increasing **sense of an ending**. Living 'happily ever after' is the traditional consequence of having set out 'once upon a time'. These conventional phrases of fairy-tales are the formulae that story has evolved to serve as landmarks for the youngest reader or listener when 'getting in' and 'ending'.

The engrossed reader feels a progressively stronger need for a fitting conclusion as the end gets nearer. The very form of story is dependent upon this sense of an ending. All of us, children most especially, make considerable imaginative investments in coherent patterns. Ending is not only the author's disposition of judgement upon his characters via the events to which he submits them; it is the reader's assurance that the fiction has organized its events appropriately. It is the evidence of a well-shaped story.

It would be a distortion to imply that these four phases of the reading process do anything more than approximate to the actual experience of the child and his book at any given time. Reading is such an idiosyncratic business that to generalize a pattern is risky. Yet, this description of the reader's journey has a practical purpose for literature teachers since, if we resist the temptation to see these phases as a fixed sequence, remembering that there may be many entries and exits made before a novel is finished, we may find a basis from which to develop a classroom methodology for handling short stories and novels (see Chapters 5 and 6). To that end, we need now to look more closely at what the reader does along his journey.

What the reader does 'en route'

An interesting exercise for groups of children (or adults) is to read the first page of a new story silently or aloud and, before going any further, to pause and jot down as quickly as possible, in 'stream of consciousness' style, '*all* the things that you can remember were going on in your mind as you were reading or listening'. If pupils jot simultaneously, without conferring, then the discussion that follows — perhaps in small groups — invariably indicates those elements of the reading experience that are shared and those that are idiosyncratic; and demonstrates not only the nature of the collaboration we make with the author whom we sense 'behind the text' but also the sort of mental activities that are common to all readers. Repeated investigations using this technique of introspective recall with readers of all ages have, without exception, generated excitement and enjoyment among the participants.

There seem to be four activities that comprise the basic elements of the process of responding. The act of reading a story involves the reader in *picturing, anticipating and retrospecting, interacting, evaluating*. These elements are intimately connected during reading and could not be used as discrete headings in the content analysis of responses. They are best seen as general characteristics of the process of reading fiction, as the principal types of mental activity that we might expect in any involved reader of stories. Our belief is that good classroom teaching constantly seeks to develop these characteristics, for from them derive the satisfactions of reading literature.

a) Picturing We have already discussed mental imagery as the primary means by which we experience the secondary world of story and argued that picturing is the most important element in the way in which a reader brings a story to imaginative life. The exercise outlined above usually demonstrates that images manifest themselves in various ways. We can distinguish, first, between those that are 'text-free' and those that are 'text-bound'. 'Text-free' images include all those associations that the reader makes which shift his focus of interest temporarily away from the text; 'text-bound' images are ones which remain directly related to the text and provide information whereby the reader is able to make meaning.

What children bring to a story is evident in the way they convey what is in their mind's eye as they read or listen. Often, they will respond to a story with stories of their own. The pictures that the reader creates from the text form themselves ineluctably into narrative sequences and the resulting anecdotal responses can be separated into three types: *retelling, analogizing* and *fantasizing* — the sorts of anecdotal responses to literature with which English teachers are familiar.

Retelling is often properly invited by the teacher as a measure of the reader's literal comprehension of whether or not the basic situation has been understood and the sequence of events followed. *Analogizing* indicates the reader's natural facility for composing stories structured upon the ones he is reading (or upon parts of them) which give an opportunity to relive or alter his actual experience or act out dramas revolving around his wishes and fears. Retellings are more frequently invited by the teacher but, by young children especially, they are less readily offered than analogies. In the classroom both these forms of anecdotal response are valid for they embody the literal and assimilative aspects of comprehension respectively. It is for this reason that, together, they provide the basis of an appropriate classroom dialogue about a novel.

There remains the *fantasizing* response where the reader allows an aspect of a story, maybe something as slight as an individual word, to lead him off into day-dream or far-ranging association. In classroom talk, many readers have learned to edit out such idiosyncracies, but the younger the children the more willing they are to share them and the delicacy of the teacher's role is, without discouraging the child, to restrain irrelevance and self-indulgence and to encourage the more fruitful departures from the text which may, given time and space, enrich the reading of that story.

b) Anticipating and retrospecting The mental activity of our second element of response can best be described as a continuous series of short- and long-term predictions and a complementary series of short- and long-term retrospections. First, let us acknowledge that there is an important retrospective element in reading where the reader's focus of attention is drawn along behind the point to which his eye has travelled as the meanings he draws from the text accumulate towards a sense of coherent form. Mechanically, via short-term retrospective activity, and imaginatively, via long-term retrospection, the reader's awareness of the story that is unravelling behind him is crucial to his response.

Nevertheless, the main thrust of the engrossed reader of fiction is forwards, anticipating what is to come. The reader's imaginative anticipation forms the driving edge of each reading. As readers, we wish to know what happens over the page, or at the end of the chapter, or when some clearly signalled event actually occurs, or when some secret or mystery is finally uncovered — and we need to place all such anticipations in the overall context of the author's final solution. To this end, we engage in a range of predictive activities including thinking through particular problems 'in advance', extrapolating, hypothesizing, speculating and guessing. Children's reading, particularly, is characterized by a sense of anticipation.

Retrospection is a more sophisticated skill. To appreciate the richness of many stories a reader has to pause and reflect, even if only momentarily, upon the events so far. On a purely narrative level, for example, the reader of a detective story is likely to enjoy looking back to see how the clues were planted. More subtly, the reader of Jane Austen will miss the irony of her writing if he is not sensitive to the tone of Miss Austen's voice or fails to hold in his mind earlier situations or conversations. The twin processes of anticipation and retrospection are thus complementary and oscillate together as the reader moves through a narrative, creating his version of the story inside his head.

In helping children to become better readers, given an appealing narrative, we can usually rely upon their willingness to look forward. Part of our function as teachers is to temper their headlong pursuit of plot with the encouragement to pause and reflect upon what has happened and so increase their enjoyment of what they have read.

c) Interacting 'Interacting' is a term we have chosen to cover a cluster of related mental activities that we engage in during reading and which comprise a third element of response. This breadth of definition is meant to incorporate all aspects of the reader's sense of himself in relation to a story and to include features that have often been conveyed in a confusing mixture of specialist and idiosyncratic vocabulary. D.W. Harding, for example, has usefully challenged us to be clear about what we mean when we talk of 'identifying' with a story and demonstrated that this catch-all term may indicate any of four notions — empathy, admiration, imitation and resemblance. (23) Literature involves the reader in projecting himself into a story and, simultaneously, assimilating the text into his own experience. When the interaction of the reader with the story is conceived in this manner, it highlights the sort of interplay that takes place. Interacting includes everything that the reader brings from his own literary and life experience to enable him to interpret a satisfying meaning from a story. Projection, as we have indicated, is clearly an important element of this activity. We interpret situations and events in a text by reading into them our own experiences and feelings. Thus our interacting with a story will cover a whole spectrum of changing relationships. A character, a scene, an atmosphere, a single phrase may touch us with unexpected power such that we feel that we can deeply understand and empathize with what is happening and that, in turn, we have been helped, however slightly, to comprehend aspects of daily life more fully. In this way, stories provide the possibility of educating the feelings and can offer their readers potential growth points for the development of a more subtle awareness of human behaviour.

Giving oneself up to story in this willing interaction may derive from all sorts of motives, from social escape to aesthetic enchantment, and may produce all sorts of effects, such as the enjoyment of fear or laughter. The relationship of these literary experiences both to the formation of attitudes and to actual behaviour is complex and largely a matter of speculation. But, if it seems to be a highly dubious proposition that stories enable us 'to live well' (24) and have the morally efficacious effects that are claimed for them by the Leavisite school, nonetheless, the process of interacting does engage the reader in a form of knowing that can be a force for good. Stories do not help us to live better; they help us to understand living better. What we choose to do about that understanding is another story.

d) Evaluating We want to distinguish between the reader's *evaluation* of a novel after it has been read and his *evaluating* of it as he is reading. If we allow ends to dictate means and the controlling purpose of reading in school becomes the production of, say, book reviews or answers to formal comprehension questions, then we are likely to distort the process and diminish its pleasure. What is important for the literature teacher is the recognition that evaluating takes place as an integral part of the process of response. Even on occasions when the exercise outlined on page 12, which by its nature excludes the specific request for value judgements, is carried out with young children, evaluative comments are nevertheless sometimes offered. They may be explicitly stated in the critical or appreciative remarks readers make, or implicitly felt. Either way, the reader's valuing of a story forms part of his impetus to continue reading it. Moreover, the valuing of one story over another starts in the very young and quickly reveals a specifically aesthetic and literary character. The awareness of story form, the knowledge of the sorts of things that go on between 'Once upon a time' and 'They all lived happily ever after', and the importance of internal consistency are all aspects of story that children can, and often do, gain before they can read for themselves.

By the time they come to master a fictional text on their own they already possess a highly developed concept of story and an instinct for what they will like and dislike. While an eight year old is likely to be less articulate about his judgements of his first book than a fourteen year old will be of his hundredth (the one preferring to savour his achievement, the other inclining to place this 'read' in the context of all his others), for both the naïve and the experienced reader, the process of evaluating is an element of their responses to a story. It is a form of committing ourselves to the experience of reading. It is a mark of discrimination and the rejection of indifference.

The reader's personal style

Every reading of every reader is unique. The variables are so many that they make the whole area of reader response both fascinating and elusive. Since much of what we have discussed so far has suggested the patterns and the variables generally experienced in *reading*, it is appropriate to remind ourselves of the constants and the variables within *readers*. For convenience of discussion rather than because they are actually separable, what the reader brings to a story can be considered under three broad headings: *experience*, *purpose* and *psychological make-up*.

Each reading is partly shaped by the words on the page, the immutable constants; but as the reader translates words into meanings, his own *experience* — the individuality of his own life, his own sense of story and the expectations he brings with him — all have a marked effect upon his interpretation.

Intimately related to his personal experience is the sense of *purpose* that the reader has. The distinction between reading for study and reading for fun is not an absolute one, but it is important when considering the processes involved. Ends do affect means. The teacher may be working at one extreme with older, practised readers on a known story, re-reading, tracking back over the details of the book. At the other, he may have offered relatively new readers a choice of books simply to read for fun, with the aim of helping the children to develop the habit of reading, knowing that the purpose here is to achieve the pleasure of being engrossed in a new story as an end in itself.

Perhaps the most influential element in what the reader brings to a story is his own *psychological make-up;* the fundamental factor, in Norman Holland's view, in deciding the 'personal style' of an individual reader. Holland's enquiries into reader response point towards a phenomenon that most literature teachers have noticed without ever being able to explain; individual children reveal personal patterns of reading behaviour which recur irrespective of the nature of the book being read. Holland summarizes his notion of 'personal style' in reading by pointing to 'the sameness one reader brings to different stories and the differences different readers bring to the same story'. (25) This concept of personal style raises the question, 'Are there different types of reader?' and, if so, what are the implications for the practice of literature teaching? Our own enquiries into the style of children's responses to stories suggest that there are indeed different emphases. Some readers seem to find more satisfaction in one or other elements of the activity of reading as we described it on pp 13–16; some most enjoy anticipating the vagaries of the plot, reading their way towards the end of the book as rapidly as possible. For others, there is more pleasure in pausing along the way to allow their own experiences to interact with those of the text or to create a clearer picture of characters and events. Yet others might reread a paragraph to relish the writer's skill in catching, say, a moment of conversation.

Broadly speaking, a distinction may be made between the *interrogative* reader and the *acquiescent* reader. The former is one who tends constantly to question the text, to predict and speculate about events and outcomes. The latter is one whose inclination is to accept what is given, to absorb the text and to bring more of his or her literary and life experiences to bear upon it in order to assimilate it more easily. There is the suggestion in identifying these two main styles of Hudson's distinction between convergent and divergent thinking; but, in view of the highly idiosyncratic nature of reading and the infinite and unpredictable variety of responses, it is truer to the nature of the experience to argue that any attempt to describe styles of reading fiction might best take the form of a continuum, with the interrogative and the acquiescent styles at opposite ends.

In practice all readers operate with both an interrogative and an acquiescent emphasis at different times during reading according to how the text provokes them, the purposes they have and their mood on a particular occasion. The danger in formulating this notion of two main emphases in personal style is the pressure it exerts towards caricature. If we can resist the temptation to fix children with one or other of these labels and use the flexibility that a continuum implies, then the idea of a reader having a characteristic emphasis in his behaviour is a helpful one. It alerts teachers to the differences between children reading the same story and helps discriminate between differences that are to do with personality and behaviour and those that reflect understanding and insight. The tendency is for literature teachers to value the interrogative emphasis as evidence of superior comprehension. In fact, this is simply a difference of style: the acquiescent reader may achieve just as full an understanding of a story but in a more covert way.

Implications for the classroom

We need a methodology for literature teaching based upon reading rather than criticism. Therefore we began with the question 'What happens when we read stories?' Our answers are an attempt to point towards such a methodology. The implications for teaching literature in school are considered in Part Three but several points are worth stressing here. They are presented below as a number of key statements of principle; these are followed by a series of questions, stated or implied earlier in the chapter, that are always applicable when talking about stories:

What principles should govern our approach to teaching stories? Reading a story is an imaginative collaboration between reader and author from which a secondary world is created. This phenomenon, as it occurs when a child is reading or listening to a story, is the fundamental subject matter of literature teaching.

The composition of this subject matter is an amalgam of individual freedom and textual constraint. The literature teacher has the delicate task of helping to maintain and develop the relationship between the reader's freely taken pleasure in a story and the discipline imposed by the text.

Given a methodology which honours the individuality of a child's response to a story, we must shift the emphasis from teaching which stresses critical analysis and value judgements about stories. We must rather concentrate on the creative act of reading and the expression of personal responses, since this is where delight in literature begins.

What questions should we ask about stories? The most fruitful questions about stories arise from the sort of mental activities that readers engage in when they are involved in the experience of fiction. Hence,

On picturing
>*What pictures do you get in your mind's eye of this character, scene or event?*

On anticipating and retrospecting
>*How did these present circumstances arise?*
>*What do you think will happen next and why?*
>*How do you think it will all end?*

On interacting
>*What do you feel about this character, setting or incident?*

On evaluating — to be asked very tentatively
>*What do you feel about the way the story is being told?*

Of course, these questions will be asked about particular texts and in words which take account of particular children. They need to be posed in an open, exploratory way to encourage a reflective response rather than a rush to judgement. Right and Wrong are not at stake. The questions will often not be asked directly, but through the kinds of classroom activities we propose in detail in Chapter 6. And where we want to encourage children to be aware of themselves as active readers and, at the same time, to signal to them that we value their individual responses, the question which underlies all the others is:

>*What is going on in your head as you are reading or listening?*

To be true to the nature of stories and to the primacy of each child's response, we must ask the right questions, then keep quiet and listen hard rather than elicit what we think are the right answers.

Chapter 2

What happens when we read poems?

Poems work differently from stories, creating their effects and evoking responses in ways that may overlap with the art of story but which are often peculiar to the nature of poetry. First impressions count a lot in our responses to literature, as we saw in relation to stories, and this is especially so with children and poems. There is no equivalent cliché to 'getting into a story'; perhaps the nearest comment that children frequently make about a poem is whether they 'get it' or not. In short, children sense immediately that there is a riddling quality to poems, something in the way words are used and laid out on the page, as if the words are saying to them 'We're special; we're the chosen few.' The problem of much current methodology is that far too often we imply that poems are riddles with single solutions which we, the teachers, happen to know rather than objects crafted in the medium of riddling word-play, yielding a range of meanings.

Our approach to a poem must be less continuously linear than to a story. The very presentation signals this. Instead of the eye being channelled along regular lines of print, themselves justified left and right and framed in predictable margins, it is suddenly invited into a more or less varied activity where the shape of the text on the page assumes a special significance. The linearity of prose presentation reflects the importance of the passage of time in fiction. Basically, the reader of a story wants to know what will happen next and how it will all end. By contrast, the infinite variety of ways in which poems are presented indicates different emphases where the sense of space is often part of the reader's response. The reader of a poem wants to move about within it, discovering what it means to him and enjoying the way it makes that meaning. The spaces around the words on the page indicate this difference of approach where poems are concerned. They are spaces we inhabit mentally as readers to apprehend the form — as it were, from various viewpoints; rather as, when looking at a piece of sculpture, we are impelled to move around the object and, in so doing, acknowledge that part of the meaning we make depends upon the vantage point we adopt and our appreciation of the way spaces have been employed. If poems cannot enjoy such three-dimensional advantages, nevertheless, by comparison with the rectangular blocks of story text, there is much greater significance invested in their two-dimensional shapes. Beyond these surface features of presentation, however, why are poems distinctive?

What poetry offers: the experience of reading a poem

In order to remind ourselves of why poetry matters and what it does better than any other kind of language use, we want to consider a single poem in detail. From a reading of 'The Stag' by Ted Hughes we can begin to answer the question of what happens when we read poems and identify four attributes of poetry that are uniquely blended to offer children the type of aesthetic experience that they will not find anywhere else: *language*, *form*, *observation* and *feeling*. The discussion is conducted under these headings.

First, the poem — please read it aloud.

THE STAG

While the rain fell on the November woodland shoulder of Exmoor
While the traffic jam along the road honked and shouted
Because the farmers were parking wherever they could
And scrambling to the bank-top to stare through the tree-fringe
Which was leafless,
The stag ran through his private forest.

While the rain drummed on the roofs of the parked cars
And the kids inside cried and daubed their chocolate and fought
And mothers and aunts and grandmothers
Were a tangle of undoing sandwiches and screwed-round gossiping
    heads
Steaming up the windows,
The stag loped through his favourite valley.

While the blue horsemen down in the boggy meadow
Sodden nearly black, on sodden horses,
Spaced as at a military parade,
Moved a few paces to the right and a few to the left and felt rather
    foolish
Looking at the brown impassable river,
The stag came over the last hill of Exmoor.

While everybody high-kneed it to the bank-top all along the road
Where steady men in oilskins were stationed at binoculars,
And the horsemen by the river galloped anxiously this way and that
And the cry of hounds came tumbling invisibly with their echoes down
    through the draggle of trees,
Swinging across the wall of dark woodland,
The stag dropped into a strange country.

And turned at the river
Hearing the hound-pack smash the undergrowth, hearing the
    bell-note

Of the voice that carried all the others,
Then while his limbs all cried different directions to his lungs, which
    only wanted to rest,
The blue horsemen on the bank opposite
Pulled aside the camouflage of their terrible planet.

And the stag doubled back weeping and looking for home up a
    valley and down a valley
While the strange trees struck at him and the brambles lashed him,
And the strange earth came galloping after him carrying the loll-
    tongued hounds to fling all over him
And his heart became just a club beating his ribs and his own hooves
    shouted with hounds' voices,
And the crowd on the road got back into their cars
Wet-through and disappointed. (*1*)

We would suggest that the reader anticipates the pattern of our discussion by pausing to record some reactions to the poem either by jotting freely for some minutes or, if some signposts help, by using the four headings that we have indicated. In this way, the reader's personal response may be set alongside our own idiosyncratic reading.

a) Language The poem is a study in monochrome: a grey, wet, November landscape, scarcely relieved by the dull colours of verse three, the blues, blacks and browns. The depressing West Country rain drips from every line. It is a poem of movement and sounds, not of colour: the running stag and the chasing hounds; people abandoning vehicles to clamber up the bank, others squirming inside their cars, shouting or leaning on the horn; other sounds as varied as kids' crying, hounds' baying, the 'bell-note' of the huntsmen's horn and the thumping beat of the stag's heart. Hughes evokes the Exmoor landscape and all the sensory effects which fill the poem in words that exemplify the two qualities that, above all, poetic language embodies: precision and concreteness. When we read of the families in the traffic jam in verse two, or hear the cry of hounds as they come 'tumbling invisibly with their echoes down through the draggle of trees' in verse four, we cannot but be aware of the close matching of words and things. This matching is achieved in a way unique to poetry. The clutter of conjunctive 'ands' in verse two suggests the claustrophobia of families trapped in their cars just as powerfully as it evokes the confusion of the hunt in verse four and the panic of the trapped stag in the final verse. Or again, as we read of the unseen hounds running through the trees, we experience the sounds and rhythm of their progress in the way Hughes separates 'down' from 'tumbling', placing the stressed word at the end of the line and filling the gap with words as insubstantial as 'invisibly' and 'echoes'. Such words are not suffering from a sort of lexical anaemia through being shut within the pages of a dictionary; they carry no mere referential meaning. These words are alive with meanings from their context, their associations and their sensory qualities; they are alive with what Hughes elsewhere calls 'the goblin in a word'. (2)

Yet, amid all the naturalistic description, one line stands out as different from all others. It signals the climax of the poem as the stag is finally trapped and we are told that the horsemen

Pulled aside the camouflage of their terrible planet.

The precision and concreteness of poetic language are suddenly thrown into a new dimension. The immediate effect of the words 'camouflage' and 'planet' is surrealistic, forcing the reader to shift perspective upon the events as they have unfolded. Yet, at this juncture, the line is finely placed, picking up the military metaphor from verse three and investing it with all the murderous intent that has so far been masked in the camouflage of 'parade'. The evil is exposed with an existential detachment. Momentarily, as the camouflage with which men cover their intentions is pulled aside, the poem reveals this incident as a symbol of man's capacity for evil on this 'terrible planet'. The language is precise and concrete but operating symbolically, challenging the reader to consider this killing as an instance of the inescapable violence with which we all have to live.

b) Form The second quality unique to poetry is the evocative role of language to convert feeling into form. The experience of form in this poem lies in the sense of the stag being caught in a clinically-laid, 'military' ambush. How is this achieved? Two examples running through the first four verses will illustrate the point. First, especially when reading the poem aloud, one is made aware of the steady momentum and pressure of all those subordinate clauses. Each verse begins with 'While ... ' and is held in suspension for five long lines until it arrives at the moving stag and marks his progress from the familiar to the strange. It is a cinematic technique; the reader's eye is invited to 'pan' across the landscape until the hunt, and the poem, are 'turned' by the impassable river. In order to reflect accurately the pace of the long, run-on lines, the reader has to hyperventilate his lungs. This is no accident. It is a remarkable example of form in poetry, for the poem insists that, to be read aloud at all, the reader must experience the *physical* stress of the subject matter. The breathlessness of the reader is the breathlessness of the stag. Secondly, the sense of form is gained through the mounting, impersonal pressure of the onlookers: the urgency of the farmers to get a good view (vs. 1), the spectators high-kneeing it up the bank (vs. 4); the waiting horsemen 'spaced as at a military parade' (vs. 3), and 'the steady men in oilskins ... stationed at binoculars' (vs. 4). All of them are figures in a landscape, some moving, others still, all waiting, with a rising sense of expectancy for the climax of a drama. Both structurally and rhythmically in the first example, and here in terms of how the human figures are placed in the development of the incident, there is a sense of formal ordering, of the poem as a made object. The form of 'The Stag' has the qualities associated with any well-wrought poem — a special tautness of structure and a sense of contained energy.

c) **Observation**   'The essential quality of poetry,' claimed D.H. Lawrence, 'is that it makes a new effort of attention and "discovers" a new world within the known world.' (3) 'The Stag' exemplifies this principle with great subtlety in the way the experience is presented. The observational eye that makes this 'effort of attention' is best understood by reflecting upon the 'onlooker role' (in D.W. Harding's phrase) that we adopt during reading. Notice the progress from *looking* to *seeing* to *perceiving* as the poem develops. In the first two verses we are looking at scenes of relative innocence and ordinariness. The stag is on its territory, in 'his private forest' and 'his favourite valley'; most of the people are confined to their territory, a traffic jam on a West Country lane in pouring rain. There is enough to catch our interest in the movements of the local farmers and the stag itself but nothing, as yet, to create unease or insecurity. On the contrary, the reader is deliberately placed in the position of looking in on another's territory. Then, in verse three, the resonances begin. The military trap is laid and, along with the crowd in verse four, we begin to see the significance of the events and to sense the threat to the stag as it moves 'into a strange country'. But it is not until the final two verses that we perceive the nature of the experience that Hughes is sharing with us. We have already noted how the last line of verse five challenges the reader to respond to the meaning of this violence. The final verse is a carefully orchestrated ending. There is no glib moral about blood sports. Instead, we are left to cope with the nature of the whole experience as one that holds in tension a number of elements: the noisy violence of the 'loll-tongued hounds', the silent threat of violence from the horsemen, the exhausted panic of the stag and the strange sense of theatre where the hunt climaxes before the crowd moves away, 'wet-through and disappointed'. Abandoning our onlooker role, we are left with our feelings, thoughts and questions about the whole experience.

d) **Feeling**   Good poems are places where thinking and feeling remain unified, avoiding the educational apartheid of so much of school that seems intent upon dividing mind and heart. Poems provide opportunities to experience and exercise the interplay of thought and emotion which Robert Witkin has vividly called 'the intelligence of feeling'. (4) How does this operate? Such exercise is gained through the reader's awareness of the sort of dialogue that is taking place between himself and the 'implied author'. (5) By making an 'effort of attention' he becomes alert to the writer's response to the experience, to his reflection upon it and the resolution of it in verbal form; and he complements this awareness with his own reading, reflection and responses. In so doing, the reader discriminates between his feelings for the efficient horsemen, the trapped and 'weeping' stag and the 'disappointed' spectators. And, in considering these two overtly emotional words in the poem, he will very probably ask himself whether 'weeping' sensationalizes the stag's predicament and why the crowd is said to be 'disappointed'. Thus the reader begins to measure his feelings beside those of the writer. Because of the very concentration of the language that the writer and reader share, feelings are *embodied* in verbal form, not merely indicated by verbal reference.

It is for this reason that a child's awareness of what language is and does will become deeper and more subtle through poetry than through any other sort of language use. A poem, as 'The Stag' shows, has the capacity to educate the feelings. To deprive children of poems is to deny them the society of clear, single voices and a range of feeling for which there is no alternative.

Language, form, observation, feeling — these are the qualities that poems uniquely embody and they are the key concepts in understanding the indirect approach to a poem that we discussed earlier that involves building up a reading from several different perspectives. One implication for teaching is obvious: if we are to enable our children's minds to take a walk around within a poem, as if looking from different perspectives at a sculpture, then the line by line approach can only be an inappropriate, inhibiting bore. Far better that the children explore a poem, respond to the bits that interest them, and slowly piece together the parts into a sense of coherent whole. Poems need to be experienced rather than explained. The main emphasis of the teacher's job is not, in fact, *explication du texte* but the cultivation of individual and shared responses to the text. If the four attributes we have discussed are fundamental to the experience of a poem then this suggests that certain recurrent, 'starter' questions will underpin our work with children. They are open, general questions inviting the reader both to attend to the words and to frame and value the individuality of his own response. We might ask:

On language
> *What words, phrases or lines stood out — for whatever reason —*
> *when you were reading or listening?*

On form
> *Can you say anything about the shape of the poem, how the words*
> *are laid out on the page?*
> *Do you notice any patterns?*
> *What effect does such a shape have on you?*

On observation
> *What is the writer really looking at, either outside or inside*
> *himself?*

On feeling
> *What feelings are conveyed during the poem at different points?*
> *Do they change?*
> *Do you share them?*

Of course, these questions will be asked about particular poems and in language which will be readily understood by a particular group of children. We shall return to them and how they are best asked in the classroom in Chapter 7.

How poems mean: 'A poem should not mean/But be'

The meaning of 'meaning' where poetry is concerned is a plural and ambiguous concept: plural because, as the discussion of 'The Stag' shows, and as you will have experienced if you teased out your own reading of it first, the meanings made in reading the poem are a result of individual exploration, idiosyncratic points of entry into the experience presented, and personal awareness of the way the words are rendering that experience; ambiguous because 'meaning' usually betokens something that can be explained or, at least, described. There *will* be matters that need explanation about many poems; there will be the need for explanatory talking or writing to hold and to represent the gist of a reader's response to a poem; there may even be the need to answer specific questions about this or that aspect of a poem; but to claim that any of these explanations resolves the 'meaning' is fatuous. As with stories, meaning is a compound of what the poem offers and what the reader brings. However, the nature of the art is such that, as we noted earlier, in the apprehension of a poem, the temporal sense of story-reading (what happens next?) gives way to a greater spatial awareness (what does this pattern of words mean to me?); and, further, in our comprehension of a poem, meaning is made as much from the reader's response to the sound, rhythm and formal ordering of the language as it is to its line of thought, syntax and lexical definition. It is these characteristics of the art of poetry that at once provide the challenge to the art of teaching it and the source of many pupils' uncertainties. For, while we may well hear many children ask of a story 'What happens next?', there will be few who ask of a poem 'What does this pattern of words mean to me?' Children have to become familiar with what sort of thing a poem is to a degree that is not necessary when responding to stories. This distinction may seem difficult to sustain at first sight, given the natural affinity children have with rhymes and jingles in their play; but oral chants are very different experiences from printed poems.

A poem by Archibald MacLeish tells the reader about the nature of poetry. It is both an assertion and itself an example of what it states. Read it aloud.

ARS POETICA

A poem should be palpable and mute
As a globed fruit,

Dumb
As old medallions to the thumb,

Silent as the sleeve-worn stone
Of casement ledges where the moss has grown —

A poem should be wordless
As the flight of birds.

*

A poem should be motionless in time
As the moon climbs

Leaving, as the moon releases
Twig by twig the night-entangled trees,

Leaving, as the moon behind the winter leaves,
Memory by memory the mind —

> A poem should be motionless in time
> As the moon climbs.
>
>   *
>
> A poem should be equal to:
> Not true.
>
> For all the history of grief
> An empty doorway and a maple leaf.
>
> For love
> The leaning grasses and two lights above the sea —
>
> A poem should not mean
> But be. (6)

The poem is a succession of images each trying to catch the essence of poetry through the medium of poetry; images that develop in sequence and lead to a strikingly simple, imageless conclusion, yet images whose essential quality is their ability to symbolize meaning, to stand for what is inexpressible in discursive language; or, as the poem puts it, to 'be equal to'.

The spatial sense of poetry is immediately evoked in the 'globed fruit'. While inviting the reader to handle this tactile object, potentially delicious to taste as well as to hold, the poem is actually saying something about how poems speak to us. A poem becomes a three-dimensional presence in the reader's imagination. It does not tell us about itself, explaining itself away, dissipating its power; instead, it literally 'expresses itself'. The images which follow suggest different sources of power and delight that poems contain: the romance and secret experience of 'medallions', the richness of human lives and histories in the 'sleeve-worn stone', the natural aspirations of the human spirit in the 'flight of birds'. And, as befits the theme of silence that unites these four images, the words that make the images are themselves examples of the principle of *ars poetica* as expressed in the last lines of the whole poem. Hence, their point is made by *how they are*, not by *what they say*. So the fruit is 'palpable' and 'globed' — the words are ripe and sensuous; 'dumb' is displayed alone on its line, its roundness reflected in 'medallions' and echoed in the rhyming 'thumb'; the lines lengthen and the sibilance increases as the slow passage of history is evoked through the sleeves which have worn away the stone over which the moss is growing; there is the flutter of wings in 'wordless'. The sensory qualities of the words are both the medium and the message, the means of expression and the idea being expressed.

The second section moves the poem on from silence to stillness; it enfolds itself by repeating the first statement as the last one, stressing the stillness, inviting us to experience permanence and stasis via the moving moon. It shifts our attention from externalized objects, the moon and the winter trees, to the internal world of the mind and hints at how poems come into being for both writers and readers. A poem becomes lodged in the mind: memory works paradoxically for, as time passes, the experience of the poem changes; it is both 'leaving' and arriving, establishing its own existence. Irrelevant details fall away leaving the symmetry and the still presence of the poem in the writer's and reader's consciousness. Such interpretations are hazardously made for the poem is operating symbolically; and again, how the words are being used is a fundamental aspect of what a poem is. Hence, we experience the enclosed atmosphere created by the repeated lines and the single focus of the moon metaphor; the imperceptible pace of the moon, caught in the alliterative reversal of what is moving and what is still, ' ... as the moon releases/Twig by twig the night-entangled trees ...'; the cunning play on 'leaving' and 'leaves'. As earlier, the words are relating to each other; they are not looking outside themselves in order to say something about poetry-making, but are contributing the whole of themselves to making a poem about making a poem.

As the last section indicates, therefore, we should not ask of a poem what it means and whether it is true or untrue; rather we experience what Eliot called 'objective correlatives', images that act as the formulae for the emotions, whether of grief or love, on the aesthetic principle that 'A poem should not mean/But be'. However we react to the nostalgic images of the first section and the clichés through which grief and love are conveyed in the last one, this principle remains valid as the point of MacLeish's poem.

There is no more severe a test for such a principle than a 'nonsense poem'. Edwin Morgan introduced the following composition on B.B.C. Radio some years ago as 'a sound poem'. Whatever we choose to call it, it highlights both the plural and ambiguous nature of how poems mean. To make a point we will come to in a moment we have omitted the title. Read the poem aloud!

Sssnnnwhuffffl?
Hnwhuffl hhnnwfl hnfl hfl?
Gdroblboblhobngbl gbl gl g g g g glbgl.
Drublhaflablhaflubhafgabhaflhafl fl fl-
gm grawwwww grf grawf awfgm graw gm.
Hovoplodok-doplodovok-plovodokot-doplodokosh?
Splgraw fok fok splgrafhatchgabrlgabrl fok splfok!
Zgra kra gka fok!
Grof grawff gahf?
Gombl mbl bl-
blm plm,
blm plm,
blm plm,
blp. (7)

It is revealing to withold the title of the poem from a class and invite their responses. Denied the language of the dictionary, there are few who can resist the instinct to create meanings. Commonly, someone will remark on the watery sounds, particularly at the beginning and end, and the harder sounds in the middle lines. Differences in line length are noticed and the significance of the punctuation is pointed out: someone or something is making exclamations and asking questions, rhetorical or otherwise; the rhythm of the writing is not that of flat statement. Pictures form in the mind's eye, speculations are made, as the readers acknowledge that there is some sort of development; an event is taking place between the opening question and the final 'blp'. Inexorably, the mind spawns its images and stories and translates them into words. Occasionally, one of the interpretations may come close to Edwin Morgan's title — 'The Loch Ness Monster's Song'.

Elements of response

What this last exercise reveals is the manner of our apprehending. In order to make the monster, we have to meet the poet rather more than half way and rely upon the fundamental signposts of poetic composition to guide us from nonsense to sense. These may be expressed in terms of four over-lapping qualities of the language of poetry which are present, in differing degrees, in the experiencing of all poems, even ones as dissimilar as 'The Stag', 'Ars Poetica' and 'The Loch Ness Monster's Song'. The four elements of the imaginative experience of responding to a poem are: words as sound, words as rhythm, words as pictures and words as story. All contribute to the meanings we make. The importance of any one element will vary from reader to reader and reading to reading. First impressions of these three poems may well give prominence to the narrative of 'The Stag', the word-pictures of 'Ars Poetica' and the sounds of 'The Loch Ness Monster's Song'. Yet our discussion of Hughes's poem demonstrates how all four elements are at work together; and, even in the other two poems where the sounds, rhythms and pictorial evocations of the words are not employed to tell a formal story *per se*, the narrative imagination is readily detectable in the ordering and development of images towards a conclusion about art, or in the sense we have of the monster coming to the surface, quizzically remarking upon the world about him, deciding that he dislikes what he sees and submerging once more into his underwater world.

These four elements need to be born in mind by every poetry teacher. The appeal of sound and rhythm is fundamental in sharing a poem with a group of children. It is a recurring testimony to the importance of what Eliot called the 'auditory imagination (which) is the feeling for syllable and rhythm, penetrating far below the conscious levels of thought and feeling, invigorating every word . . . ' (8). Teachers know from personal observation as well as from the work of the Opies that children possess this auditory imagination from infancy and develop it in their play. These aspects of a poem's meaning, as we suggested earlier, are the ones with which children have a natural affinity. Repetition of key words, the significance invested in particular word sounds and rhyming patterns are all sound effects that appeal to children. Similarly, children bring an innate sense of rhythm to poetry. Youngsters especially prefer rhythm to be strongly-marked, a clear beat that is regularly accented. Older readers may develop a liking for both the buoyant, rhythmical character of a Causley ballad and the slow down-beat of an introspective lyric by de la Mare and be able to discriminate between their tastes. Just as Eliot's phrase 'auditory imagination' incorporates the elements of sound and rhythm, so the notion of the 'narrative imagination' includes the elements of picture and story. 'Words as pictures' covers a range of visual effects that poet and reader share through the medium of a poem, from the mental imagery that is provoked in the reader's mind to his awareness of the haiku poet's genius for miniature or the concrete poet's sense of fun. In poems our pictorial sense may be exercised in response to form and lay-out or in the picturing that we find the words evoking as we read. Just as we are proliferators of images, so we are of stories. Again, the sense of narrative may be no more than the natural propensity to link pictures into sequences, the ordering of experiences to represent them to ourselves more coherently. Yet the enthralling power of story in poetry can go beyond this. Stories in verse hold children in a double spell: the enchantment of the fiction and the form. It is a power that is felt most richly in the traditional literature of narrative and ballad verse arising directly from the oral heritage. Words as sound, rhythm, picture and story: these verbal elements of the art are the carriers of feelings and ideas in poetry.

Implications for the classroom

We need a methodology that enables us to translate this plurality of meaning into classroom activities.

a) Three questions to keep in mind The singular nature of poems and the unique way that they convey meaning demand that the teacher of poetry must ask:

> *What is my* knowledge *of the poetry written for and accessible to children?*
> *What* time *do I give to poetry?*
> *When the voices of poet, children and teacher are talking about a poem*
> *in my classroom, is the discussion based on the primacy of the individual child's* response?

Knowledge of the poetry available for children is our fundamental professional commitment. If we are not readers of poems we can scarcely expect to become teachers of poems. The corrective, if one is needed, is easy and pleasurable: it is simply to read as many slim volumes of individual poets' work as possible and not merely to confine ourselves to school anthologies. Such a reading programme is often best carried out along with one or two colleagues: likes and dislikes, stock responses and personal reading habits are usually challenged in this way and strong recommendations are more likely to be followed up, leading to a sharing of 'how things went' in the classroom. The bibliographies of poetry written for children given in Chapter 4 (pp 85 and 92) suggest a starting place.

Time is a significant factor in the teaching of poetry. After all, most poems are so short that they take no time at all to read and enjoy by comparison with novels or plays. There ought to be plenty of time for poetry, then, even if the poems only survive in the gaps between other activities. Examine your own practice. How much time per week do we give to poetry? Children (all of us) develop as readers by keeping in continual practice. It follows that, if we and they expect to take this aspect of English seriously, all children should have the chance to hear, and when appropriate talk about, several poems each week. Secondly, what do we do with the time? If poetry lessons repeatedly fall into a 'read–discuss–write' sequence then it is not surprising that the majority of children will lose interest. Poems are unpredictable; we should try to emulate this quality in the patterns of our lessons. The implication for our teaching is to be flexible in the ways we work and, above all, to allow the singular nature of a particular poem to dictate to us how it should be handled. **Responses** to poems are often oblique in nature and hesitant in expression if they are genuine efforts to come to terms. Conversely, they are usually uncompromising, not to say blunt, if they are simply a means of indicating a dislike of the whole business. Enough is known about the operation of all-class lessons and discussions in small groups from two to five pupils to suggest that the latter have a particularly significant role to play in poetry tea-ching. (9) Again, if the answer to our question about time suggests the need for a change of emphasis, the direction is clear: put the onus more squarely upon the children to explore the poems and talk out their responses in a variety of differently structured tasks (see Chapter 7). Inevitably there will be more *talk* about matters unconnected with the task in hand but this does not mean that there will be less attention given to a poem than in an all-class lesson directed by the teacher. On the contrary, if groups are given a clear goal to achieve, a physical arrangement conducive to discussion and the urgency of a time limit then, with most classes, the teacher's fears about time-wasting, irrelevance or anarchy largely disappear. When talking about poems, as about anything else in schools, the paradox applies that free speech demands a firm framework. Small group work is not an instant panacea. A class unfamiliar with it will need to be trained, and there are as many dangers in over-use as neglect. Nonetheless, there are clear advantages.

The sorts of benefits that accrue in pair and group discussions of poems and which are much harder to achieve in all-class discussions, are: the willingness to tolerate uncertainty, misunderstanding and ignorance; the sense that whatever they make of the poem it will be uniquely theirs; the awareness that, since they are in control of the talking, they can return to parts of the poem when they like and so fit their sense of the details into a growing appreciation of the whole. Such benefits, of course, are not only to be gained in poetry lessons; but, in view of the nature of poems, the advan-tages of small group discussions are particularly helpful in eliciting individual responses.

b) Meeting, sharing and studying poems
Meeting Most children meet most poetry either on sheets of duplicated paper or in anthologies. It is a curious fact that, while we know that if

children like a story by Enid Blyton or Robert Leeson they are likely to seek out another by the same author, we deny them the possibility of this social bond with poets by the way we mediate between the writer and the reader. How children meet poems in school is the area of work that requires most attention. It ought to be self-evident, but it often strikes teachers as a novelty, that the single most important resource in poetry teaching is a collection of three or four dozen slim volumes of poems by single authors. This collection can be augmented by anthologies, so that there is a variety of voices and styles and an eye-catching presentation. The main purpose of such a collection is not as a staff room resource but as the basis for classroom activity. For one of the best ways for a class to meet poems is by spending ten minutes regularly set aside to browse through a wide variety of books, dipping and skipping, and finding out what they like and dislike. Individuals may well discover they prefer one person's poems to those of another and the social bond thus begins to develop. Given a wide and varied choice of poetry books, the most reluctant pupils are hard-pressed to claim that there is nothing of interest. After this browsing time, it is generally an easy transition to reading poems aloud as individuals choose them. Discussion may follow some poems and not others: close scrutiny is certainly not required. The purpose, especially in the early weeks with a class, is to put everyone at ease with poems by reading a lot and saying little. Regular exposure to a wide selection of poems in an informal way is the best grounding we can give children if we want to cultivate a liking for poetry.

Sharing   The key to a proper sharing of poetry is performance. It is easy to set children to work at 'improper' sharing by sending them on metaphor hunts and simile chases, by exhorting them to collect examples of assonance and alliteration (or, as one of our pupils said with more truth then he knew, 'illiteration'), or by asking them to think about a poem as evidence supporting a project on, say, 'Water' or 'The Wild West', rather than as a totality in itself. This is not to outlaw the use of figurative and technical language or to decry project work. It is simply to plead for activities that are appropriate to the nature of poems. If 'A poem should not mean/But be', then the sharing children do should focus not on worrying out its meaning but on celebrating its being. This is why performance is important. It may imply copying out and illustrating favourite pieces for display purposes, public readings, dramatizations and the like where groups of children concentrate upon presenting poetry in such a way that it may be enjoyed and savoured for its own sake.

A cassette tape-recorder is an indispensable aid in this area of work. A simple demand upon small groups of children might run along these lines: 'You have a ten minute slot to fill for BBC Radio's *Poetry Please* series. Your producer wants you to catch the interest of a young audience and to include a minimum of four poems read by different voices. You must introduce and link the poems in a suitable way. Choose your poems, script your introduction and linking passages and then record your programme.' This activity requires reading and discrimination, the exercise of personal choice, ordering and relating poems in sequence, comment upon the selection and, above all, rehearsal of the presentation with the decisions about voices, pace, intonation and mood that this entails. The tape-recording of such mini-anthologies provides a class with a pleasurable activity in itself, a source of material for future use and the exacting discipline of performance. If a 'real audience' in another class or school can be arranged, so much the better. In this sort of work the art of teaching poetry comes closest to the art of poetry itself, for both are based upon a common principle: playing with words within the discipline of form. This maxim should inform our teaching just as it does the poems themselves.

Studying From time to time, even with young groups, the teacher will want to concentrate upon a poem in some detail. Close study will only work, and can only be justified as an occasional activity, if it is rooted in the pattern of meeting and sharing poems outlined above. By 'close study' we do not mean the formal criticism of a poem: this has no place in poetry lessons with children in the years before public examination courses. But, if children are exploring poetry in an atmosphere that encourages them to develop their own tastes and articulate their own responses, then there will be times when it is right to pause over a particular poem. Three questions may provide a useful framework within which to plan detailed work:

> *What does the poem say to you?*
> *How does it do it?*
> *Does it work?*

The first requires the reader to hold on to his own response, (for example by jotting down his reactions prior to discussion) and to articulate his thoughts and feelings about the poem. Among any group of children these will be very varied and the teacher's role here is to collect something from as many as possible, delaying judgement and being content to let the descriptions of mood, idea and atmosphere gather round the reading of the poem. The second question, too, will produce a scatter of reactions and the teacher may well end up with a blackboard-full of all the things the class has noticed about the shape of the poem, its sounds, rhythms, individual words and images — again, details which are to be collected for fun 'to see what we can find', not worried over for judgement. The third question must remain until last. It invites the reader to say whether a poem succeeds for him and to offer a judgement of personal value about his sense of the whole piece. If the question is put prematurely it may invite the rejection of poetry that comes from ill-considered and inaccurate reading or insufficient opportunity for reflection. It is important for the teacher to be receptive to hostile feelings and judgements about a poem that develop from careful reading.

L.A.G. Strong reminds us of the central principle of poetry teaching and provides a challenging conclusion:

> Remember, the object at every stage is to keep and develop the
> child's liking for the music of words. Explanations and annotations
> do not matter. A child's misconception may be of much greater
> value to him than the explanation which destroys it. (*10*)

Chapter 3

Narrative lines

Reading development is the subject of many whole books (*1*), most of which are concerned with 'reading' as a set of skills to be deployed across the curriculum and consider 'development' as the progress from learning to read to reading independently. We have a narrower focus on literature and learning and a conviction that involving children with poems and stories is the key to development in reading during their middle and secondary school years. In Part Two we shall focus on a range of genres that are important in the child's literary progress. Some brief contextual comments about the literature published for the 9–14 age range and about the idea of development itself are a necessary preamble.

First, there is a consensus in all the approaches to reading development about the importance of a book-saturated environment as the way in which children will be encouraged to discover their own tastes in reading. Variety in provision, via the use of local and school libraries, classroom collections of books, school bookshops and the like, is essential. Encouraging children to buy books and develop their own mini-libraries is important for, as most teachers know, whatever efforts schools make, there is no substitute for books in the child's home. Even in the age of video culture and rapidly changing patterns of family life, home is still where youngsters are most likely to find the spare time and the most conducive places in which to read for pleasure.

Secondly, there is the vexed question of quality. It appears in various guises. C.S. Lewis's three ways of writing for children consist of two of which he approves and one of which he does not (*2*). The best children's stories, he claims, arise either from the method adopted by Carroll, Grahame, Tolkien and many others whence 'the printed story grows out of a story told to a particular child with living voice and perhaps *extempore*'; or they emerge in the way Lewis himself worked which consisted 'in writing a children's story because a children's story is the best art-form for something you have to say'. Both are qualitatively different from the third way of writing for children 'as a special department of "giving the public what it wants"', catering to the supposed desires of a young audience on the market principle. Similar discriminations appear in Townsend's distinction between children's literature and children's reading matter (*3*) and in Whitehead's survey of children's reading interests, which turns upon the differences between 'quality' and 'non-quality' books. (*4*)

All these sources demonstrate a concern for the serious study of the children's book as an art-form in itself, a sub-division of literature proper, like the short story, with its own conventions and characteristics. Some efforts have been made to define these features (5) but, as yet, no clear criteria have emerged. Besides, from the point of view of a child's development in reading, a convincing case can be made out for the inclusion of a fair portion of roughage in the young reader's diet, as Peter Dickinson has suggested (6). As long as children are reading and showing some personal development in their choices and tastes, and as long as English teachers continue to test the quality and suitability of the books they offer children against their own critical judgement, then debates about the status and value of particular books can be seen in their proper relative terms and not as a means of placing novels and poems in rank order on some supposed scale of absolute worth. This is neither an attempt to undermine the importance of, say, Hardy and the Brontës in school literature nor an effort to elevate Mills and Boon into the curriculum. It is merely to urge that, against the contemporary background of book production and marketing, it is crucial for teachers to keep their own judgements about quality and suitability under constant review. When deciding about a new book two simple questions may suffice. Do I think it is well written? Do I think it is appropriate for my particular group of children? For, as Terry Eagleton has pointed out, 'value terms in literature are always transitive terms. Value means value for somebody, in a particular situation' (7).

Thirdly, there is the neglect of poetry. Handling poetry is an area of the primary/middle school curriculum and the secondary English curriculum where many teachers feel uncertain of their knowledge, uncomfortable about their methods and guilty about both. The older the children the less likely is their teacher to spend time on poetry in school (8). It is not sufficient for literature teachers to acquiesce in the common view that poetry is a minority art and that concern about its neglect is misplaced.

Fourthly, it is necessary to ask how development actually operates. At any point, a child has a past, present and future to his reading development. In other words, he needs books he *has read* already — familiar favourites, easy to relate to, predictable and secure; books he *is reading* — a catholic selection of books appropriate for his current stage of development; and books he *is growing into*, ones that are mentally and emotionally stretching and which we may judge have some elements that are beyond him. Development does not mean leaving one sort of literature behind for ever as one moves on to another. Certainly, children who become habitual readers do experience the feeling of growing out of childish things that no longer satisfy ('growing out' of the series books, for example, is common in early adolescence); but, generally, development operates in a less clearly defined manner than this. For children, like their parents and teachers, use books for various purposes and to satisfy diverse needs. Depending upon a host of variables in a child's life at any one moment, he may turn to books that are known to be undemanding because they are familiar, exciting because they are new and unknown, or challenging because they are known to be rather 'old' or 'difficult' for someone of his age. When this stage has been reached the child has begun to see himself as a reader. When a thirteen year old is reading in rapid succession — or even concurrently — a Famous Five story, a new book by Nina Bawden or Philippa Pearce, and a novel by Hardy after seeing it on T.V., then the past, present and future are in a reassuring and often amusing relationship. Peter Hollindale quotes a delightful example of this stage of development from Michael Innes's book, *The Journeying Boy*. The youthful hero of this novel writes home from boarding school:

> Please deliver at once by special messenger one pair of binoculars for bird-watching and a good camera (not box). Please send also these books: *Biggles Flies East*, *Biggles Flies West*, *Biggles Flies North*, *Biggles Fails to Return*, Bertrand Russell's *History of Western Philosophy*, George Moore's *Daphnis and Chloe*, *Biggles and the Camel Squadron*, Bleinstein's *More and More Practical Sex*, Blunden's *Life of Shelley*, also *Atalanta in Calydon*, *Biggles in Borneo*, *Women in Love*, and any *close* translations of Caesar's Civil Wars. (*9*)

If the growth of literary competence and satisfaction are most likely to be nourished by wide and catholic reading and by honouring the individuality of each child's development, it nevertheless remains true that literature teachers have a special responsibility for widening and deepening children's knowledge and experience of stories and poems. The following sections indicate ways in which this might be achieved. We have attempted to provide three types of comment:

> to characterize the different kinds of literature;
> to say what they offer to children; and
> to indicate the range of material available including short reading lists.

In this chapter we consider four genres which depend largely upon linear narrative: fairy tales, myths and legends; fantasy and science fiction; short stories; and novels written for young people moving into adolescence. In Chapter 4, our emphasis is upon literature which depends more for its impact upon the reader's awareness of visual qualities, shapes or patterns, as well as language: picture books and poetry.

Fairy tales, myths and legends

Why are fairy tales, myths and legends so important? What do they offer children that is different from anything else they encounter? These two openings serve as reminders of the characteristics of traditional stories. The first is the beginning of *The Juniper Tree*, in the version by the Brothers Grimm. (*1*)

> A long while ago, perhaps as much as two thousand years, there was a rich man who had a wife of whom he was very fond; but they had

no children. Now in the garden before the house where they lived there stood a juniper tree; and one winter's day as the lady was standing under the juniper tree, paring an apple, she cut her finger, and the drops of blood trickled down upon the snow. 'Ah!' said she, sighing deeply and looking down upon the blood, 'how happy should I be if I had a little child as white as snow and as red as blood!' And as she was saying this, she grew quite cheerful, and was sure her wish would be fulfilled. And after a little time the snow went away, and soon afterwards the fields began to look green. Next the spring came, and the meadows were dressed with flowers; the trees put forth their green leaves; the young branches shed their blossoms upon the ground; and the little birds sung through the groves. And then came summer, and the sweet-smelling flowers of the juniper tree began to unfold; and the lady's heart leaped within her, and she fell on her knees for joy. But when autumn drew near, the fruit was thick upon the trees. Then the lady plucked the red berries from the juniper tree, and looked sad and sorrowful; and she called her husband to her, and said, 'If I die, bury me under the juniper tree.' Not long after this a pretty little child was born; it was, as the lady wished, as red as blood, and as white as snow; and as soon as she had looked upon it, her joy overcame her, and she fainted away and died.

After the death of his wife, the husband remarries and, some time later, a daughter is born, half-sister to the little boy who is 'red as blood and as white as snow'. The story then tells of the brutal stepmother decapitating the boy, putting the boy's head back on his shoulders, implicating her daughter in the murder and serving the boy to his father in a gruesome black soup! These horrors are offset in the second part of the tale when the sorrowful daughter places the boy's bones under the juniper tree; her heart lightens, and the boy is transformed into a beautiful bird that flies out of the tree. The bird/boy flies round the village, happily singing a song about its own killing, and bargaining with the goldsmith, the shoemaker and the miller for suitable presents for the family. The father gets a gold chain, the daughter a pair of red shoes; and the haunted, evil stepmother receives a millstone that crushes her to death. At the end the juniper tree bursts into flames and the little boy is reunited with his father and half-sister. The tale is horrific and compelling — but not more so than our second example from the legend of Beowulf.

There are many versions of the story of Beowulf; here is the opening of a recent prose translation by Kevin Crossley-Holland (2).

'Stranger!' called Hygelac.
The men near the king stopped talking and picking their teeth and swilling stonecold mead over their gums.
'Stranger!' called Hygelac.
In the hall of the king of the Geats, a hundred men listened.
Almost silence. The cat-fire hissed and spat, golden-eyed tapestries

winked out of the gloom. Silence. The man rose from the stranger's seat.

'Your name?' demanded Hygelac.

'Gangleri,' said the stranger. 'In your tongue: Wanderer.'

'All right, Wanderer. It's time you sang for your supper.'

Men on the mead-benches shifted their buttocks, and stretched out their legs. The gathering faced inwards towards the fire.

Wanderer stood in the poet's place by the hearth and rubbed his one gleaming eye. 'I'll fuel you,' he said, 'with a true story, and one close to my heart. This story of past and present and future.'

'True?' called out a young man, the king's nephew, Beowulf by name. 'How can it be true if it's in the future?'

'Because it is not finished,' said Wanderer. 'You must finish it.'

Beowulf, how old was he, not more than twenty, felt his cheeks flush with quickening blood.

Wanderer stooped and scooped up six-stringer, the harp that always stood in the poet's place. Gleaming maplewood, white willow pegs, white fingertips, a quivering face.

'Listen!' said Wanderer. 'A story of heroes!' Now he plucked the harp with a plectrum. 'A story of monsters!' And plucked it again. 'A story of Denmark!'

The storyteller arrests both Beowulf's attention and ours and we follow the warrior hero in his three battles. As a young man he fights Grendel and the monster's even more loathsome mother and journeys home loaded with gifts. Fifty years on, king of his own people, he fights and kills a dragon but receives a fatal wound in the battle. The tale ends with the ceremonial burning and burial of the dragon-slayer along with all the treasure he had captured from the dragon's hoard.

From two brief examples it is clear that youngsters are being offered a quite different sort of reading experience from that of the conventional children's novel. Below we have identified the main characteristics of such stories since we need to think about the nature of these tales in order to share them more effectively with children.

Definitions For Elizabeth Cook, 'myths are about gods, legends are about heroes, and fairy tales are about woodcutters and princesses'; and she adds that

> ... myths are about the creation of all things, the origin of evil, and the salvation of man's soul; legends and sagas are about the doings of Kings and peoples in the period before records were kept; fairy tales, folk tales and fables are about human behaviour in a world of magic.... (3)

For teachers and children differences are less important than the qualities that these stories have in common. What essentially distinguishes fairy tales, myths and legends from other literature is that they all deal with universally felt experiences — themes, ideas and emotions which cross boundaries of culture, language and age group and seem to reflect the very nature of *homo sapiens* in story form. The importance of these traditional stories cannot be over-estimated. They are a way we represent ourselves to ourselves in cultural terms; individually, they are a means of reconciling within ourselves the inner world of our single psyche with the outer world of objects in which we must live. Ted Hughes speaks of the imaginative exercise we all need to maintain healthful relationships between inner and outer worlds and sees the role of traditional stories as 'laying down blueprints for imagination'. (4).

Just why the child reader may find such 'blueprints' more accessible and powerful in these stories than elsewhere we must move on to consider.

The anonymous author Perhaps the most obvious thing that is common to fairy tales, myths and legends and which separates them from other fiction is the remoteness of an author. True, children may have a hazy awareness of a man called Homer who tells the stories of Odysseus's travels, or a sense of the Gawain poet; but such tales have been translated and told in so many versions over the centuries that they acquire the aura of anonymity. The social relationship that the child develops with these traditional stories during reading is more with a culture and a genre than with an individual author working at a particular time. This is even clearer in the case of fairy tales. Tolkien sees 'the primal desire at the heart of Faerie ... (as) ... the realization, *independent of the conceiving mind*, of imagined wonder' (5) (our italics). When a story has been realized in this way, the reader can plunge into the first page of *The Juniper Tree* or *Beowulf* to find that the imaginative possibilities of the stories are immediate and inviting because of their existential detachment; they are free from the sense of an individual author and strong through the sense of a whole culture at work.

Narrative voice The voice of the traditional story is distinctive. Because the author is anonymous the narrator can never be self-conscious. He will avoid reflection, seldom offer a direct interpretation of events and even decline to dwell upon particular details of his tale. If we open Andrew Lang's *Tales of Troy and Greece* and read, 'Long ago, in a little island called Ithaca, on the west coast of Greece, there lived a king named Laertes ... ' (6); or hear the quiet tones of the undramatized narrator of *The Juniper Tree*; or encounter the dramatic technique of the story within a story at the start of *Beowulf* — the voice is always definite; this is how things were. Whether the style is that of calm exposition or a piece of theatre, the tone is one of flat statement. The uncompromising power of these stories derives directly from a narrative voice that says simply and clearly to the reader: 'These are the facts of the tale; take them or leave them'

The sense of audience Fairy tales, myths and legends are for the whole community. Fairy tales did not originate as children's stories but as oral tales shared amongst ordinary folk; and some of these people, particularly the nurses and servants who had such an important role in bringing up the children of the upper and middle classes, would naturally share their stories with these youngsters. Myths and legends were even more clearly adult in origin, with their roots in religious rituals and courtly entertainment.

Certainly, there are no indications of a child audience in the traditional stories themselves. There is no avoidance of violence, sex or emotional trauma as one would expect in stories written specifically for children; on the contrary, traditional tales are as abundant in these respects as many a contemporary adult novel. What distinguishes these stories is their telling. The clean lines of the narrative, the simple presentation of character, the clarity of the language and the proper resolution of the ending all characterize the sort of tales 'which holdeth children from play, and old men from the chimney corner'. Traditional stories grip the childlike imagination that dwells in all of us.

Plot The strongest means that these stories have to arrest and keep the reader's attention lies in the power of their plots. Events are simplified though beneath them may lie complex issues. Plots are single-minded, an uncomplicated sequence of incidents. There is a remorseless inevitability about the stories, as though they are following the laws of nature — whether it is the course of natural justice as in the treatment of the stepmother in *The Juniper Tree*, or that of heroic leadership in *Beowulf*.

The two openings quoted above exemplify the power of plot. The start of *The Juniper Tree* is like a miniature fairy tale itself in its form and development; and both openings contain within themselves the main elements of the story to come. In the first, birth and death, sorrow and joy, the motifs of blood, snow and the tree are all held within the natural, inevitable unfolding of the seasonal cycle — almost in the manner in which a short dumb-show might foreshadow the more elaborate playing out of events. The opening of *Beowulf* achieves parallel effects by different means. When Wanderer speaks it is to tell us that the story has already begun:

> 'I'll fuel you,' he said, 'with a true story, and one close to my
> heart. This story of past and present and future.'
> 'True?' called out a young man, the king's nephew, Beowulf by
> name. 'How can it be true if it's in the future?'
> 'Because it is not finished,' said Wanderer. 'You must finish it.'

The artifice of the storyteller is practised to implicate the reader and enchant the protagonist; Beowulf is caught up in the current of history; and for the rest of the tale we acquiesce in the supposed truth of the legend.

Character The people in traditional stories are typical rather than unique. Stereotypes abound. The oppositions of goodness and wickedness, stupidity and cleverness, beauty and ugliness recur and are frequently seen within the members of one family. One of the peculiarities of myths and legends is that while the storyteller may want to persuade us of the uniqueness of Odysseus or Robin Hood — their unsurpassed bravery or unrivalled courage — the way the tales are told serves to emphasize the typicality of these heroes. One of the peculiarities of fairy stories is that *their* typicality does not derive from the high incidence of tiny creatures with magical powers, for there are hardly any fairies in them, but rather from the human characters being subject to strange incidents in enchanted regions. Common to all is the absence of any overt investigation of motive or feeling; there is none of the psychological exploration of the novel. Instead of reflection upon the ideas or emotions behind a character's behaviour, we are given direct statement. Thus the mother of *The Juniper Tree* is either 'sad and sorrowful' or she feels unalloyed joy. Beowulf is a noble and brave fighter and a wise and respected ruler. No further explanations are required or expected.

The subtlety of the characters in traditional stories lies rather in their patterning; not in what characters think and feel but in the way they are deployed in the overall texture of the narrative. The Grimms do not even tell us that the mother is pure and good, let alone justify the assertion. Instead they allow us to feel the natural goodness of her character, partly by the fondness her husband shows, but mainly by presenting her as a flower of the seasons that blossoms and dies. Her natural creation contrasts sharply with the unnatural creation of the stepmother as the story proceeds. Beowulf, too, is a symbol of man's nobility and courage; dragon-slayer, a warrior to defeat the unnatural forces of darkness on behalf of all of us, and in so doing to assert that, though Grendel exists (like other monstrous images of evil throughout literature), Grendel can be beaten.

Setting   The settings of traditional stories, whether in unnamed places or in far-off landscapes in the North or the Mediterranean, are remote; and the events for which they are the context happened long ago. It is very often the exotic objects and attributes of the lands of fairy tale, myth and legend that are memorable. The power of the juniper tree, Jack's magical beans; the great swords — Hrunting of *Beowulf* or Excalibur and Joyeux of Arthurian romance; Scylla and Charybdis or the dragon's teeth that grow a harvest of warriors to be cut down that Jason encounters in his quest for the Golden Fleece — all are arresting images in themselves and signal to the reader that, in these stories at least, the rules of the workaday world are suspended. The secondary worlds of traditional stories are governed not by the surface features of time and place, cause and effect, imported from the primary world but by the conflicts of human experience. After all, so-called realistic fiction is a comparatively recent phenomenon, associated with the rise of the modern novel in the mid-eighteenth century. These ancient stories, with their settings in remote lands, come down to us from earlier times and speak more directly of the desires which drive people and the terrors that beset them.

Theme   In fairy tales, myths and legends, situations are set up swiftly, as in *The Juniper Tree;* tasks or problems are introduced in succinct terms, as in

Beowulf. The direct, unelaborated style of the stories allows children to face the basic human predicaments of food, shelter, survival, death, loss, identity and the like with a concreteness and immediacy that are unavailable elsewhere in literature. Paradoxically, these stories also deal with our sense of the numinous, with our feeling for the unreality of existence as opposed to such basic needs. In their refusal to make a clear distinction between the real and the magical, fairy stories incorporate a dimension that readers describe variously as religious or spiritual, or simply by reference to a sense of unseen forces and powers that lie behind the realities we live by. The themes of fairy tales, myths and legends are the timeless ones, the big issues of man's existence; yet they are presented in frameworks that distance these matters from the social and personal worlds that their readers inhabit. They also cut down the story to a manageable size so that the theme is exposed starkly, without all the literary embellishment of the novel. Elizabeth Cook makes the point in terms that are familiar to us from Chapter 1:

> The Secondary World of myth and fairy tale is a world of
> fighting, of sudden reverses of fortune, of promises kept and broken,
> of commands obeyed and disobeyed, of wanderings and quests, of
> testing and judgement, gratitude and ingratitude, and light and
> darkness. It is clearly impressed with patterns that anyone can trace
> more uncertainly in his own experience of the primary world. The
> realistic, localized story of Mrs Hodgson-Burnett's *The Secret
> Garden* shows a child what it is like for one little girl, very different
> from himself, to feel afraid: the story of *Beowulf* shows him fear in
> itself. (7)

If, however, we leave aside the 'distancing' framework in which these traditional stories are cast and ask how they speak to the individual reader in personal terms, it is possible to generalize their themes around the two complementary ideas of man's wishes and fears. The variations on these themes are powerfully exemplified in *The Juniper Tree* and *Beowulf* and endlessly elaborated in the wealth of traditional stories hinted at in our bibliography.

Teaching the tales   Given the variety of avenues to explore with these stories, it is best to remind ourselves of the importance of a straightforward, literary approach; that is, of steeping oneself and the children in as many stories as possible and trusting the individual's responses in the context of a growing awareness of a lot of tales. The approach we would urge concentrates on the stories themselves. It accepts the take-it-or-leave-it voice of the narrator, resists explaining the tales, delights in performing them and insists on reading plenty of them. Teachers might expect to involve children in some of the following activities:(8)

1 Retelling   This activity is central to the tradition. Thirteen or fourteen year olds retell these stories in simple terms for children at the local primary school, while middle school pupils retell them for infants. Brief notes on the plot as an *aide memoire* could precede a live, oral retelling to younger children or a tape-recorded anthology of several tales. Both are demanding tasks for the older pupils and provide enjoyable experiences for both tellers and listeners.

2 Picture story Since these stories often lodge in the mind as a series of still images, children can often tell a story in pictures either as a sequence of drawings, maybe in comic strip style; as a collage; or, with the Greek and Egyptian myths as a shaping influence, as a more stylized frieze; or they could devise a map, inset with small pictures, to show the main images of the story.

3 Modern tales Traditional stories put a handful of characters through a brief, clear series of events; they are relatively easy, therefore, for twelve to fourteen year olds to write. It is essential that they are exposed to a number of tales first; and it may be sensible to read some stories by Oscar Wilde or Ted Hughes to give them the feel of old tales in a modern idiom. Again the goal of writing for younger children is helpful. A possible way-in is to take the underlying situation and conflict of a tale like *Hansel and Gretel* or *Cinderella*, list the elements on the blackboard and ask the children to write their own stories in a modern setting around these elements. Anthony Browne's visual interpretation of *Hansel and Gretel* (Julia MacRae Books, 1981) would be helpful here.

4 Drama Confrontations of characters (Beowulf and Grendel), dilemmas to work your way out of (Odysseus's men in the cave of the Cyclops), oppositions between the forces of good and evil so permeate these stories that movement work (possibly against a spoken narrative) and improvization will often be more exciting activities than ones that stay close to the printed text.

5 Diaries or logs Traditional stories frequently involve journeys or quests. Keeping the diary of a knight or warrior-leader on his travels, or writing up the ship's log of a voyage, has two advantages. It gives children a means of recording the sequence of events in a tale and thus of understanding its structure better; and it takes children inside a character and a situation to look at events imaginatively from a different viewpoint.

Recommended reading So much of the success of work on these traditional stories depends upon what activities are chosen, the experience and ages of the particular children and the editions used. Teachers would be wise to 'shop around' among the many versions of these tales, particularly with the guidance of Elizabeth Cook's *The Ordinary and the Fabulous* (C.U.P.)

We have referenced books here and elsewhere in the way which seems of greatest use to teachers with limited funds to spend:
a) paperback publisher
b) educational hardback publishers, where they exist
c) hardback publisher only where (a) or (b) does not exist — hardback editions are indicated by an asterisk.

Fairy tales

Katharine Briggs   *British Folk Tales and Legends: A Sampler*   (Paladin)
Angela Carter (ed)   *Sleeping Beauty and Other Favourite Fairy Tales,*
                      illus. M. Foreman   (Gollancz★)

Helen Cresswell   *The First* and *Second Armada Lion Books of Fairy Tales*
    (Collins)
Jacob and Wilhelm Grimm   *Grimms' Fairy Tales*   (Puffin); and *Grimms'*
    Fairy Tales, trans. Peter Carter,
    illus. Peter Richardson   (O.U.P.★)
Erik Haugaard (ed)   *Hans Andersen: His Classic Fairy Tales,*
    illus. M. Foreman   (Gollancz★)
Joseph Jacobs   *English Fairy Tales*   (Dover)
Naomi Lewis (ed)   *Hans Andersen's Fairy Tales*   (Puffin)
Ruth Manning-Sanders   *A Book of Dragons* (and other titles)   (Methuen)
Geraldine McCaughrean   *One Thousand and One Arabian Nights*   (O.U.P.★)
Jennifer Mulherin (ed)   *Favourite Fairy Tales*   (Granada)
Iona and Peter Opie   *The Classic Fairy Tales*   (O.U.P.)
Charles Perrault   *Perrault's Fairy Tales*, illus. G. Doré   (Dover)
    Complete Fairy Tales, illus. W. Heath Robinson
    (Kestrel★)

Greek myths and legends
Leon Garfield and Edward Blishen   *The God Beneath the Sea*
    The Golden Shadow   (Carousel)
Roger Lancelyn Green   *Tales of the Greek Heroes*   *The Tales of Troy*
    (Puffin)
Andrew Lang   *Tales of Troy and Greece*   (Faber)
Kathleen Lines   *The Faber Book of Greek Legends*   (Faber★)
Barbara Leonie Picard   *The Odyssey of Homer*   (O.U.P.★)
James Reeves   *Heroes and Monsters*   (Blackie)
Ian Serraillier   *The Way of Danger*   *The Clashing Rocks*   *Heracles the Strong*
    (Heinemann New Windmill)
Rex Warner   *Men and Gods*   (Heinemann New Windmill)

Northern myths and legends
Sheila Banfield   *Leif the Lucky: A Vinland Hero*   (John Murray)
Jim Budd   *Loki: A Mischievous God*   (John Murray)
Kevin Crossley-Holland   *Beowulf*, illus. Charles Keeping   (O.U.P.★)
    The Norse Myths   (Penguin)
Roger Lancelyn Green   *Myths of the Norsemen*   (Puffin)
Barbara Leonie Picard   *Tales of the Norse Gods and Heroes*   (O.U.P.★)
Rosemary Sutcliff   *Dragon-Slayer: The Story of Beowulf*   (Puffin)
Henry Treece   *Vikings' Dawn*   (and other titles)   (Puffin)

Arthurian romances
Roger Lancelyn Green   *King Arthur and His Knights of the Round Table*
    (Puffin)
David Marigold   *Lancelot and Elaine: a Lost Love*   (John Murray)
Barbara Leonie Picard   *Stories of King Arthur and His Knights*   (O.U.P.★)
Anne Reyersbach   *The Grail Quest: From Frost To Flower*   (John Murray)
Ian Serraillier   *The Challenge of the Green Knight*
    (Heinemann New Windmill)
Rosemary Sutcliff   *The Light Beyond the Forest*   (Bodley Head★)

Modern fairy tales, myths and legends

Joan Aiken   *The Kingdom Under the Sea*, illus. Jan Pienkowski   (Puffin)
Sara and Stephen Corrin (eds)   *The Puffin Book of Modern Fairy Tales*
        (Puffin)
Ted Hughes   *How the Whale Became   The Iron Man*   (Faber)
Terry Jones   *Fairy Tales*, illus. Michael Foreman   (Puffin)
Rudyard Kipling   *Just So Stories*   (Piccolo)
George MacBeth   *Noah's Journey* in *Collected Poems 1958–1970*
        (Macmillan)
Antoine de Saint-Exupery   *The Little Prince*   (Piccolo)
James Thurber   *The 13 Clocks*   (Puffin)
Oscar Wilde   *The Happy Prince and Other Stories*   (Puffin)
Jay Williams   *The Practical Princess and Other Liberating Fairy Tales*   (Hippo)

Science fiction and fantasy

A familiar dictum for literature teachers requires that we should 'start where the kids are'. In the areas of science fiction and fantasy, the difficulty is that they are ahead of most of us; or at least, somewhere else. For many of our pupils, these particular kinds of story are almost addictive. Dr Who, Luke Skywalker and the rest may have first captured their young devotees on the screen, but children also follow their adventures avidly through proliferating series of paperbacks; or they may themselves adventure with sword and sorcery, dungeons and dragons on their V.D.U.s; or, armed only with sword and shield, paperbacks, 'adventure sheets', pencil and dice, they may confront the hazards of their quests in the best-selling story-games of the 'Fighting Fantasy' series devised for Puffin by Steve Jackson and Ian Living-stone. It may be that a new generation will dare to boldly range the galaxies with Captain Kirk and Mr Spock — but this time as members of the crew of the 'Enterprise' — for the old heroes (witness Flash Gordon and Superman) have a splendid capacity for periodic reincarnation.

The D.I.Y. stories offer an experience which differs essentially from that of reading a novel. Through the consistent use of the second person singular narrative, the relationship between author and reader is radically altered. (The Bantam Books' 'Choose Your Own Adventure No. 12', *Inside UFO 54–40*, in which 'You're the star of the story', informs the reader, in these random examples, 'You tell Mopo not to worry . . .', 'You interrupt yourself to catch a rope . . .', 'Kim Lee and you look at each other in the dim light . . .'.) The demand for decisions on almost every page means that the reader's picturing of a secondary world is fragmented and subordinated to the activity of problem-solving. The processes of anticipating or interacting are different in kind from those offered by a consecutive narrative. This is not to dismiss the possible value of these books for children as decision-making games; but we doubt whether the activity involved in determining upon a route forward is as deeply, or as diversely, active as that of reading a novel which, in the sense we proposed in Chapter 1, leaves space for the reader.

There has been a committed adult following for SF and fantasy literature, of course, long before *Close Encounters, Star Wars, E.T.* and the advent of story-games. We are aware that by grouping SF and fantasy together we may excite the derision of the devotee; there are separate audiences for the two genres. However, it seems that SF and fantasy can usefully be considered together here because they draw comparable responses from readers and so invite similar treatment in the classroom.

In the discussion which follows, we are thinking of stories in which a writer might decide to carry us across to a parallel world, into the past or the future or out into space; or he might decide that time stands still, animals talk, sorcery threatens or that worlds collide. Having adjusted, broken or ignored the natural laws or circumstances of Earth to create a setting for his story, a writer retains plausibility by being consistent within his newly ordered universe. Although we may be at some remove from our own familiar world, the writer may use his different vantage point to offer clear, if oblique, insights concerning ourselves and our own world. SF or fantasy fictions may connect more precisely with some readers' unspoken or half-formed thoughts and imaginings than a naturalistic narrative set in familiar surroundings.

We consider first those whose settings do not directly impinge upon our own, though what happens may illuminate or be parallel to our experiences; such settings we have called 'other worlds'. Secondly, we turn to settings which are recognizable as our own familiar Earth, but an Earth in which one or more natural laws or circumstances have been changed; these we have called 'our world with a difference'.

Other worlds   Writers who invite a flight of fancy through the galaxies or to the forests and mountains of an imaginary continent must first secure their readers' seat belts. 'Other worlds' must be credible in their own terms. An author may establish his world through detail about its geography, history, customs, lore and language to convince us of the plausibility and consistency of his invention. The younger the reader, the more important it is that stories contain their plots within a stable framework. Especially with such readers, however, security lies within the inner rhythms of a story rather than in its setting. Themes often play upon the preference of these younger readers for clear-cut moral codes; and in that respect they are often extremely conservative in character. Both SF and fantasy for the younger reader may be literatures of exploration; but the discovery is finally that of the familiar in what is, on the surface, the highly unfamiliar world of spaceships and lasers, wizards and dragons and the like. In the majority of these stories, Good plays Evil and wins. We know our hero will triumph much as we knew that Beowulf would defeat Grendel. The interest lies in how the task is carried out and the price to be paid.

Three examples will illustrate how apparently dissimilar heroes of this kind of tale are in fact driven by similar moral values.

The 'other worlds' of Dr Who may seem light years away from the earth of the 1980s, though with his floppy hat, multi-coloured scarf and insouciant jokes, the good doctor perhaps still owes a little to the period of his first incarnation, the 1960s. On television and in the novels, children are offered swift action, ingenious plots, some excellent scientific hocus-pocus and a nicely-judged line in understated humour. Literary style inclines to the functional. There is no doubt about the Doctor's ethical stance; he is on the side of the angels, though his own religious affinities are less than specific. Interest concentrates on *how* he will defeat the Daleks, or whatever, not on *whether* he will win this time. Not only are we unequivocally on the side of Good, we are implicitly, but clearly, on the side of Humanity (warm, irrational and spontaneous) and against Machines (cold, calculating and predictable). An exception to the rule, the Doctor's robotic dog K9, transcends its machine-like qualities by its very dogginess, slightly fussy voice and its long-suffering stance towards its zany master.

The time-honoured virtues of courage, self-sufficiency and single-minded commitment to Right are also the watchwords of Keill Randor, hero of some of the most entertaining recent SF for young readers — Douglas Hill's series which began with *Galactic Warlord* (1). Randor stands in a tradition which could be traced back as readily to the sons of the Empire beloved of G.A. Henty and R.M. Ballantyne, as to the space travellers of H.G. Wells or Jules Verne; for this is unabashed blood and thunder stuff. Randor, last of the Legionaries of Moros, is a finely-honed fighting man, 'once the youngest and, some said, the finest Strike Group Leader in the 41st Legion'. The mysterious Overseers, struggling to maintain order among the warring planets, have equipped Randor with a kind of bionic impregnability, including unbreakable bones. This is just as well, it turns out, for he is subjected to consistent assault by janglers, beam guns and whatever further terrors his enemies can devise. Readers are in little doubt, however, that Randor is as likely to win through against all odds as, in their day, Bulldog Drummond, Biggles, Dick Barton or Dan Dare.

The personal qualities which enable Bilbo Baggins to survive a hazardous quest in *The Hobbit* (2) (or which sustain his nephew Frodo in *The Lord of the Rings* trilogy) are in essence much the same as those of Dr. Who or Keill Randor. Bilbo may be fearful and comfort-loving in physical matters where Randor is brave and careless of bodily well-being; and Bilbo is diffident where the Doctor is vain. But when it matters, all three are personally courageous, loyal to ideals, know their own limitations and willing to sacrifice themselves for the sake of others. The shift to Middle Earth, with its emphasis upon clear-cut virtues, allows Tolkien to offer a critique of modern society. The special quality of such secondary worlds lies in their capacity to deal obliquely — at one remove — with complex themes of both personal and universal concern.

Ursula Le Guin's Earthsea trilogy (3) is an example of a fantasy which absorbs us in the lives of characters in an 'other world' while providing insights about ourselves and our own world. The trilogy also takes us on to a probably older readership and shifts our discussion from those 'other worlds' which 'comfort and conform' to those which 'challenge and disturb', to adopt a helpful distinction made by Rosemary Jackson. True fantasy, she argues, is a literature of subversion whose purpose is to present people and events in such a way as to question the accepted and familiar. In their different ways, some books with which children may become acquainted as they grow up do this: *Dr Jekyll and Mr Hyde* and Kafka's *Metamorphosis* are examples which Jackson discusses. For her, many of the fantasies that achieve cult status in our society celebrate, rather than challenge, traditional values, and are often coloured by nostalgia for a vanished paradise:

> From Walter de la Mare, Beatrix Potter, A.A. Milne, to Richard
> Adams and J.R.R.Tolkien, a tradition of liberal humanism spreads
> outwards, covering with its moral, social and linguistic orthodoxies
> a world of bears, foxes, wolves, rabbits, ducks, hens and hobbits (4).

We would argue for the appropriateness of books which 'comfort and conform' for the younger end of our age range. The literary progress of a child within the genres of SF and fantasy seems to us to be precisely a movement from such books to those which 'challenge and disturb'. The reading list on p. 51 is arranged in this way.

Ged, the hero of the Earthsea trilogy, is confronted by difficulties which none of Ursula Le Guin's readers can themselves escape. The underlying conflict in which Ged is embroiled is still between Good and Evil; now, however, those terms can be defined with no more certainty than in our own world. In *A Wizard of Earthsea*, the hero's quest takes him throughout the archipelago to learn and practise the craft of wizardry. He pits his lore against that of dragons and wrestles with illusions. Ged may face such enemies without, but the true battleground is within himself. He must find, and maintain, a sense of personal balance; he must clearly recognize his own power to harm before he can use his power for good. In *The Tombs of Atuan*, Ged teaches the young priestess Tenar to work towards the responsible delight in life which he himself has claimed as his adulthood. In *The Farthest Shore*, Ged comes to understand what it means to release his hold upon his own life and to acknowledge the talents and differences of those who follow. An acceptance of our own mortality is necessary for the wise use of the time and gifts we have. Ursula Le Guin expresses through her fantasy beliefs which, if they are to become tenets for the practice of a life, demand constant watchfulness. For example, Ged learns that simplicity and love are at the heart of wisdom; that humility and respect towards men and knowledge are the keys to the kind of power worth having; and that the essence of humour is seriousness.

All this could become ponderous and bewildering to young readers and pretentious to adults. Certainly, these are not themes which could be overtly introduced to early adolescents. They are embedded within the narrative of the fantasy, however, and through the grace of its language, and the inevitability of the story, the Earthsea trilogy carries many readers along with its own steady impulse. It is a remarkable, even a sustaining, achievement.

Our world with a difference   Readers who are lukewarm about invitations to voyage through space or join a band of intrepid wayfarers venturing along paths where trolls lurk or dragons smoulder, often prefer books where they can, as it were, keep one foot on familiar ground. They may enjoy stories which play along the boundary line, shifting to and fro between the real and the supernatural — perhaps by way of the back of a wardrobe or the ruins of a church. Beyond the wardrobe, C.S. Lewis developed a Christian allegory in the *Narnia Chronicles* (5) whilst Alan Garner — starting from a bomb-site in Manchester — explored legendary themes which link the quest with the growth of self-knowledge (*Elidor*) (6). The time-slip fantasy (*Tom's Midnight Garden* (7), *A Traveller in Time* (8)), and the psychological fantasy (*A Game of Dark* (9), *Marianne Dreams* (10)) are examples of the kind of story which flickers between our world and the supernatural.

Authors who choose to make such modifications to normality are often interested in what the new viewpoint will reveal. Natalie Babbitt, in her marvellously shaped tale, *Tuck Everlasting* (11), invites us to consider what might happen if, in a wood somewhere, there were a spring whose waters conferred everlasting life (in this world, not the next). From this, a story is derived which implicitly shows its readers the cycles which turn through so much of human experience. Suppose, as Penelope Farmer does in *Charlotte Sometimes* (12), that you go to sleep in bed at boarding school and sometimes wake up as another girl in the same bed half a century ago. Annabel Andrews wakes up in even more startling circumstances in Mary Rodgers's *Freaky Friday* (13), when she discovers she is wearing her mother's body. These exchanges allow a particularly sharp focus upon a concern fundamental to the imaginative development of children — what *is* it like to be in someone else's shoes? Such stories are very teachable for this reason, often inviting the young reader's laughter of recognition and presenting frequent cues for improvization and writing which draw readers enjoyably closer to the stories and clarify their own speculations.

Other writers have also remained in our world, but have reordered things on even more dramatic hypotheses. What if animals could talk? Consider *The Wind in the Willows* (14), *Charlotte's Web* (15), *Mrs. Frisby and the Rats of NIMH* (16) or *The Mouse and His Child* (17). Wonderfully funny and inventive though these books are, much of their strength stems from serious themes which bring us back to our own world: the value of roots, the acceptance of change, the nature of pride and of compassion.

Or, what if an alien arrived among us? The popularity of *E.T.* suggested that the film touched upon a speculation which both children and adults find intriguing. Nicholas Fisk's *Grinny* (18) is presented by eleven year old Tim as extracts from his diary - with a consequent informality:

> *Jan. 14* Astonishing news! I had come back from Mac's house and
> had just been shouted at as usual by Mum (TAKE YOUR BOOTS
> OFF), when I heard . . . the station taxi . . .

The occupant of the taxi, who claims to be Great Aunt Emma, is in fact a visitor from another planet whose intentions are far from benign. She is the forerunner of a colonizing force, able to nullify the intelligence of adults and indifferent to her human victims.

More global issues have preoccupied writers who have extended the 'What if ... ?' to 'What will society be like if, one day in the future ... ?' Several authors have developed scenarios which confront their readers with a future earth suffering severe shortages of resources or the effects of a catastrophe. John Christopher's 'Prince-in-Waiting' trilogy (*19*) considers a world returned — apparently — to a medieval pattern after machines have wrought their carnage. In the same author's *Empty World* (*20*), Neil Miller is orphaned, then watches his grandparents die from a lethal virus which devastates the South of England. He sets off for London where he finally meets two survivors. This is a bleak fable for our times, far more convincing than those television series in which doughty bands of post-holocaust pioneers march towards a braver, cleaner world (or perhaps a more romantic, older world) where the wheel waits to be rediscovered. In Christopher's stories, questions are implicit about the way we live *now*. If we are stripped of polite convention, material comfort and legal restraints, are there any alternatives to greed, mistrust and despair?

Novels which pose such sombre questions are parallel to the Earthsea trilogy in their power to disturb and challenge and, like Le Guin's books, they are appropriate for the older readers in our age range. Younger readers will have found much that 'comforts and conforms' and much to be amused by in SF and fantasy set in 'our world with a difference', for the invitation to join in upsetting the natural order of things can be a ticket to the dimension of Non-Sense.

Roald Dahl's books are well-known examples; children who have enjoyed his swift humour will probably also enjoy Chris Powling's *The Mustang Machine* (*21*) about the exploits of an amazing riderless bike, recounted with the kind of irreverence and muscular junior school dialogue which reads aloud well to a whole class. Robert Leeson's Abu Salem (in *The Third Class Genie*) (*22*) is discovered living inside a beer-can near the railway arches. His rather uncertain competence brings his young discoverer, Alec, almost as many problems as solutions in his disaster-prone life. Marmalade Atkins's talking donkey, Rufus, (in Andrew Davies's *Marmalade and Rufus*) (*23*) whirls her off in his chauffeur-driven car on riotous expeditions to the El Poko night club where he does the occasional gig impersonating a man impersonating a talking donkey. Philip Curtis's Brain Sharpeners' series combines a school story with SF when, in *Mr Browser and The Brain Sharpeners* (*24*), Mr Browser's difficult class undergoes a transformation when their brains are sharpened by aliens looking for subjects to colonize a new planet.

Stories like these which enable their young readers to make ready connections between the secondary worlds of fantasy and SF and everyday environments are especially welcome, since readers with limited confidence and experience of stories often react with indifference or hostility to narratives requiring a trusting initial leap into space or the realms of high fantasy.

Teaching ideas   The derivation of 'fantasy' suggests literally 'a making visible' and our teaching of both SF and fantasy might well aim to allow young readers to see both the distant fictional worlds and their own circumstances more clearly. (Many of the teaching ideas we propose in Chapter 6 are applicable to SF and fantasy stories.)

1 Quests   Whether in space or over more solid terrain, quests can be charted — perhaps in the 'Here Be Dragons' kind of illustrated map. They lend themselves also to graphic work in friezes, board games, or tableaux and mime work reflecting episodes to be set alongside readings from the text.

2 Sword and sorcery   Although we wonder how much inventiveness is required of the participant in the D.I.Y. adventures (whether in book or computer program form), they do offer an interesting model. Having watched young 'dungeon masters' at work writing their own scenarios, we suggest that it is well worth encouraging able children to devise such games, based on models such as the Puffin Fighting Fantasy series. Children might use the plot of an existing story or, (perhaps freer), a ready-made environment such as the Earthsea Archipelago or Middle Earth, or a world of the children's own invention.

3 Points of entry   Examples of literary and personal 'points of entry' to imaginary worlds are collected from the class. Attention might be drawn to early picture books (*Where the Wild Things Are*), to *Alice* (rabbit holes and looking glasses) or the garden door in *Tom's Midnight Garden*. Some references with illustratioris to adults' fascination in this area could also be interesting (e.g. the Brontë family's worlds of Gondor and Angria). Some children may be able to ask their parents about childhood equivalents. This collection of 'points of entry' could be complete in itself or be developed through stories or drama.

4 Comic strip   Some of the most exciting SF and fantasy stories, especially for younger readers are very similar to comic strip stories in their emphasis upon rapid action (for example, Douglas Hill's Keill Randor series). Rather than trying to turn a whole story into a comic strip (a daunting task), readers might concentrate upon a large illustration for a single episode. The class might thus build up a wall display based on the book. Some models from SF and fantasy comics could be considered to show both graphic style and the arrangement and compression of 'speech balloons'.

5 What if ...?   Since suppositions initiate so many 'our world with a difference' stories, it seems worth while making stories (written, spoken, improvized) which start from a single hypothesis. Some ideas can be 'borrowed' from stories. For example, 'What if ... you shrank to be only 50 cms high? ... you could hear through brick walls? ... your television set showed tomorrow's news? ... your pet suddenly started talking? ... you could be in two places at once? ... you are allowed to travel, just once, for one hour only, to any period in the past or in the future?' If existing novels are used as the source of an idea, it can be valuable to do this kind of work *before* reading the book as a way of heightening interest in the text itself.

Recommended reading We have sub-divided titles into two sections which, broadly, reflect the progress from stories which 'comfort and conform' to those which 'challenge and disturb'. As we have argued, the experience of both kinds of stories seems to us valuable in the literary progress of the reader.

For 9–11

Philip Curtis *Mr Browser and the Brain Sharpeners* (Puffin)

Roald Dahl *Charlie and the Great Glass Elevator* (Puffin)

Andrew Davies *Marmalade and Rufus* (Grasshopper)

Brian Earnshaw *Dragonfall 5* (and sequels) (Magnet)

Florence P. Heide *The Shrinking of Treehorn* (Young Puffin)

Douglas Hill *Galactic Warlord* (and sequels) (Piccolo)

Ted Hughes *The Iron Man* (Faber)

Norton Juster *The Phantom Tollbooth* (Fontana Lions)

Robert Leeson *The Third Class Genie* (and sequel) (Fontana Lions, Collins Cascades)

Mary Rodgers *Freaky Friday* (and sequels) (Puffin, Collins Cascades)

E.B. White *Charlotte's Web* (Puffin, Macmillan M Books)

For 12–14

Natalie Babbitt *Tuck Everlasting* (Fontana Lions, Collins Cascades)

John Christopher *The Guardians* (Puffin, Heinemann New Windmill)
  The Prince in Waiting (Puffin, Collins Cascades)
  Empty World (Puffin, Heinemann New Windmill)

Peter Dickinson *The Weathermonger* (Puffin, Longman Pleasure in Reading)

Nicholas Fisk *Grinny* (Puffin, Collins Cascades)

Alan Garner *Elidor* (Fontana Lions, Macmillan M Books)

Monica Hughes *The Keeper of the Isis Light* (Magnet)

Penelope Lively *The Ghost of Thomas Kempe*
  (Piccolo, Heinemann New Windmill)

Ursula Le Guin *A Wizard of Earthsea* (and sequels) (Puffin, Heinemann New Windmill)

Robert C. O'Brien *Mrs Frisby and the Rats of NIMH*
  (Puffin, Heinemann New Windmill)
  Z for Zachariah (Fontana Lions, Heinemann New Windmill)

Philippa Pearce *Tom's Midnight Garden*
  (Puffin, Heinemann New Windmill)

John Rowe Townsend *The Islanders* (Puffin, Oxford Archway)

Classics Several of the older children's classics fall into these genres; they tend to defy classification by age-group. For example: *Alice in Wonderland, The Secret Garden, The Wind in the Willows, The Wizard of Oz,* and *The Hobbit.*

Short stories

Short stories are a boon to the literature teacher. In the busy school day, where the novel is intractable the short story is amenable. Even a story of about five thousand words is not too long to tax the stamina of the youngest listener or reasonably competent reader and offers the satisfaction of a whole fiction at one sitting.

For teachers, particularly those whose undergraduate English courses gave scant attention to the short story, this is an area where a reading programme can be enjoyable and realistically set up in much the same way as we suggested for poetry (p. 29). The aim should be to develop, perhaps with one or two colleagues, a personal anthology of stories for each age group. The bibliography on p. 59 is a place to start.

For children, it is important to recognize that short stories are not a substitute for novels but a supplement to their literary diet. There are advantages in short stories that are beyond the utilitarian considerations noted above and which focus upon the peculiar qualities of this literary form.

a) Variety An immediate bonus in sharing a selection of short stories with children is that they will rapidly gain a sense of the diversity of fiction. If, as we believe, a varied diet is important in helping children to become readers then short stories clearly offer the most practical way of introducing children to many different types of fiction in the shortest time. *Authors' Choice* (1), in which Kaye Webb collected favourite stories chosen by seventeen contemporary children's authors, illustrates the range of voices and styles that this genre adopts. Frank O'Connor's hilarious 'First Confession' rubs shoulders with Jane Austen's 'History of England', a piece of juvenilia written with all the artfulness and fun of an alert fourteen year old. The urban setting, straight talking and uncompromising realism of Bill Naughton's 'Spit Nolan' contrast sharply with the rural romanticism of the stories by Arthur Ransome and Rudyard Kipling. Such an anthology is a bag of sweets — a pick-and-mix selection of flavours, textures, shapes and sizes, perhaps not all to one's taste but mostly delicious in their different ways. Infinite variety is the hallmark of the genre; it is also one of the best ways to tempt the palates of potential readers.

b) Brevity The most obvious characteristic of the short story is its very brevity; but how long is short? Stephen Leacock's farcical 'My Financial Career' or several of Ernest Hemingway's laconic tales, for example, fill no more than two or three pages; E.M. Forster's 'The Machine Stops' or Scott Fitzgerald's 'A Diamond as Big as the Ritz' stretch to a five figure wordage. More important than the mere word count, however, is the use to which such brevity is put by the writer and what effect it provokes in the reader. Rather like the lyric poem, the length and delicacy of the short story (when compared with the novel) mean that it centres typically on the significant moment, the revelatory incident, the instant perception; and it aims to give significance to this particular focus. Often this will mean concentrating on the fortunes of a single character at a crucial juncture in his personal history, as William Golding does in 'Billy the Kid', or at a moment of crisis, as Maupassant does in 'A Vendetta', or at a time of challenge, as Doris Lessing does in 'Through The Tunnel'. All are stories to read to twelve year olds; each will have its sharply individual impact. Short stories lodge in the mind as complete entities where novels are harder to retain because of their spread, their inclusiveness. It is not simply that the reader's memory for the details of the novel is inadequate; but, more positively, that the short story often catches that which is intrinsically memorable — the intensity of a particular experience, the turning-point in a life, the odd combination of circumstances, the unusual string of events. Or again, a story may become memorable because it focusses on a place or an object that holds within itself the symbol of a way of life, as happens so powerfully in Alan Garner's 'The Stone Book'; or simply because it offers, as Roald Dahl's 'The Hitch-hiker' does, a tale of the unexpected.

c) Structure Another peculiarity of short stories, clearly related to their brevity, is that they offer an immediate sense of narrative structure. The three phase movement of fiction, of beginnings, middles and endings, is here stripped down to its essentials. It is not that such phases are necessary or invariably present in short stories. It is rather that short stories offer so many examples of this pattern — from the Rule of Three in shaggy dog stories or traditional tales of bears or goats gruff to the pattern of exposition, complication and resolution in more recent and sophisticated stories — that there would seem to be an aesthetic preference for it. Our expectation of simple structure modifies the nature of our process of response: where short stories are concerned we experience not so much 'the sense of an ending' as *'the sense of the whole'*. For when the reader starts on a story he knows it can be read in one 'go'; gratification may come within minutes. The pleasures and elements of response that we defined in relation to the novel (p. 13) are contracted and the process is speeded up. In particular, anticipation and retrospection may be quickened to the point of becoming what V. S. Pritchett calls an 'implicit intelligence test'. Picking up the clues to predict the ending is part of the pleasure; filling out the details of setting, character and the like is equally important, given that the author has space for a lightning sketch rather than an elaborate picture; responding to the single situation that the short story focusses upon may well mean that we put ourselves imaginatively into the tale more urgently than with the novel; and our evaluating of the plausibility and consistency of the plot is sharpened to such a point that an awkward sentence or inept word will puncture the credibility of the whole. The adjustments we feel in the elements of our response when we read a short story are a direct result of a form of narrative that prunes away and telescopes in order to achieve concentration within an enclosed space. This tight structure often produces one of the chief attractions of the short story — the 'twist in the tail'. It makes short stories eminently teachable, since predicting the ending on the basis of the story so far is considerably more interesting if you know there is likely to be a sudden, unexpected turn of events on the last page. Yet, whatever the pattern, the structure and brevity of the short story mean that the reader has a stronger sense than with a novel of being in control of the form. V.S. Pritchett catches what we have called this 'sense of the whole' in these remarks:

> A few minutes, an hour, a day, a few days are often given their
> indwelling value ... A portion of life has been isolated; it has not
> been lost in some large continuity. It is not the missing chapter of a
> novel but a thing standing on its own. It has the sustained,
> undispersed energy of the writer at the time. (2)

d) Narrative imagination   There is a rider to this point about narrative structure. If short stories offer children an immediately accessible sense of beginnings, middles and endings in a formal, literary mode, they also offer them the realization that stories in books are close to the stories they might hear at the meal table or on the bus. Short stories are primarily concerned with anecdote, that is, with a clearly defined event which can be handled and presented within a limited space. The wit of the delimited form is shared by the successful raconteur and the good short story writer. Granted we may have higher expectations from a written text — we look for the writer to do something with the anecdote, to distil from it implications and significance of a more general kind — nonetheless, the *narrative imagination* is common to both. The relationship between the way our thinking operates from moment to moment and narrative as a literary form is one that storytellers have long known. Isaac Bashevis Singer makes the point in *Naftali the Storyteller and his Horse, Sus:*

> When a day passes, it is no longer there. What remains of it?
> Nothing more than a story. If stories weren't told or books weren't
> written, man would live like the beasts, only for the day. ...
> What's life, after all? The future isn't here yet and you cannot
> foresee what it will bring. The present is only a moment and the past
> is one long story. Those who don't tell stories and don't hear stories
> live only for that moment, and that isn't enough. (3)

It is paradoxical that what appears to be the slightest and humblest form of fiction, often neglected in literature courses in higher education, should remind us most potently both of the essential nature of narrative and that stories — whether spoken or written — are the single most important element in the education of children.

e) Three stories   Three examples of the short story writer at work will illuminate what we have said about the variety, brevity, structure and narrative imagination characteristic of the form. 'The Stone Book' (4) is about seven thousand words long and, unless given support by prepared readings and imaginative activities, is probably best regarded as a story for committed readers to enjoy on their own. By contrast, 'The Hitch-hiker' (5), though only a little shorter, is ideal for reading aloud to a middle school class. 'First Confession' (6) is different again. It exists in two versions: a first person narrative told with great subtlety in *My Oedipus Complex and Other Stories*, which is the better one to use with fourteen year olds; and a third person account which is shorter and more accessible to ten year olds, anthologized in *Author's Choice* and *People and Diamonds, Book 3* (7). Either version is likely to provoke much amusement; and the teacher can choose whether to give children the pleasure of half-stifled chuckles during silent reading or to dust off his Irish accent and enjoy the laughter of the whole class.

The opening sentences of 'The Stone Book' arrest the reader's attention in a quiet, undramatic way. They are a fine example of precise, concrete language which, like that of poetry, aims to evoke rather than explain.

> A bottle of cold tea; bread and a half onion. That was Father's
> baggin. Mary emptied her apron of stones from the field and
> wrapped the baggin in a cloth.
> The hottest part of the day was on. Mother lay in bed under the
> rafters and the thatch, where the sun could send only blue light. She
> had picked stones in the field until she was too tired and had to rest.
> (p. 11)

In a few deft strokes we are given three main characters, the sense that this is to be Mary's story, the feel of hard, rural labour and of a way of life that is being looked at through the lens of history. The five objects of the first paragraph — a bottle, some bread, a half onion, some stones and a cloth — have the presence of a still life painting, except, of course, that they cannot be still since they are starting a story. There is movement in the text as Mary empties her apron and wraps the baggin; there is movement in the reader as this unusual word registers. The images, information and sense impressions of the second paragraph widen the focus but retain the same clarity. The alert reader is already drawn into a secondary world far distant from the primary one.

The action of 'The Stone Book' takes place on a single day and the three phases of the story are carried forward in some memorable symbolism. The exposition, focussing upon the relationship between Mary's aspirations and her father's craft as a stonemason, is conveyed through Mary's breath-taking climb up the church spire to deliver the baggin. Here she is, the baggin between her teeth, reaching the top:

> The spire narrowed. There were sides to it. She saw the shallow
> corners begin. Up and up. Tac, tac, tac, tac, above her head. The
> spire narrowed. Now she couldn't stop the blue sky from showing at
> the sides. Then land. Far away.
> Mary felt her hands close on the·rungs, and her wrists go stiff.
> Tac, tac, tac, tac. She climbed to the hammer. The spire was

thin. Father was not working, but giving her a rhythm. The sky was
now inside the ladder. The ladder was broader than the spire. (p. 18)

Mary's awareness of her own family history and possible futures is apparent
both before the climb (p. 15) and as her father spins her on the weathercock
(pp 22–24). The story is explicit that this is to be a memorable day: as her
father lifts her down from the weathercock he says:

'You'll remember this day, my girl. For the rest of your life.'
'I already have,' said Mary. (p. 24)

The development of the story is then immediately signalled in Mary's desire
to read. A second archetypal image of human journeying and progress, this
time through the labyrinth of caves and tunnels under Glaze Hill from which
the stonemason quarries his materials, invests this desire with a greater
significance than that of Mary simply wanting a prayer-book like those of her
friends. Her subterranean quest for knowledge intensifies the action as she
threads her way under the hill, unwinding the silk behind her; and the vivid
images of the bull, the hand and her father's mason mark drawn on the rock
wall are both memorable in themselves and evocative of the lesson that Mary
learns about the continuity of her family's history. The resolution of the story
is embodied in the stone book that Mary's father makes for her. This gift
is much richer than a book made of paper which has but one story to tell:

And Mary sat by the fire and read the stone book that had in it all the
stories of the world and the flowers of the flood. (p. 61)

'The Stone Book' has the sense of wholeness and well-wrought form; its
story is told quietly and intensely; Mary's experience has a generality that lifts
it far beyond the merely anecdotal; and yet it is the 'indwelling value' of this
single day in Mary's life in 1864 that remains with the reader after 'The Stone
Book' has been closed.

In 'The Hitch-hiker' the reader is led by the nose. The situation could not
be simpler: a writer driving to London in a brand new car picks up a hitch-
hiker who urges him to see if the car will do the 129 m.p.h. its makers boast
for it. The car is stopped for speeding, the driver booked and, during the rest
of the slow-motion journey to London, we focus upon the speed of the
passenger's fingers as he demonstrates his skill as a pickpocket, or finger-
smith as he prefers to be called. The *coup de grâce* is when this master craftsman reveals on the last page that he has picked the policeman's pockets of the
two note-books in which their names and all the details of the offence had
been recorded.

The cleverness of the story is in the way Roald Dahl places the reader in
the course of the telling. Through the first person narrative we may relate
easily to the driver, sharing the enjoyment of his new toy, empathizing with
his generosity to the hitch-hiker, feeling apprehension and exhilaration when
he puts his foot down, and guilt by association when he is caught. While the

reader is swept along by the speed of events in the opening few pages, he also shares the driver's curiosity about the identity of the hitch-hiker and, in particular, about his job. The development of the story concentrates first, upon the booking, in order to set up the ending and, secondly, upon the slow, teasing, revelation of the hitch-hiker's skills. With such dexterity, pickpocketing is elevated into art or magic and we need to believe this if the ending is to work. For it is a measure of Dahl's skill that he inveigles us on the the side of the pickpocket so that we are delighted that the elegant, skilful fingers have defeated the gloating ponderousness of the law and happily acquiesce in the criminal act of burning the evidence of the books at the end. Equally cheerfully, we overlook the implausibility of even these fingers being able to reach through a car window, unbutton two breast pockets, remove the books and rebutton the pockets all while being questioned by a police-man! Thus Dahl exploits the reader's suspension of disbelief and the reader has the feeling that a joke has been played upon him. We are left in the posi-tion of the writer in the story, namely, that the writer of the story — like the pickpocket — has used us as a means to exercise his technical skills. We may feel a bit manipulated in the process but we cannot help admiring and enjoying the way the deception is pulled off.

In Frank O'Connor's story all the terrors of childhood fall upon the slight shoulders of a small boy, Jackie, as he prepares to make his first confession. Into this single event O'Connor has concentrated many of the potent elements of childhood and blended a solemn subject with a farcical wit to make one of the most entertaining short stories that we know. In fewer than three thousand words, in the shorter version, Jackie is dragged to church by his elder sister, attempts to make his confession while — for perfectly plausible reasons — hanging upside down in the box, catapults out of the box into the aisle when the strain becomes too great, confesses his plan to dismember his grandmother to a most understanding priest and, finally, emerges triumphant from church with a mere three Hail Marys and a bag of bull's-eyes.

The ingredients that make this incident memorable and significant, apart from the humour with which the tale is told, all reflect the child's view of the world. It is a story that looks at life from knee-height yet avoids being either patronizing or sentimental. The elements of childhood that Jackie's experi-ence so amusingly dramatizes and illuminates are the need for appropriate behaviour, particularly in social rituals such as church-going; the need to sort out truth from falsehood in the advice, explanations and actions of older children; the need to exorcize the nameless terrors of the imagination and the destructive feelings towards nearest and dearest; and the need to come to terms with personal failures and successes. All this may sound rather serious for what is, after all, a very funny story; but its appeal is not only in the humour but also in O'Connor's sharp eye for the details of the children's reactions to each other and to the adult world around them. Amongst other things, this is what makes the two versions of the story so interesting, for they represent decisions on the author's part about the narrating voice to use and its place within or at a distance from events. This leaves a decision for the teacher, too.

What characteristics do these three very different examples have in common? In its own way each story shows the three related qualities which typify the genre: first, a short story makes a single impression on the reader; secondly, it does so by concentrating on a crisis; and thirdly, it makes this crisis pivotal in a controlled plot (8). It would be foolish to insist on too precise a definition of these traits, given the varieties of fiction, but collectively they do indicate the overriding strength of the short story form: it puts all its energies into one direction.

Teaching ideas   The best thing to do with short stories is to read them. Work on short stories can easily become 'top-heavy' and the enjoyment of the story lost. It can be entertaining (and focussing) if the reading of a short story is interrupted (very briefly) whilst the class speculate about how it will end. The activities below may help children to be responsive to the *form* of the short story, often by engaging in telling or writing stories themselves.

1 Bags of sweets   Children make up their own class/group selection. Unless the children have read a great number of short stories, this will probably work best as a class anthology with a purpose such as helping the teacher collect together their most enjoyed stories to use with next year's class or as an exchange with a parallel class (not necessarily in the same school).

2 Telling tales   Children are provided with a basic structure (see our discussion of the Rule of Three on p. 53) and try to fit a story they know (from local or family sources, perhaps) into that pattern. They practise telling that story in pairs or small groups (possibly with the use of a tape recorder). It may be feasible to work towards a class anthology or to select a few stories for an all-class 'story-time'.

3 The most ...   As a way of appreciating how a short story writer often works from a single incident or character (see pp 52–53), children select some *extreme* moment or very memorable person known to them (e.g. the most important 60 seconds of my life, a place I'll never forget, the most surprising person I've known, the worst/best present I've ever had, the coldest/hottest I've ever been). They use this material to shape a story to be told to a particular audience — a real or imagined person/group, two or three years younger than themselves.

4 How did it all begin?   A group talks about surprises they've read about, heard about or experienced. From this, they devise the *last* paragraph of a short story (word and time limits may help). These endings are then exchanged with another pair/group who decide what has preceded this ending.

5 It's obviously a ...   Groups are provided with objects about which to tell a story. There are numerous ways of using objects; for example, they could be items brought back by the children (who are star-ship captains) from other planets, where the objects are very important — the captains make their reports to each other; they could be exhibits in an 'Antique Show' on television where the pupil-experts pronounce upon their histories; or, three objects could be integral to a story. What has interested us is the fluency often generated when children tell stories whilst physically handling an object — partly because they concentrate on that and not on an inhibiting audience, but also there is an inventiveness that seems to be released through the tactile contact itself.

Recommended reading

For 9–11

Alan Coren   The 'Arthur' series   (Puffin)
Sara and Stephen Corrin (eds.)   *Stories for Nine-Year Olds*
  Stories for Tens and Overs   (Puffin)
Richmal Crompton   *Just William* stories   (Macmillan)
Marcus Crouch (ed.)   *The Whole World Storybook*   (O.U.P.★)
Judith Elkin (ed.)   *The New Golden Land Anthology*   (Puffin)
David Jackson and Dennis Pepper (eds.)   The 'Storyhouse' series, especially
  'Orange', 'Yellow', and 'Red'   (cassettes also available)   (O.U.P.)
Rudyard Kipling   *Just So Stories*   (Piccolo, Macmillan M Books)
Philippa Pearce   *What the Neighbours Did*
  (Puffin, Longman Pleasure in Reading)
Chris Powling   *Daredevils or Scaredycats*   (Fontana Lions)
Paul Theroux   *A Christmas Card   London Snow*   (Puffin)

For 12–14

Joan Aiken   *A Harp of Fishbones and Other Stories*   (Puffin)
Douglas Barnes (ed.)   *Short Stories of Our Time*   (Harrap)
Graham Barratt and Michael Morpurgo (eds)   *The Story-Teller*
  (Ward Lock)
Steve Bowles   *Jamie*   (Fontana Lions)
Aidan Chambers (ed.)   *Haunted Houses*   (Piccolo)
Robin Chambers   *The Ice Warrior and Other Stories*   (Puffin)
Roald Dahl   *The Wonderful Story of Henry Sugar*
  (Puffin Plus, Heinemann New Windmill)
Farrukh Dhondy   *Come To Mecca*   (Fontana Lions, Collins Cascades)
  East End At Your Feet   (Macmillan Topliner)
John L. Foster (ed.)   *Gangs and Victims*   (Nelson Getaway)
Alan Garner   *The Stone Book Quartet*   (Fontana Lions)
Alfred Hitchcock (ed.)   *Ghostly Gallery*   (Puffin)
George Layton   *The Fib and Other Stories*   (Fontana Lions)
Michael Marland (ed.)   *First Choice*   (Longman Pleasure in Reading)
Bill Naughton   *The Goalkeeper's Revenge*
  (Puffin, Heinemann New Windmill)
Philippa Pearce   *The Shadow Cage*   (Puffin, Macmillan M Books)

★indicates hardback edition

Dennis Pepper (ed.)   *Ends and Escapes*   (Nelson Getaway)
Edgar Allen Poe   *Tales of Mystery and Imagination*   (numerous editions)
Eric Williams (ed.)   *Great Escape Stories*   (Puffin)

Growing up through stories

What are adolescents looking for in fiction?   Much will depend on how
active they are as readers: how skilled they have become in anticipating,
retrospecting and picturing as they move through a story; how receptive they
are of variety and subtlety of form; whether or not they are able to respond to
complex narrative structures or to the voice of a writer saying more than
appears on the surface of a story. Much will also depend on who they are
themselves during what can be a turbulent phase of experience; on what
qualities of personality and range of experiences they bring to the text. We
shall develop this last point, since it is here that the adolescent reader seems
most open to exploitation.

As secondary teachers notice every day, adolescence is a time when a
circle of relationships is expanding, often to include both sexes. It seems
particularly crucial to be accepted by your community of peers. At the same
time, a sense of individuality is emerging more distinctly. Whilst new and
exciting independent experiences become possible, or at least desired, there is
often a need to reach back to touch an older security which some have been
able to find in family relationships. Some adolescents begin also to recognize
the shifting frailties and strengths of the adults they know — if we are lucky,
they may tolerate and even come to value both qualities. There is often a
growing recognition of moral, social and — for a number — political
ambiguities and an awareness of the need to make choices. There may be a
recurring anxiety about who they are to become in the contracting world of
work, and the realization that it may not be possible to retrace false steps
taken in the next few years. Often such disturbances are painful and over-
whelming, prompting adolescents to rebel against the adults who, from their
perspective, constrict their freedoms; or to opt out of anything that seems —
and may well be — irrelevant to their purposes. (Reading itself may be a
permanent or temporary casualty here; we return to this specific problem on
pp 94–100.)

In short, early teenage readers might hope to meet experiences comparable with their own at a time when life is often confusingly charged with
excitement and tedium, pleasure and threat. They might hope for a preview
of possibilities which their own expanding worlds seem likely to present.
They may also gain a glimpse of people, places and experiences they are unlikely to encounter at first hand. They might find clarification of their own
relationships through insights into fictional characters — whether adolescents
or adults. They might also seek distractions from their own primary world
which may seem — and be — frustratingly problematic or limiting.

Committed readers may not find too many difficulties if they are lucky enough to have on hand respected teachers, librarians or parents who know both the readers and the literature. Even then, there can be phases when adolescents become preoccupied with fresh concerns and reading stops for quite lengthy periods. Such readers, when they are ready, often choose to move on to books written without any specific age group of readers in mind, as well as books published on lists for young people.

Practised readers tend to have already well-developed personal styles, and generalizations about what will appeal to them are unreliable. Both girls and boys incline towards novelists who offer a strong narrative line with characters facing clear-cut decisions; we have included a list of authors often enjoyed by readers moving on to adult literature on p. 68 (List A). Tentatively, we suggest that, if it is possible to generalize about the tastes of the sexes, girls may well prefer novels where there is an emphasis on the development of character, whilst boys continue to be most interested in what characters actually do; this interest in action often leads boys to turn away from fiction to reading about hobbies, sports and accounts of exploration or military daring.

Able readers need their literary roughage too. They may find it in a range of comic-books, romantic novels, sexual adventures or tales of the occult and horror. Some of these books will seem worthless, even pernicious, to teachers; but it is arrogant to ignore them and counter-productive to condemn them. If time and trust allow, it is best to be attentive where adolescents clearly want to talk about them; and to offer recommendations within a genre if possible.

What is on offer?   In recent years, publishers have worked hard to define and satisfy a market of readers not yet interested in substantial adult fiction. Following the evident success of American books for 'Young Adults', several publishers in Britain have produced their own lists, often including many American titles, with the early adolescent reader specifically in mind. Penguin have found a successful balance in their Puffin Plus series; and Collins's Fontana Lions have perhaps the surest feel for this market among paperback publishers. Among hard back publishers, Bodley Head (with their 'New Adult' series) Gollancz and Oxford are the three for teachers to watch most closely.

One particular assumption about potential readers seems to have shaped publishing policy: that teenagers want to read about teenage characters in contemporary settings in the belief that they could thus bring their own lives readily into interaction with the text. It may well be that this line of thought has been accepted too easily. Adolescents, whatever their reading ability, may want to spend much of their reading time, if they read at all, exploring what it is like to be an adult rather than in confirming what they already know, perhaps all too well.

Many of the authors choose to write about characters who face a problem, or who are alienated in some way from the cultural or social mainstream. The difficulties range from feeling separate from one's peers because of a physical disability or personal gaucheness to feeling isolated for reasons of social class or ethnic origin. The emphasis upon alienation is not altogether new. It was to be found, for example, in the stories of the D.C. Thomson comics, *Rover, Hotspur, Wizard* and *Adventure* along with their prewar stable companion, *Skipper* — all avidly read by children of widely differing social and intellectual backgrounds. Here in weekly episodes, each three or four thousand words long, sustained over several months, one might revel in the exploits of 'Alf Tupper, the Tough of the Track', a working-class athlete sleeping rough under the railway arches, training on fish and chips and regularly defeating more privileged, but less sporting, opponents; or 'Smith of the Lower Third', whose eponymous hero had won a scholarship from South Street Central School, Ironboro', to Lipstone, one of the most distinguished public schools in the land. But if the theme of alienation was similar, the treatment of it was not. The comic story writers dwelled less earnestly on the problems and retained a kind of cheerful optimism that all would eventually turn out well. Whilst it is true that they never flinched from the improbable, and their attitudes sometimes seem dated and even distasteful to us now, they did write lively and well-crafted stories. It could be argued that Thomson's decision to turn to pictures in their comics in the fifties, coinciding with the rival attractions of widespread television, left a vacuum in printed stories for the whole ability range of early adolescent readers which has never been filled. Each weekly issue of a Thomson comic contained fifteen to twenty thousand words, and many children read three or four comics a week.

Contemporary lists reflect a more anxious era. Writers for the age group now are very specific about the problems of their young heroes and heroines, whose lives are rooted in the real world; or in some cases, as we shall presently see, in a glamourized version of the real world. Paul Zindel's *The Pigman* (1968) (1) is sometimes regarded as the first of the genre, though Salinger's *The Catcher in the Rye* (1951) (2) is perhaps the real progenitor. *The Pigman* charts the relationship of a boy and a girl with an elderly recluse and ends with the old man's death. In this and subsequent Zindel novels, young characters rarely have enough personal security to exercise cheerful commonsense. His stories are almost without adults who can talk, or simply *be*, with their kids. In the end, Zindel's young characters seem to come to a clearer sense only of their own impotence.

American authors have usually been more exploratory than British writers in probing sexual and social issues. In *Forever*, (1975) (3), Judy Blume, whose popularity is world-wide, is usually hailed as the first writer to get sexual intercourse onto the pages of a book published on young people's lists. Robert Cormier's *The Chocolate War* (1975) (4) is a relentless account of physical and psychological bullying in a High School. Alice Childress's thirteen year old Benjie in *A Hero Ain't Nothing but a Sandwich* (1973) (5) is well on the road to being destroyed by heroin pushed on the streets of Harlem. Rosa Guy has treated lesbian relationships with a dignity and sensitivity which must have increased the understanding of many of her readers. These explorations have not been without adult complaint. Judy Blume, for example, is under regular fire in the States and sometimes in the U.K. Parental objections have led to several of her books being removed from the shelves of school and community libraries.

These American stories — and many others — have been widely read in British schools, especially by those sometimes described as 'reluctant readers'. British teachers have also turned to America in the absence of a body of British books with black people in central roles: for example, the novels of Virginia Hamilton, Mildred Taylor and Rosa Guy.

American novels are often characterized by a raciness of language, a sense of the sometimes dangerous excitement of being a teenager and are set in a separate teenage culture which adults do not understand, whether of the street or affluent suburbia. Presumably, British readers were in part acclimatized to a different culture through the television version of the States; or the attractions of the stories may have lain in their very remoteness. One of the most frequent and puzzling comments from British readers of these books in the early seventies was 'these people talk like we do', which was palpably not the case. What they may have meant was that the characters did not speak, think or behave like most of the people in the books they were usually given to read.

In Britain in the early sixties, John Rowe Townsend ventured away from the polite middle-class family adventure into the working class environment of *Gumble's Yard* (1961) (6). His later *Goodnight, Prof., Love* (1970) and *The Summer People* (1972) are sensitive explorations of mid-teen relationships whilst his *Noah's Castle* (1975) (7) invites consideration of social and political questions in a bleak Britain of the near future. Joan Lingard in her 'Kevin and Sadie' books examined relationships which crossed barricades between religions in Northern Ireland, as did Peter Carter in *Under Goliath*(8). At last, by the start of the eighties, there were several British novelists whose work had much to offer to the young adolescent. Later in this section we shall consider two novels (Rukshana Smith's *Sumitra's Story* (9) and Robert Leeson's *It's My Life* (10)) which are distinctively British both in tone and content; and we have included a selection of titles to serve as an introduction to recent work in this field in List B on p. 69.

Good and bad books Books for young adolescents are no more immune from 'admass' than records, television or clothes. The commercial channelling of children's tastes starts before they even begin at school, but it is nowhere more skilfully engineered than in the early years of secondary education. Peer group conformism exploited by commercial interests produces, in the words of Raymond Williams, a 'culture of the disinherited' — one that has not grown from roots in a particular, living community but has been manufactured by the electronic media. It is easy to see this exploitation in television programmes or pop music; as economic pressure on the publishing world becomes more severe year by year, it is apparent in the stories produced for young adolescents.

The outward manifestation of this pressure is in the way books are marketed. The specialist bookshop has now to contend with the high street stores — not only W.H. Smiths, but Marks and Spencers, Woolworths, Boots and Sainsburys. This development is obviously not malign in itself. The day when a youngster can slip a Tesco 'own brand' Roald Dahl Reader into the family trolley during the weekly shopping expedition may not be far away. Yet, when books are marketed as commercially as beefburgers, there is the risk that what will sell — swiftly and in very large numbers — is what gets published. The recipe fictions take over, offering blatant tastes to satisfy adolescent appetites — a kind of literary fast food. Plots may seem to depend upon combining shoplifting, rape and acne with racial tension and pre-marital intercourse, preferably involving a biker. The very titles — *I Think I'm Having a Baby, You Would if You Loved Me* — suggest the flavour.

The inner manifestation of the exploitation of the adolescent reader is another kind of soft sell; it lies in the content of the stories themselves. Consider the appetiser proffered on the inside cover to the potential reader of *Bad Apple* by Larry Bograd (*11*):

> Fifteen year old Nicky has never had it easy. He lives in a run–down apartment in New York with his parents and his crazy Uncle Eli. Bored both at home and at school, he becomes drawn unthinkingly into crime, almost as an extension of his lifestyle. Drugs, junk food, easy sex and the total aimlessness of his life, all lead him inexorably to commit an act of senseless violence that has devasting consequences.
>
> In this chilling and thought-provoking novel, Larry Bograd describes one teenager's struggle to exist in a world that seems out of control . . . and is.

'Fifteen year old Nicky' is the narrator of the story, and the book ends with him in detention awaiting trial for the shooting of an elderly couple in a robbery. Nicky is virtually a psychopath. After he has shot his victims, he tells us:

> I haven't felt this good in a long while. And, funny, I feel nothing. I look at the back of my hands — they're shaking — and I start to laugh as the air lifts them easily above my head. Prune grabs me just before I can rise into the sky. For the moment, I feel free and fancy.
> (p. 131)

There is no overt authorial comment made upon the narrator's actions or attitude. There cannot be, since events are seen through Nicky's eyes. He greets his lawyer thus: 'You can get me out of here. I don't belong here. I didn't do anything wrong. It wasn't my fault.' He revels in the attention paid to him by the media. Bograd is playing a precarious game. Perhaps his readers are implicitly invited to make their own judgement upon his repugnant hero, but it may well be that his life's-a-load-of-crap-so-why-give-a-damn attitude has a meretricious appeal to young readers. Such an attitude offers an easy way out from a morally confusing and economically hostile world. To be less severe, a young reader's personal circumstances might indeed be so bleak that Nicky's plaintive stance has its own kind of reasonableness. Such a book may do little more than confirm its readers' belief that things just aren't worth the effort — it invites an easy acceptance of life's impossibility. Consciously or not, Bograd may be exploiting the susceptibilities of his adolescent readers.

Bad Apple has been very precisely matched in Europe by Olivier Beer's prize-winning novel, *Le Chant des Enfants Morts*, published in the United Kingdom as *Pas de Deux* (12). It is a Bonny and Clyde story in French dress. Francois and Isabelle meet at an exam, which they fail. Life offers nothing, so they embark on a career of burglary which culminates in several murders, a pursuit and a shoot-out with the police. The publishers claim on the fly-leaf that 'the violence is redeemed by innocence, and in particular by Francois' anguish and compassion'. The first part of this defence is at best inscrutable and, as for the second, Francois' anguish and compassion extend no further than himself and his deeply dislikeable girlfriend. Marcel Marceau, who broke silence to recommend this novel, is quoted on the front cover — 'I read this beautiful thrilling novel through the night. A book that made me see the new generation'. A bleak prospect.

The worlds of these novels do not allow the reader to engage in what we called in Chapter 1 the activity of 'interacting' any more than the worlds of a Travails-of-Tracey style of photo-story or the comic-book strip of Sergeant Rock Granite v. the Panzer Division, Round 28. You cannot bring your real life into play with texts which ignore the intractable, jagged nature of actual experience and caricature the difficulties of being young; what you do probably bring into play are tendencies to self-centredness and self-dramatization which ignore the feelings and needs of others. In Ursula Le Guin's words 'to praise despair is to condemn delight, to embrace violence is to lose hold of everything else'.

It would be naïve to deny that many early adolescents are encountering some demanding circumstances for the first time, though as teachers well know, blackmail, protection rackets, theft, racial victimization and glue sniffing are hardly unknown in junior schools. Most classes include children desperately anxious about relationships within their own families and with some of their peers. In principle, then, it is entirely valuable that writers have not avoided the problematic. What is culpable, however, is the stance of a writer who seems to be drawing young readers into a kind of conspiratorial relationship. The underlying suggestion is that he, the writer, knows what hell it is to be young even though other adults, particularly teachers and parents, do not. In such stories, teenagers themselves tend to be romanticized and their difficulties exaggerated or distorted. As a consequence, solutions to problems are often glib. Adults are almost always seen as fossilized, no longer capable of growth, often authoritarian or ridiculous. There is usually an absence of the kind of humour which reminds us at least of our humanity and our capacity to confront difficulties. In the last analysis the criticism of this kind of book is that in terms of plot and character, the writer is pandering to an adolescent's inclination to self-absorption.

If our point concerning exploitation of adolescent readers has validity, we need to have some means of deciding which books to offer to young adolescents — books which provide genuine possibilities for 'growing up through stories'. The checklist below is not concerned with a broad range of literary qualities; it is a means of deciding if a book, in our sense, exploits its readers. These questions may be useful:

☆ Is the relationship the author extends to the reader little more than a kind of knowing wink — an invitation to a conspiracy against a harsh, uncaring world? This seems to us a kind of condescension and, ultimately, a betrayal.

☆ Is the counsel of the book one of despair? Books such as Golding's *Lord of the Flies* or Cormier's *The Chocolate War*, for example, may adopt a pessimistic view of human nature, but in our experience they do not leave readers feeling that it is worthless to combat difficulties, or evil itself, with as much strength as possible. We cannot see any value in offering young readers books which are nihilistic.

☆ Is the book essentially a problem with a story grafted on to it — a kind of novelization of a magazine agony column? For example, if violence or racial tension are involved in the story, is their treatment gratuitous or integral to the novel?

☆ If readers bring their own experiences into play with the text, will they find clichés of plot and character or events and people with which they can readily engage?

☆ Is there the possibility that the book will expand or open some area of understanding — concerning character, place or social, moral and political circumstances?

☆ Are the adults in the story two-dimensional, devoid of any sympathy towards teenagers and incapable of growth themselves?

☆ Is the dialogue synthetic? For example, does it tend towards the frenetic zaniness of some teenage magazines?

Two books worth reading   We turn now to two novels which seem to us to offer young readers many satisfactions: Rukshana Smith's *Sumitra's Story* and Robert Leeson's *It's My Life*.

Sumitra's Story describes the fortunes of a Ugandan Asian family compelled to come to Britain by the policies of Idi Amin. Sumitra is the oldest of four daughters. The values which her parents had based their family life upon in Uganda conflict with those of their new country. In Africa, her father had been the prosperous owner of a shop selling electrical goods; in London, with no English at his command, he works in a factory making components; he feels constantly belittled, and becomes sullen and depressed. Sumitra settles in to her new life more readily than her parents, but finds herself constantly caught between the cultures of home and school. Her Saturday job confirms the self she has discovered in England:

On Saturdays Sumitra became Sue, in swinging skirts and bright
blouses, with a tailored jacket tossed casually over her shoulders. She
wore her hair loose, hanging down her back. From nine to five Sue
was liberated, smart and cheeky, like the other girls at work. Sue
was part of the adult world, responsible for running the office while
the rest of the staff served in the shop. (p. 113)

The issues of loyalty to parents, of racism, of a woman's control over her
own life are integral to the plot — they develop from the interaction of
characters in a contemporary circumstance. Sumitra is eventually forced to
face a choice of one life or the other. The decision is complex:

'It's not only my parents,' insisted Sumitra, wondering if
Gwynneth really did understand. 'You see, it's my sisters too. There
are three of them — my parents would never allow me to leave
home, which means that if I do leave I'll have to run away — and I
might ruin my sisters' lives by doing so. You don't know what some
Indian parents are like. My sisters may never marry because I've
disgraced the family name.' (p. 156)

Her confusion is all the greater since she is sympathetically conscious of the
diminution of her parents; her father's loss of identity and the bewilderment
of her mother.

There is no suggestion of condescension towards the reader; things are
not distorted to romanticize Sumitra's situation; there are points of entry for
readers of any culture and both sexes. Asian readers may identify more easily
with the challenges faced by Sumitra and her need to find a solution to the
dilemmas posed by different value systems. For the majority of young
readers the story gives particular insights into the ways of thinking and
feeling of people whom they may otherwise meet only superficially or
through the distorting sensationalism of the media. There are white pupils —
and teachers and librarians — who initially reject novels by or about blacks
and Asians on the grounds that these stories are 'not relevant to us', an
objection never raised against *I am David*, *The Silver Sword*, *Tom Sawyer* or
the American settings of many popular titles. *Sumitra's Story* is primarily
worth reading because it is a well-written novel; it also offers the possibility
of helping its readers make more sense of the world in which they live.

Robert Leeson's *It's My Life* is also about a girl. Jan finds herself caught in
a domestic trap. Her mother suddenly leaves home. Her father cannot cope
on his own account and he certainly cannot manage to look after Jan's young
brother, Kev. Eventually, Jan comes to understand just why her mother left
home and that 'what had happened to Mum was what really mattered.
Because that had everything to do with what was going to happen to Jan'.

Like so many novels for adolescents, *It's My Life* is concerned with
acquiring self-knowledge. What distinguishes it from 'recipe fiction' is
Leeson's uncompromising account of a domestic breakdown; it is a mess,

with no easy answers. Understanding both her parents is Jan's principal route towards adulthood. She learns also through her dealings with Kev, her grandparents and her boyfriend. Peter is neither a young god nor a devil — he's a boy not quite able to catch up with events, and Jan's recognition that someone she has fallen for has clay feet contributes to her ability to take responsibility for her own life. Through her father, Peter and Kev, Jan is recognizing what it is to be the prisoner of male dependence and male possessiveness. Readers can trust Leeson because he is faithful to the ambiguous nature of experience. A single incident does not lead to a cascade of scales falling from the eyes. Jan learns through accretion and erosion — the way people do learn in this kind of circumstance.

The book involves fundamental questions about being a father; about the alternatives facing a woman trapped in a claustrophobic marriage; about how other people's expectations may shape our behaviour; about social and regional stereo-typing (for 'Northerness' is important in the book); and the hypothesis that 'blokes were always looking out at things, girls were always looking in at themselves' (p. 62).

Of course, that is not the whole story. Leeson has also a keen eye and ear for the comic, tells his story with compelling pace, catches dialogue convincingly and creates a Northern town where you can smell the wind off the moors.

Recommended reading

List A Many able early adolescent readers are ready for novels published on adult lists. They may reach back for an Enid Blyton one day, and forward to Charlotte Brontë the next. We thought it would be useful to provide a short list of authors whose work has given pleasure to such readers. We note only *one* work by each writer, as a possible aid to selection for class libraries. Some titles are selected with only the most accomplished readers in mind; such children can sometimes be left marking time and so tend to lose interest in reading altogether.

Stan Barstow   *Joby*   (Heinemann New Windmill)
Pierre Boulle   *The Bridge on the River Kwai*
                      (Fontana, Heinemann New Windmill)
Ray Bradbury   *Fahrenheit 451*   (Granada)
Charlotte Brontë   *Jane Eyre*   (Various Editions)
Margaret Craven   *I Heard the Owl Call My Name*
                      (Picador, Heinemann New Windmill)
Daphne du Maurier   *Jamaica Inn*   (Pan)
C.S. Forester   *The African Queen* (Penguin)
Ernest Hemingway   *The Old Man and the Sea*
                      (Granada, Heinemann New Windmill)
Jack London   *The Call of the Wild*
                      (Penguin, Heinemann New Windmill)
George Orwell   *Animal Farm* (Penguin, Heinemann New Windmill)

Jack Schaeffer   *Shane*   (Methuen, Heinemann New Windmill)
John Steinbeck   *The Red Pony*   (Piccolo, Heinemann New Windmill)
J.R.R. Tolkien   *The Lord of the Rings*   (Allen and Unwin)
P.G. Wodehouse   *Carry On, Jeeves!*   (Penguin)
John Wyndham   *The Day of the Triffids*   (Penguin)

List B   We offer here a selection for the teacher unfamiliar with recent books published specifically for the early adolescent reader — the kind of fiction we have touched upon in pages 61 to 63. We have not repeated titles mentioned in the body of this section and have tried to choose books of quality comparable to *Sumitra's Story* and *It's My Life*. Most of the books are worth consideration as all-class readers.

Bernard Ashley   *Break in the Sun*   (Puffin, Oxford Archway)
Judy Blume   *Tiger Eyes*   (Piccolo, Heinemann New Windmill)
John Branfield   *The Fox In Winter*   (Fontana Lions, Collins Cascades)
Peter Carter   *Under Goliath*   (Puffin)
Gerald Cole   *Gregory's Girl*   (Fontana Lions, Collins Cascades)
Rosa Guy   *The Friends*   (Puffin, Macmillan M Books)
Tim Kennemore   *The Fortunate Few*   (Puffin Plus, Collins Cascades)
Julius Lester   *Basketball Game*   (Puffin Plus)
K.M. Peyton   *A Midsummer Night's Death* (Puffin Plus,
            Oxford Archway)
Moreton Rhue   *The Wave*   (Puffin Plus)
James Watson   *Talking in Whispers*   (Fontana Lions)

Chapter 4

Pictures and poems

Picture books

Infants have picture books as a crucial element in coming·to terms with reading; adults have books of pictures in which photographs, paintings and illustrations may well be more important than words. In between, in the earnest world of school, picture books are given scant regard, children's visual education goes underground into comics and sideways into television, and the developing reader is consigned largely to the medium of print by his well-meaning teachers.

The idea that picture books are 'babyish' has become outdated since the success of *Asterix*, *Tintin* and the books of Raymond Briggs; the indications are that picture books can be exploited more fully than at present with older children. In an excellent guide to picture books for the 9–13 age range, Elaine Moss (1) stresses four points fundamental to the successful use of such books. First, the teacher should know them and enjoy them himself. Secondly, the books should be available in sufficient quantity in the classroom or library to enable choices to be made and for the format to be familiar. Thirdly, if the books are in the school library, there should be a separate location and identifying mark for picture books for older pupils: 'a top shelf close to the novels is the best place'. Finally, picture books are a 'great unifier in mixed ability classes' — a point that indicates one of their main teaching virtues in that the combination of visual and narrative appeal allows children of different abilities to enter the stories in their own way and at their own level.

The modern picture book originates in the last third of the nineteenth century with Walter Crane, Randolph Caldecott and Kate Greenaway who were followed a little later by Beatrix Potter and Arthur Rackham. It is worth reminding ourselves of their pictures and stories not least because their work maintains its appeal and continues to appear in modern editions. The definition of what constitutes a picture book, even among these five, is a variable one. We take it to mean a book in which the art work is more than illustration and has, at least, a role equal to that of text. A minority of picture books are wordless, two of the best examples being Raymond Briggs's *The Snowman* (2) and Shirley Hughes's *Up and Up* (3), but most are made in the mixed medium and the best are often created by the single imagination of an author/artist. Reading a picture story, with or without words, is a subtly engaging process which has certain similarities to the fiction reading discussed in Chapter 1; for, though a single picture offers the reader the aesthetic experience of colour, line and shape just as a painting does, it is also part of a narrative sequence. The spatial and temporal dimensions of the picture story are thus tantalizingly interfused in our responses. The phenomenon is not unknown in painting, especially where the artist had an educational purpose. Hence, whether as adults reading one of Hogarth's anecdotal series, *The Rake's Progress* or *Marriage à la Mode*, or as children reading, say, the Ahlbergs' *Each Peach Pear Plum* (4), we are simultaneously exploring the details within the still frame *per se* and also interpreting the frame itself as a detail within the whole narrative. This experience of, at once, making local meanings and fitting them into the larger pattern of the story is the imaginative exercise performed by all readers — whether of text or picture-books — and constitutes *the* essential element of reading development.

The classic text to demonstrate picture story reading is Pat Hutchins's *Rosie's Walk* (5), but because this is more suited to younger children, we have chosen to concentrate upon John Burningham's *Come Away From The Water, Shirley*, Figure 1, (6) and Arnold Lobel's *Frog and Toad All Year*, Figure 2, (7). Each has a degree of sophistication beyond that of the simpler picture books for infants and makes demands upon middle school readers that will introduce them to some of the narrative techniques frequently deployed in prose fiction.

John Burningham's book consists of ten double-page spreads, 'landscape' in lay-out, which encourage the reader to pause and look rather than to read and hurry on. The left page of each spread depicts Mum and Dad in their deckchairs on the beach, the right page relates the imaginary adventures of Shirley and her dog as they fight a band of pirates, escape with a map, discover the buried treasure and sail home with the loot. This sequence is bounded by two single page pictures of the family as they arrive and depart from the beach which serve the formulaic function of 'Once upon a time' and 'They all lived happily ever after'. The left-hand pages are relatively static, two seated figures who read, knit, smoke, drink tea or fall asleep; the colours are pale and unvaried, the drawing is light and repetitive. Mum is the only character to speak, her series of warnings to Shirley culminating in several comments about and to her husband where both words and pictures are reminiscent of Thurber. The right-hand pages are full of action as Shirley becomes the heroine of her own daydream. The colours are richly applied and vary from the patchwork effects of the fight scene, to the dominant yellow and orange as the treasure is found, to the black, blue and silver of the night-time journey home. The perspective varies, too, from close-ups to longer shots as the wordless half of the narrative demands.

Younger children will largely ignore the left-hand pages but for eight and nine year olds there is the tacit acknowledgement that they live an inner and outer life simultaneously and that ironies abound between the two. Hence, when Mum, eyes down over her knitting, says 'Your father might have a game with you when he's had a little rest', the reader links the equivocal 'might' to the snoozing Dad and at once juxtaposes the dim possibility of a routine beach game with the excitement of Shirley's imaginary game of

That's the third and last time I'm asking you whether you want a drink, Shirley

Figure 1   Facing pages from *Come Away from the Water, Shirley* by John Burningham

digging up the treasure shown on the facing page. The mixed medium is threefold throughout this book. The two halves of the pictorial narrative complement each other through a series of wryly observed parallels and the text acts as a humorous counterpoint to both.

The text plays a bigger part in Arnold Lobel's *Frog and Toad All Year*. The book consists of five tales, one for each of the seasons plus a Christmas story to conclude. The words and pictures are finely integrated: the brown and green illustrations, entirely appropriate to these two creatures, themselves convey the story-line; the words are precise and apt, show a good ear for dramatic and humorous dialogue and read fluently. The characters are consistent throughout: Toad is beset by the fears, disasters, wonderment and unpredictability of childhood; Frog has the steadiness, knowledge and manner of a resourceful parent. The first tale, 'Down The Hill', turns upon Toad's changing feeling towards a sledge-ride. Initial reluctance changes to fear, excitement, bravado, disaster and self-righteousness in rapid succession. The cleverness of the telling is that the reader is 'in the know' at the point where Toad is hurtling downhill oblivious of the fact that Frog has fallen off. This sort of dramatic irony, cementing the bond between author and reader, is an important experience in reading development. Irony draws the reader in. 'The Corner' too engages the young reader through a favourite literary device. It is a story within a story based upon the cliché of 'the corner that spring is just around'. 'Ice Cream', perhaps the funniest of the tales, builds up an imaginary monster from the most unlikely of resources — two chocolate ice creams. The organization of the slap-stick is carefully handled, again through a basic literary technique of taking the reader half way through the tale of Toad's problems with the melting ice cream and juxtaposing this

incomplete knowledge with the signs of imminent disaster that the waiting Frog sees before the climax is reached. 'The Surprise' is the cleverest tale. Here Frog and Toad are kept apart throughout and set out on identical, altruistic missions — the secret good deed of clearing the other's fallen leaves. Despite the wind rendering their work useless, each is left with his delusion of worthwhile endeavour and a consequent sense of virtue and happiness. As in the first tale, there is the irony for the reader of being 'in the know' and the

Figure 2　From *Frog and Toad All Year* by Arnold Lobel

There was Frog.

"Hello, Toad," he said.

"I am very sorry to be late.
I was wrapping your present."

"You are not at the bottom
of a hole?" asked Toad.

"No," said Frog.

"You are not lost
in the woods?" asked Toad.

"No," said Frog.

"You are not being eaten
by a big animal?"
asked Toad.

"No," said Frog. "Not at all."

"Oh, Frog," said Toad,

"I am so glad to be
spending Christmas with you."

superiority conferred because the joke is on the characters. There is also a satisfying aesthetic experience in the pattern of narrative development: the symmetry in both words and pictures is finely judged. The last tale, 'Christmas Eve', relies upon the build up of imaginary fears as the story of the ice cream had done. This time, however, the substance of the fears is in Toad's mind rather than on his person. He imagines the horrifying fates that may have befallen Frog since the latter is so late arriving for Christmas, collects various implements of rescue, goes outside to begin his mercy mission only to be confronted by Frog on the doorstep. The deflation of Toad's fears in the ensuing dialogue is an excellent example of the way anti-climax is used to resolve narrative.

What do such picture books offer children in their reading development? Clearly those that achieve a successful integration of text and pictures in telling their stories are capable of giving their readers an aesthetic experience comparable to that gained through reading other forms of literature. More-over, in the best of these books the narrative skills characteristic of the mature novel are to be found in simplified but effective forms. The use of juxtaposition, daydream, irony, the story within a story, climax and anti-climax that we have noted in the stories of John Burningham and Arnold Lobel are also present in many of the books recommended on pp 75–76. Such books provide not only a good, attractive introduction to more demanding literature; they are simultaneously an imaginative complement to stories that are told primarily through print alone. For the picture book is a different sort of reading experience: whether the words are read aloud or rehearsed in the head, picture book reading tends to be audio-visual. The relative sparseness of the words, with their caption-like appearance and tendency to dialogue, invites the reader to speak them. Picture books, too, are sociable; they ask to be shared and may be read by two or three readers of widely differing abilities at once. The advantages of picture books are thus threefold from the literature teacher's point of view: this mixed medium has its own aesthetic value, it employs many sophisticated narrative techniques in immediately accessible ways, and it encourages children not only to discuss the stories but also to share and talk about the actual process of reading. No other literary genre gains the willing collaboration of its readers so readily.

Teaching ideas

1 *Putting words to pictures* Provide a group or an individual with a picture book in which the words have been removed or covered over. The task is to write the story to accompany the pictures. This can be done as a complete class if the film-strip from Weston Woods is used (see p. 153). It is easy enough to 'grade' the difficulty of this task, e.g. *Rosie's Walk* for nine year olds, *How Tom Beat Captain Najork* for thirteen year olds. It is as well for pupils to look through the entire story before they begin devising accompanying text.

2 *Talking pictures* The pictures from wordless picture books are provided separately and in random sequence. The task is to order the pictures into a narrative sequence — in the process, children talk through possible versions of the story and are ready to justify their decisions to others.

3 *Storytelling* Using the Weston Woods filmstrips children prepare a reading of the story either 'live' or on tape (possibly to be presented to younger classes or at an assembly).

4 *Alphabet books* Children are shown several different alphabet books and then invited to create their own. This works best if the original books are *not* open during the children's work (they provide too strong and daunting a model). Children working in groups might be allocated four or five letters, with the whole alphabet making up a wall-display. Alphabets can be unified by their themes (animals, children's names, horrific accidents) and by the form of the words (e.g. rhyming couplets).

5 *D.I.Y.* A class spends some time browsing among a selection of picture books — if possible, about 80 books borrowed from a library. After a lesson spent in this way, when children often become very animated as they meet old favourites, meet a book for the first time or decide on the suitability of a book, the class moves on to making their own books. Some children worry about the inadequacy of their art-work, and we find it necessary to convince them that simple representations of their ideas (for example, stick men) will be fine. This work is capable of much development, depending on available time. For example, stories can be read to younger children in draft form, then revised; or the scheme can be carried through to the point where the authors bind their own books.

Recommended reading We recommend a minimum age for some of these books, as shown in the brackets. Others can be read to three or four year olds. This does not invalidate their use with older children. There are no hard and fast rules about the suitability of a picture book for a particular age; as indicated in *Teaching ideas* much depends upon how the book is used.

Mitsumasa Anno   *Anno's Alphabet*   (The Bodley Head★)
Raymond Briggs   *Fungus the Bogeyman*   (Hamish Hamilton) (*12+*)
                 Father Christmas Goes on Holiday   (Puffin)
                 The Snowman   (Hamish Hamilton)
                 Gentleman Jim   (Hamish Hamilton) (*14+*)
                 When The Wind Blows   (Hamish Hamilton) (*14+*)
Anthony Browne   *Hansel and Gretel*   (Julia MacRae Books★)
John Burningham   *Come Away From the Water, Shirley*   (Picture Lions)
Lewis Carroll   *The Pig-Tale*, illus. L.B. Lubin
          (Little, Brown and Co. Distributed Hutchinson)
Russell Hoban and Nicola Bayley   *La Corona and the Tin Frog*   (J. Cape★)
Russell Hoban and Quentin Blake   *How Tom Beat Captain Najork and His
                          Hired Sportsmen*   (Puffin)
Shirley Hughes   *Up and Up*   (The Bodley Head)
Edward Lear   *The Pelican Chorus and The Quangle Wangle's Hat*,
          illus. Kevin W. Maddison   (Ash and Grant★)

Arnold Lobel   *Frog and Toad Tales*   (World's Work★)
Alfred Noyes and Charles Keeping   *The Highwayman*   (O.U.P.) (*12+*)
Michael Rosen and Quentin Blake   *You Can't Catch Me*   (Deutsch)
Maurice Sendak   *Where The Wild Things Are*   (Puffin)
                 In The Night Kitchen   (Puffin)
                 Outside Over There   (The Bodley Head★) (*12+*)
Rosemary Stones and Andrew Mann   *Mother Goose Comes to Cable Street*,
                 illus. Dan Jones   (Puffin)

Teachers wishing to explore the use of picture books will also find the following helpful:

Robert Cumming   *Just Look*   (Kestrel★)
This is a book about paintings addressed to children and written in a clear, uncomplicated way. It is lavishly illustrated and, through asking its readers to look closely at details and techniques, it achieves many insights into the ways in which pictures gain their effects.

Robert Cumming   *Just Imagine*   (Kestrel★)
This is a companion volume to its predecessor in the same style. It is concerned with how ideas and emotions are conveyed in paintings. There is rather more text and exposition than in the earlier book. It is suited more to children over 12 years of age.

M.C. Escher   *The Graphic Work of M.C. Escher* (Macdonald and Jane's★)
A fascinating book celebrating the work of a master draughtsman and artist. Escher's visual experiments in perception have a wide appeal, often to mathematically-minded children.

Norbert Lynton   *Looking at Art*   (Kingfisher★)
This book concentrates chiefly on painting, providing first a historical survey and then a closer look at some eighty artists by moving from a single painting to a broader introduction to each painter. It is modest and conversational in tone, assumes a lively curiosity among its readers and is appropriate to children over 12 years.

Serge Prokofieff   *Peter and the Wolf*, illustrated Warren Chappell, (Kaye and Ward★)
This edition combines the text with illustrations and the melody line for each character. Used in conjunction with a recording (especially, L.S.O. conducted by Sir Malcolm Sargent and narrated by Sir Ralph Richardson on Decca, SPA 90) it can provide a powerful audio-visual experience. See also the edition, illustrated Charles Mikolaycak, Granada.★

Giles Waterfield   *Faces*   (Wayland★)

> A fascinating portrait gallery — paintings, sculptures, masks, cartoons — with comments often preceded by the kind of question which feels like a genuine enquiry for an opinion rather than a threat. Interesting contrasts are brought out through juxtaposition. There are many pictures which themselves ask implicit questions about their subjects.

Poetry for children (9–11)

There has been a marked increase in the number and variety of poetry books published for children in recent years. Established poets such as Charles Causley and Ted Hughes have continued to write for children and to edit anthologies with youngsters in mind; new voices such as those of Michael Rosen and Kit Wright have been added to the Mersey Sound and their informal idioms, often spiced with a wry humour, have gained immediate response from children; and children's verse from past generations continues to be reissued, notably that of Edward Lear and Lewis Carroll (often single poems in picture book form), Walter de la Mare and Eleanor Farjeon.

What can such poets offer children? The priority must be the experience of poetry as fun. If 'poetry begins in delight....' then it should certainly retain this delight in the classroom. The power to evoke ready enjoyment is common to all the recommended books listed at the end of this section. Enjoyment comes in many forms and it is vital that children become aware that poetry can be written about anything from dustbins to the cosmos, that it has many different voices and reflects many different moods; that it is often jokey and not too different from the rhymes and jingles, jokes and puns that are part of every childhood — yet, in its mystery, it can also command stillness and wonder. When children have this kind of awareness and the confidence that accrues from the frequent sharing of poems, poetry sheds any air of preciousness that may have gathered around it. Such foundations are crucial for these poets offer, in easily accessible ways, aesthetic experiences that provide the basis for children's later literary development. Poetry has unique qualities, as we have argued in Chapter 2; and, if children are reading and sharing poems regularly, then they will be experiencing language at its most condensed and imaginative; they will be impelled to look at the world the poets describe with 'a new effort of attention'; and they will gain a sense of how feelings are not only expressed in words but how they can be shaped and made comprehensible in aesthetic forms. These may seem grandiose claims; but, if poetry is handled in the ways we outline in Chapters 2 and 7, they are claims that can be met in most classrooms in the course of work that is often entertaining and, sometimes, magical.

How can we best equip ourselves in this area? First, we should know

★*indicates hardback edition*

what is available and, secondly, what classroom approaches are most likely to reflect the singularity of each individual poem. Accordingly, we have derived our teaching ideas (see p. 84) from the discussion of particular poems written for children. In Chapter 7, we mention many more approaches that can be adapted to particular poems.

Songs, ballads, rhymes, chants, the oral inheritance of all our literature, are the spring from which much subsequent children's verse draws life. When it comes to printed poetry for children at least three strands are discernible in the tradition: didactic verse, nonsense poetry and lyrical poetry. Each has its echoes in the work of contemporary poets who address a young audience.

Teaching them a lesson   Until the end of the eighteenth century, children were regarded as miniature adults rather than as persons with a mentality peculiar to their years. Moral instruction had to be imparted and verse helped children to remember the lessons. It is in this area that children's poetry has changed most radically. Compare the moralizing solemnity of Isaac Watts with the chirpy good-humour of Michael Rosen. They are both writing about children quarrelling:

> Let dogs delight to bark and bite,
>   For God hath made them so.
> Let bears and lions growl and fight,
>   For 'tis their nature, too.
>
> But, children, you should never let
>   Such angry passions rise:
> Your little hands were never made
>   To tear each other's eyes. (1)

> I'm the youngest in our house
> so it goes like this:
>
> My brother comes in and says:
> 'Tell him to clear the fluff
> out from under his bed.'
> Mum says,
> 'Clear the fluff
> out from under your bed.'
> Father says,
> 'You heard what your mother said.'
> 'What?' I say.
> 'The fluff,' he says.
> 'Clear the fluff
> out from under your bed.'
> So I say,
> 'There's fluff under his bed, too,

you know.'
So father says,
'But we're talking about the fluff
under *your* bed.'
'You will clear it up
won't you?' mum says.
So now my brother — all puffed up —
says,
'Clear the fluff
out from under your bed,
clear the fluff
out from under your bed.'
Now I'm angry. I am angry.
So I say — what shall I say?
I say,
'Shuttup stinks
YOU CAN'T RULE MY LIFE.' (2)

Overt, paternal preaching in the language of the hymnal where the advice is direct and uncompromising is replaced two centuries later by rumbustious dramatizing in the informal voice of home or playground where advice is neither sought nor given. Michael Rosen is in no way didactic yet, in the treatment of his major themes of family relationships, children's behaviour and interests, there emerges a humorous tolerance of human difference, an empathy with the concerns of others, an assertion of the worth of the individual against the mass, a sense of the fun and the tension of friendship, all of which speak a morality to today's children as clearly as Isaac Watts did for past generations. The voice is utterly different: Christian words like 'God', 'sin', 'evil' and 'praise' which the didactic poet can wave as rhetorical flags confident that their signals will be understood, have no place in present day agnosticism; but the implied messages of kindness, understanding and fair-dealing in Michael Rosen's poems achieve similar effects by subtler means.

Humour has always been an important adjunct to didactic verse and, for children, the blacker the better. There are modern examples — one thinks of Roald Dahl's poem about 'That nauseating, foul, unclean, /Repulsive television screen' in *Charlie and the Chocolate Factory* — but, for the most part, contemporary poems are rarely more than off-white compared with the black humour of the Victorians. Michael Rosen's, 'My dad's thumb . . .' (3) looks like mere sycophantic nostalgia at the powerful digit possessed by his father in comparison with the bleeding stumps of little Conrad who has his thumbs cut off by 'the great long red-legg'd scissor-man' in Heinrich Hoffman's 'The Story of Little Suck-a-Thumb'! (4) If we are less certain of the advice we give children in general, we seem more certain that poetry is not the best means to proffer it. In children's poetry, open didacticism has died; advice is a matter of flippancy:

Caterpillars living on lettuce
Are the colour of their host;
Look out, when you're eating a salad,
For the greens that move the most. (5)

Or, as in two other poems by Roy Fuller — 'The National Union of Children' and 'The National Association of Parents' (6) — advice wittily acknowledges the compromises that parents and children negotiate each day. Contemporary children's poems, whether they tell of the traditional Christianity of Charles Causley, the gentle humanity of James Reeves, or the relaxed agnosticism of Michael Rosen, convey their morality in the oblique and implied ways befitting their time.

The best means of engaging children with such poems is by their presenting them in spoken form. Indeed, when teachers or students, as well as children, have worked in groups rehearsing a reading of, say, Charles Causley's 'Mary, Mary Magdalene' or Michael Rosen's 'If you don't put your shoes on', their awareness of the way poems are made, literally, as 'spoken forms' is greatly sharpened.

To take two examples already mentioned, one approach to 'I'm the youngest in our house' (p. 78) is to cast groups of four as mother, father and the two children and have them prepare a reading of the poem for live or taped performance. If the class can choose among a selection of poems about similar topics, so that different groups are working on different pieces towards 'an instant poetry show' in half an hour's time, then so much the better.

Roy Fuller's pair of poems 'The National Union of Children' and 'The National Association of Parents' involves wider arguments and suggests a different treatment. The class might be divided in two: one half are the children, the other the parents. As a preparation for the reading, each group lists and discusses its own arguments and attitudes and considers how it will counter the points raised by the opposition based upon the information in the poems. A ten minute debate with nominated speakers from each side (or a free for all), is not only enjoyable in itself but gives the children a chance to rehearse the tone of voice and weight of feeling they will give to different lines of the poems. A public reading of the two poems, perhaps staged as a television interview as the second one suggests, rounds off the work in a satisfying way largely because this teaching sequence takes children behind the language to grasp the attitudes and feelings involved. In short, it enables them to do what all poetry teaching should encourage — to lift the words off the page and make them their own.

'There will be nonsense in it!'   So commanded one of the 'cruel three' little girls who made up Lewis Carroll's first audience for *Alice* — or so he tells us in the verses which precede the story. Humour was an antidote as well as an adjunct to Victorian moralizing verse. The solemnity of Christian teaching could not be undermined, least of all in children's poetry, but the solemnity of language was fair game. The nonsense verse of Edward Lear and Lewis Carroll bubbles up like a brightly coloured anodyne amidst the dull medicines administered by the eighteenth- and nineteenth-century moral versifiers. Irreverence is a quality of childhood; irreverence in the children's poet towards the seriousness of poetic expression, whether in Lear and Carroll or Milligan and McGough, is a quality gleefully seized upon by youngsters. The zany word-play, the delight in the whimsical and the sheer sense of fun in Edward Lear's verse and in the nonsense poems of the Alice books remain unsurpassed.

Subsequent humorous verse for children took different forms: Belloc's voice was more witty, James Reeves's *Prefabulous Animiles* (7) more measured. Only in relatively recent years, in the world of The Goons and The Goodies, has anything like the authentic voice of nonsense been heard again. It is present in the anguish of Spike Milligan's prisoner in 'Ye Tortures' (8), who is 'Bluned on ye Grunions/and Krelled on his Grotts', in the verbal trickery of Roger McGough's *In the Glassroom*, (9) and in the occasional piece by Michael Rosen, notably his dotty tannoy poem which begins:

> The train now standing
> at Flatworm's heaven
> will not stop or start
> at Oldham, Newham
> You bring 'em, We buy 'em,
> And all stations to
> Kahalacahoo, Hawaii. (*10*)

These recent verses have 'been put through the mind-mangle' in Lewis Carroll's vivid phrase with the same cheerfully idiotic effects as those of their nineteenth-century predecessors, but, as yet, without the technical mastery and ear for poetry that characterizes much of the work of Lear and Carroll. The poems of Carroll from *Sylvie and Bruno* not only show the gap that remains between the skill of a fine craftsman in nonsense and that of his modern counterpart but also remind us that in our enthusiasm for popular contemporary writers we must not neglect the continuing appeal of earlier verse. Read Carroll's splendid piece 'The Pig-Tale' with a superior Gielgud voice for the camel, a peremptory Barbara Woodhouse voice for the frog and a doleful Clement Freud voice for the pig. Or, try this in a Milligan voice:

> In stature the Manlet was dwarfish —
> No burly big Blunderbore he:
> And he wearily gazed on the crawfish
> His Wifelet had dressed for his tea.
> 'Now reach me, sweet Atom, my gunlet,
> And hurl the old shoelet for luck:
> Let me hie to the bank of the runlet
> And shoot thee a Duck!' (*11*)

As the story of the duck-shoot proceeds, to the notes of the 'Outlandish guitar', towards the hilarious bombardment 'from toplet to toelet/with Nursery-Songs!' by the fairy Voices, Carroll's control over his medium is consummate. The surreal absurdity of the poem is caught in these lines:

> On he speeds, never wasting a wordlet,
>> Though thoughtlets cling closely as wax,
> To the spot where the beautiful birdlet
>> So quietly quacks.

The subtle mix of the wordless man beset by clinging thoughts and the brainless duck emitting its unsuspecting quacks is pointed up cleverly by the rhythm and by the audacious rhyme of 'wax' and 'quacks'. The note of universal sadness that lies behind the nonsense picture of 'the spot where the beautiful birdlet' quacks is unmistakeable: Lewis Carroll's handling of severely end-stopped and finely run-on lines to communicate this feeling produces some of the best verse ever written for children.

> Where the Lobsterlet lurks, and the Crablet
>> So slowly and sleepily crawls;
> Where the Dolphin's at home, and the Dablet
>> Pays long ceremonious calls:
> Where the Grublet is sought by the Froglet:
>> Where the Frog is pursued by the Duck:
> Where the Ducklet is chased by the Doglet —
>> So runs the world's luck!

Nonsense poems depend on word-play — puns, invented vocabulary, comical rhymes; from the 'portmanteau words' of Lewis Carroll to the topsy-turvy phrases of Charles Causley in 'As I Went Down Zig Zag' and '"Quack!" Said The Billy-Goat' (*12*), language is a plaything. Dramatized readings, including some choral speaking and musical backing, can be especially helpful in pointing up the sounds, rhythms and word-play of nonsense poetry. Children could add some modern entries to a field-guide based on Lear's 'Nonsense Botany' (*13*); present Roger McGough's 'The Lesson' (*14*) either as a series of tableaux to accompany a reading (taped or live) or as a wall-display comic strip with the verses as captions; or create their own images of the 'Jubjub bird' and the 'frumious Bandersnatch', in words and pictures or through movement, to complement Carroll's and Tenniel's portrait of the Jabberwock.

'Rhymes that, like bells, the mind may chime and ring to.' The spirit of song, whether joyous or sad, is the one that invests the work of many of the best poets for children: William Blake, Robert Louis Stevenson, Eleanor Farjeon and Walter de la Mare, from whose 'Words' we take the title for this section. De la Mare's eminence in children's poetry stems from his unique combination of qualities: an ability to look with an innocent eye; a talent to cast things in words of childlike spontaneity; and a technical skill which is characterized by a fine ear for the music of poetry and facility in a wide variety of verse forms. To the present day reader, a cursory glance at his poems may give an overall impression of quaint delicacy, but a closer look at half a dozen pieces taken at random easily demonstrates that de la Mare's range in mood, viewpoint and language is as varied as are the forms in which his poems are made. Read aloud 'Somewhere', 'Two Deep Clear Eyes', 'The Ship of Rio'; notice the witchy incantation of 'The Little Creature', the quiet introspection of 'Ever', the sharp sarcasm of 'Hi!'Perhaps a poem that shows as well as any the childlike sensibility of de la Mare's work and seems to catch some Blakean echoes in its vision and craftsmanship, is 'The Magnifying Glass' which begins:

> With this round glass
> I can make *Magic* talk —
> A myriad shells show
> In a scrap of chalk;
>
> Of but an inch of moss
> A forest — flowers and trees;
> A drop of water
> Like a hive of bees. (*15*)

Since the war, James Reeves and, more recently, Charles Causley and Ted Hughes have dominated children's verse. In Reeves's poems a studied tone is always evident: the technical variety is there, so is the childlike focus; but the poems seem to offer more than they actually give. There are few pieces to reread and savour; but, of those that do more than merely arrest the attention, the most successful is 'Cows'. A brown cow and a white exchange bovine remarks as they chew the cud like the two seasoned rustics they are:

> 'Rain coming,' said the brown cow.
> 'Ah,' said the white.
> 'Flies is very tiresome.'
> 'Flies bite.' (*16*)

The dialogue throughout is brief and humorous and the cows' exchanges are backed by a rhythmical refrain. A group of three children rehearsing the poem aloud can have great fun with the voices, pace and intonation. Their presentation of the poem could be enhanced by the use of masks or simple puppets.

At first sight, Charles Causley and Ted Hughes seem to represent quite antithetical approaches in their poetry for children. Causley, a skilled ballad-writer, often on Christian themes, seems far distant from the hard, uncompromising images of Hughes's predominantly free verse poems. Causley often celebrates creation and seems to compose his poems in neat patterns like reflected miniatures of some grander design. Hughes is always locked in struggle with creation, 'mixing it' with the pain of birth and death and, in his later anthologies, *Season Songs*, *Moon-Bells and Other Poems* and *Under The North Star* (*17*) making few concessions to the child reader. The black voice of *Crow* is never far distant: indeed, it is raised once in the second of these anthologies to sing a sardonic death-chant, entitled 'Horrible Song'. Yet, for all their differences, there is often a sense of loss at the end of Causley's poems and a feeling of hard-won achievement in Hughes's that suggest an ambivalence that is common to both. Two poems, each characteristic of its author, which catch this quality are Hughes's 'March Morning Unlike Others' and Causley's 'The Forest of Tangle'. These pieces, along with, say, Hughes's 'Work and Play' and 'Leaves', and Causley's 'Mary, Mary Magdalene' and 'Miller's End' from the anthology *Figgie Hobbin* (18) are the kinds of contemporary poems which are continuing the main tradition of children's poetry and, in doing so, blurring the borderline between adult and children's verse in just the same way that the work of Blake and de la Mare did in earlier periods.

What such lyrical poems offer children is a quality that appears only incidentally in didactic or nonsense verse: a sense of mystery. Often in these stories and songs there is the ghost of some strong emotion or powerful idea lying beneath the surface which, while it may not be fully understood, will be felt through the language and rhythms of the poem.

Teaching ideas   We have argued here and in Chapter 2 that both *hearing* and *performing* a wide variety of poems are vital. Many of the ideas suggested in Chapter 7 are appropriate here. Some particular activities might be:

1 Poem per day   Each child in turn chooses a poem to read out or put on the display board. Usually this takes no more than a couple of minutes a day and, at the very lowest, you will know that the class has been exposed to over 200 poems between September and July! Take copies and your class can build up its own version of Kaye Webb's anthology, *I Like This Poem* (Puffin) (19).

2 Reading aloud   The teacher selects poems which pose problems for reading, or invite different interpretations, or require two or more voices. The following are all printed in *Watchwords 1, 2* or *3*, ed. M. & P. Benton.
'Cows' James Reeves
'Mary, Mary Magdalene' Charles Causley
'Noah's Journey' George MacBeth
'The Late Passenger' C.S. Lewis
'The Animals' Carol' Charles Causley
'Jabberwocky' Lewis Carroll
'The train now standing' Michael Rosen
'I'm the youngest in our house' Michael Rosen
'If you don't put your shoes on' Michael Rosen
'The Little Creature' Walter de la Mare
'Goodbat Nightman' Roger McGough
'The Loch Ness Monster's Song' Edwin Morgan
'Ballad by Hans Breitmann' Charles Leland
'Nooligan' Roger McGough

Pairs/groups rehearse and present readings of their chosen poems.

3 Collecting   Children in this age range are usually collectors of something — so why not poems? Poems about things they are interested in — cats, horses, sport ... Helen Morris's *Where's That Poem?* (*20*) is a useful reference book. Poems could be collected on file cards into thematic anthologies.

Recommended reading
Individual poets
Hilaire Belloc   *Cautionary Verses*, Collected illus. album edition
           (Duckworth★)
Alan Brownjohn   *Brownjohn's Beasts*   (Macmillan★)
Lewis Carroll   *The Humorous Verse of Lewis Carroll*   (Dover)
Charles Causley   *The Tail of the Trinosaur*   (Beaver Books, Hamlyn)
           Figgie Hobbin   (Puffin)
Roald Dahl   *Revolting Rhymes*   (Picture Puffin)
Walter de la Mare   *Collected Rhymes and Verses*   (Faber)
T.S. Eliot   *Old Possum's Book of Practical Cats*   (Faber)
Eleanor Farjeon   *Invitation to a Mouse and Other Poems*   (Pelham Books★)
Roy Fuller   *Seen Grandpa Lately?*   (Deutsch★)
Ted Hughes   *Moon-Bells and Other Poems*   (Chatto and Windus★)
Edward Lear   *The Complete Nonsense of Edward Lear* ed. Holbrook Jackson
           (Faber★)
           A Book of Bosh, chosen by Brian Alderson   (Puffin)
Roger McGough and Michael Rosen   *You Tell Me*   (Kestrel)
Spike Milligan   *A Dustbin Full of Milligan*   (Dobson)
           Silly Verse For Kids   (Puffin)
Sylvia Plath   *The Bed Book*   (Faber★)
James Reeves   *Complete Poems For Children*   (Heinemann★)
Michael Rosen   *Mind Your Own Business*   (Deutsch)
           Wouldn't You Like to Know   (Deutsch)
           Quick, Let's Get Out of Here illus. Quentin Blake
           (Deutsch★)
Kit Wright   *Rabbiting On*   (Fontana Lions)
           Hot Dog and Other Poems   (Puffin)
General anthologies
Jill Bennett (ed)   *A Packet of Poems*   (O.U.P.★)
Michael and Peter Benton (eds)   *Watchwords, Vols. 1 and 2*
                          (Hodder and Stoughton)
Charles Causley (ed)   *The Puffin Book of Magic Verse*   (Puffin)
           The Puffin Book of Salt-Sea Verse   (Puffin)
           Stories in Verse For Children illus. C. Keeping
           (Batsford★)
Robert Fisher (ed)   *Ghosts Galore*   (Faber)
John L. Foster (ed)   *A First Poetry Book*   *A Second Poetry Book*
           A Third Poetry Book   (O.U.P.)
Iona and Peter Opie (eds)   *The Oxford Book of Children's Verse*   (O.U.P.★)
Adrian Rumble (ed)   *Have You Heard The Sun Singing?*   (Evans★)
Ian Serraillier (ed)   *I'll Tell You a Tale*   (Kestrel★)
Geoffrey Summerfield (ed)   *Junior Voices Vol. 1–4*   (Penguin)

★*indicates hardback edition*

Poetry for children (12–14)

Rites of passage Even when pupils have enjoyed poems up to the age of twelve, they often seem to lose interest in poetry — even become hostile to it — as they move towards adolescence. We consider here two reasons for this: first, the choice of material; and second, how that material is introduced.

One of the commonest features of adolescent writing, whether it takes literal or metaphorical form, is the idea of the journey. Whether the writing is a quest for truth or about the journey to school, the sense of purposeful and significant movement recurs with a frequency that suggests that journeys have a symbolic importance in the minds of young people. In the development of literatures, too, the journeys of Odysseus, Sir Gawain and the other Arthurian knights provide the archetypal patterns for many subsequent quest narratives. The journey movement thus has both a long literary heritage and an appeal to young readers who are living their lives forward, aware, however dimly, that they have to negotiate their own rites of passage into adulthood.

Teachers of this age group need little reminding that these journeys are often not a smooth forward progression. Both literally and figuratively, pupils thrash about under the pressure of new experience. They may well be wary of anything which invades vulnerable feelings. Nevertheless, poetry for such pupils must begin to take account of the personal journeys that adolescents are making through their early teens and to match them with poems that feed their slowly acquired abilities to empathize with others' feelings, to cope with abstract ideas, to understand the complexity of moral judgements and to develop a sense of pleasure in the ways in which poetic language operates. Many teachers choose material intuitively according to these criteria and delay, say, poems about war or intense suffering until children are thirteen or fourteen years old, poems about love relationships or religious experience until a year or two after that, and poems of satire and protest until the fifth or sixth form. Such decisions, rough and ready as they are, show the teachers' acknowledgement of the journey through adolescence. Given the variety of routes that children take and the differences in their pace of development it is especially difficult to match the right poetry to the right child at the right time. If in doubt about the choice of poems two guidelines are worth observing: first, go for material of real imaginative power where the language and feeling compel a response; secondly, do not underestimate the pupils' capacities — err on the side of difficulty.

Some contemporary poets writing for children appear to operate on these principles and offer poems that make considerable demands upon their readers by facing them with the complexity of themselves and the world they inhabit. If children have had experience of the themes and style of traditional ballads and perhaps some of the longer narrative poems (for example, 'The Pied Piper of Hamelin', 'Horatius' or 'The Tail of the Trinosaur') in addition to the poetry we discussed in the previous section, then they will be well prepared for more demanding fare. Ted Hughes's *Season Songs* (1), itself a journey through the year, is shot through with images and observations that force the reader to look afresh at familiar things and to exercise his own feelings. Many of Charles Causley's poems, too, have an elusiveness and air of mystery that make them, at once, both engaging and disturbing. Look, for example, at the enigmatic 'Nursery Rhyme of Innocence and Experience' with its echoes of Blake and Coleridge in its treatment of the journey away from childhood.

One of the great poems that children of around twelve years of age should meet is 'The Ancient Mariner'. This voyage is one to catch the imagination through its romance and mystery just at the time when children are most prone to lose interest in poetry. Coleridge's poem has a peculiar ability to enchant: the fact that a work of such power and complexity is so accessible to twelve year olds through its language and narrative style means that 'The Ancient Mariner' is potentially a major literary experience in children's reading development. We have chosen, therefore, to devote most of this section to 'The Ancient Mariner' because it exemplifies, more completely and powerfully than any other poem we know, all that is unique to the art of poetry and it embodies the ideas that we have discussed in Chapter 2. In this sense, one poem can stand for all the others.

'The Ancient Mariner'

Teller and listener   We said earlier that stories in verse hold the reader in a double spell: the enchantment of the fiction and the form. Nowhere in English literature is this more true than in 'The Ancient Mariner'. The poem dramatizes the relationship between teller and listener. The compelling presence of the mariner and the menacing power of his 'glittering eye' which subdues the wedding guest so that 'He cannot choose but hear' are calculated to arrest the reader's attention at the outset. The theatrical way the poem is presented as a dialogue between teller and listener runs throughout Part 1 where the mariner is no more than an eccentric, if threatening, nuisance to the wedding guest. But the overt exchanges between the dramatized narrator and this hapless passer-by are important in the poem's development both to underline the moral and educative purposes behind the mariner's compulsion to tell his story and to reinforce the terrifying atmosphere that the account generates. At the opening of Part 4, after the description of the spectre ship and the death of the sailors and, again, midway through Part 5, when the angelic spirits enter the corpses of the crew and 'work the ropes', the wedding-guest's terror at the events is evident. Finally, in Part 7, after the tale is told and the mariner explains that the act of telling is his only existence, the wedding celebrations reassert themselves as the controlling context. An explicit sense of the art of storytelling thus frames the whole poem. Moreover, it is the sort of narrative with a ready appeal to a young audience — a tale of mystery and horror. Yet, even the young reader does not have to move far into the story before he senses the symbolic nature of events.

A sense of movement   The choice of significant detail, the telling image, the fresh, clear diction are hallmarks of the ballad and contribute to making the poem immediate and accessible to relatively inexperienced readers. The ways in which a sense of movement is conveyed demonstrate this. The journey occurs in highly particularized settings which are invested with such generalizing weight that they come to represent a backdrop of the whole of creation. Hence there are constant details of the sky and the planets, of the changing speed and navigation of the ship, and of the powers that work in the unseen depths. Our perspectives upon events are subtly orchestrated to give us a simultaneous sense of the immediacy of the mariner's story in close-up and the universal setting within which his fate is both a detail and a symbol. There is a brightness and clarity in the words and the images they evoke: the shapes and colours are those of a child's picture book.

> And ice, mast-high, came floating by,
> As green as emerald.

Yet, in the following stanza, the same clear pictorial technique not only conveys absence of movement but, in the last two lines, shifts the reader's perspective to a more distant vantage point.

> Day after day, day after day,
> We stuck, nor breath nor motion;
> As idle as a painted ship
> Upon a painted ocean.

The poem is full of memorable lines in which physical movement and sensuous states are given in vivid, concrete images, cardinal colours, and simple rhythms all of which speak directly to young readers and invite a visual response. Activities which engage children in speaking the lines aloud, perhaps for a taped performance, will highlight the narrative movement and the powerful images more directly than any amount of discussion about the poem.

The appeal of the supernatural   The supernatural machinery of the poem also has a ready appeal. Children perhaps find it easier to accept the supernatural in the poem simply as an essential narrative device than do adults, who often look to interpret and explain away the spirits and visions. The children are right: after all, the *action* of the poem depends upon supernatural forces once the mariner has committed his crime. Spirits begin to take over the ship as early as Part 2, they possess the bodies of the crew (save that of the mariner), propel the ship to its home port and finally sink it in the harbour. For much of the poem the mariner is inactive; things happen to him under the control of supernatural agencies and are conveyed through fantastic symbols. A voyage of mental and spiritual discovery, plotted with such imagery, is a natural development from the worlds of fairy tale, fantasy, myth and legend that should be the landmarks in a child's literary education. At a narrative level, then, children will take the supernatural elements in their stride. Equally important, however, is the haunting quality they produce. The spectre ship with its figures of Death and Life-in-Death, the Voices in the air and the Polar Spirit combine with changes in geography and weather to produce a ghostly, dream-like world; and the feelings that readers are asked to share with the mariner are of loneliness, guilt, longing, horror, fear — all the abstract monsters of the child's imagination which are here given form and substance. Indeed, the depression and isolation that the poem focusses upon in its central sector speak readily to pupils in early adolescence.

Beneath the surface   Beyond the narrative movement and the supernatural machinery to which most children can readily respond are aesthetic matters and conceptual issues which, while young readers may not talk about them without prompting, nevertheless form inevitable elements in their unspoken apprehension of the poem. No attentive reading can fail to notice, however hazily, the parts that the sun and moon play in the pattern of the poem's imagery. The sun is often red, burning, threatening, bloody, merciless; the moon is white or pale, cool and enchanting, casting a healing light on events in contrast to that of the aggressive sun. There are other oppositions in the poem, too; for example, killing the albatross and blessing the water snakes, the powers of water and those of the air. Here, as with the planetary images, 'The Ancient Mariner' involves the reader, whether he knows it or not, in a pattern of symbolic incidents and archetypal images that invest this seafarer's tale with an elemental strength. The way to coax children's awareness of such matters is not so much by direct questioning (though this may form part of the procedure) but rather through involving them in a creative response to the poem such as the frieze suggested below. In deciding how to represent the sun and moon, where to place the killing and blessing in the sequence, what prominence to give to the oceans, the storm blast and the supernatural winds, children are ineluctably caught up in the aesthetic patterns and energies that control the whole poem.

Similarly, with twelve year olds, as opposed to sixth formers, questions of the overall theme and interpretation of the poem are not a prime concern. This is not to say that they will not arise: twelve year olds have a highly developed sense of crime and punishment and may well want to talk about the justice of the events. Some will sense the mystery with which the poem leaves us: the cycle of crime, guilt, suffering and the possibility of redemption are clear but the eccentric, wandering life of continual penance that is the mariner's lot is scarcely in tune with the uplifting Christian moral with which the poem ends. The formal closure of the ballad, however, quite properly overrides such questions with young readers and it is the emergence from suffering into a state of grace, represented in the sequence with the old hermit, that is important as it is reflected in the salvation the mariner finally achieves and his acceptance into the community of the 'Kirk'.

Teaching sequence   'The Ancient Mariner' is thus able to deepen children's sense of story through this double spell of the fiction and the form; but children will only fully come to terms with the poem through an imaginative classroom presentation. In the following sequence the recommended edition is *The Rime of the Ancient Mariner*, illustrated by Gustave Doré, Dover/

Constable paperback. The first two activities are seen as essential, the remaining ones are optional extras.

1 A sense of the whole   Children hear the poem read aloud either by the teacher or by a recording. (2) The poem is presented as a serial in three instalments:

Parts 1–3:   journey out — killing the albatross — the spectre ship — death of sailors

Parts 4–5:   mariner's isolation — blessing water snakes — ghosts of sailors work the ship — Polar Spirit speeds ship to Northern waters

Parts 6–7:   journey back, accompanied by voices of two spirits — angels over the corpses of the sailors — ship sinks in the harbour — mariner's life of constant penance.

2 Mapping the voyage   Children make a map/frieze depicting the mariner's progress (perhaps groups to work on different sections of the poem). Ship's log, diary entries of the mariner (individual or group work).

3 Words and pictures   Vandalize two copies of the recommended edition, delete page numbers, mount (and laminate, if possible) as 76 cards. Children, in three groups as above, match the text to the Doré pictures. (The cards, of course, would be a resource for other occasions.)

4 Tellers and listeners   Children rehearse sections of the poem for a public reading or taped recording, perhaps to be used in conjunction with the map/frieze above. Background music can enhance the performance.

5 Movement   Stylized mime or tableaux to accompany extracts of the poem, e.g.

the mariner's meeting with the wedding guest
killing the albatross and the changing reactions of the sailors
the dead men working the ropes.

6 Board Game   See illustration of Kirstie Campbell's version p. 91 designed on the snakes-and-ladders principle, to explore the mariner's changing fortunes. Children lay out the board, with picture squares and number squares and quotations from the poem. Decisions about forward and backward movements should relate to the events of the poem: e.g.

shoots albatross — go back 7
becalmed — miss a turn
blesses water snakes — go forward 5

7 Cartoon   A version of major incidents with the children's own captions.

8 Mural   A group of children create a single picture to depict the three levels — air, sea, underwater — combining the major images of the poem in one design. The picture should be 3-tiered and stylized.

9 Writing   The mariner's message in a bottle, giving his account of what has happened, where he is and a plea for help.

Recommended reading   Few poems can offer such literary experiences with the richness of Coleridge's masterpiece but, on a smaller scale, many of

Figure 3 'The Ancient Mariner' boardgame based on an original design by student-teacher Kirstie Campbell

the poems in the list of recommended books will challenge the feelings and develop the sensibility of readers over twelve years old. Many anthologies (with the notable exception of *The Rattlebag* (*3*)) group poems together by themes either openly or covertly. While these arrangements may be useful in the initial selection and presentation of material, it is important to remind ourselves that our main effort should be to go for the memorable experience rather than feel that we are doing anything significant by attempting to cover a theme. For, whatever is done to them, poems remain obstinately miscellaneous creations: they do not take easily to being fitted into thematic collections appropriate for particular age groups.

The journey through adolescence is so idiosyncratic that just when and with which class the English teacher introduces particular poems must be an individual choice. Ideally, what should be happening is that our own reading of the poets becomes sufficiently wide and eclectic that we feel able to make up our own anthology of poems, one that will be in a continuous state of change due, in part, to the effects of sharing our choices with our pupils.

Recommended reading

Individual poets

William Blake *Songs of Innocence and Experience*
           (Illuminated edition, O.U.P.)
Charles Causley *Collected Poems, 1951–75* (Macmillan)
Samuel Taylor Coleridge *The Rime of the Ancient Mariner*
           Illustrated edition, G. Doré
           (Dover/Constable)
Walter de la Mare *Collected Rhymes and Verses* (Faber)
Robert Frost *Selected Poems* (Penguin)
Thomas Hardy *Selected Shorter Poems* ed. J. Wain (Macmillan)
Seamus Heaney *Selected Poems* (Faber)
Adrian Henri, Roger McGough, Brian Patten *The Mersey Sound,*
      Penguin Modern Poets, No. 10 (Penguin) *New*
       Volume (Penguin)
Ted Hughes *Season Songs* (Faber★)
           Under the North Star (Faber★)
           Selected Poems 1957–1981 (Faber)
Brian Jones *The Spitfire on the Northern Line* (Chatto and Windus★)
D.H. Lawrence *Selected Poems*, ed. W.E. Williams (Penguin)
Brian Lee *Late Home* (Kestrel★)
Roger McGough *In the Glassroom* (Cape)
Gareth Owen *Salford Road* (Kestrel★)
Vernon Scannell *New and Collected Poems 1950–1980*
           (Robson Books)
Alfred, Lord Tennyson 'The Lady of Shalott' in his *Collected Poems*
           (O.U.P.)
Edward Thomas *Collected Poems* (Faber)

Anthologies

Michael and Peter Benton (eds) *Touchstones Vols. 1–3*
                Watchwords Vols. 2 and 3 (Hodder and Stoughton)
John L. Foster *A Fourth Poetry Book* (O.U.P.)
Michael Harrison and Christopher Stuart-Clark (eds) *Poems 1 and Poems 2*
                The New Dragon Book of Verse (O.U.P.)
Ted Hughes and Seamus Heaney (eds) *The Rattlebag* (Faber)
David Mackay (ed) *A Flock of Words* (The Bodley Head★)
Roger McGough (ed) *Strictly Private* (Puffin)
Geoffrey Summerfield (ed) *Voices Vols. 1–3* *Worlds: Seven Modern Poets*
           (Penguin)
David Woolger *The Magic Tree* (O.U.P.)

★*indicates hardback edition*

Chapter 5

A methodology for teaching

Chapters 1 and 2 examined the activity of the reader. Chapters 3 and 4 considered what different kinds of literature offer their readers and pointed towards classroom practice. The rest of this book relates those chapters to the teaching of literature in schools though, for the moment, our path to the classroom door may seem circuitous.

Some of the qualities of this poem by Wallace Stevens (1) will, we think, be most evident if it is read aloud:

THE HOUSE WAS QUIET AND THE WORLD WAS CALM

The house was quiet and the world was calm.
The reader became the book; and summer night

Was like the conscious being of the book.
The house was quiet and the world was calm.

The words were spoken as if there was no book,
Except that the reader leaned above the page,

Wanted to lean, wanted much most to be
The scholar to whom his book is true, to whom

The summer night is like a perfection of thought.
The house was quiet because it had to be.

The quiet was part of the meaning, part of the mind:
The access of perfection to the page.

And the world was calm. The truth in a calm world,
In which there is no other meaning, itself

Is calm, itself is summer and night, itself
Is the reader leaning late and reading there.

Most experienced readers will recognize this mood of absorption. The poem evokes it as much by the measured repetitions of certain phrases that seem to pad the house with their dull monotones, merging its reality with the unreality of the book, as by the explanation of what happens when 'the reader became the book'. The four key words of the title are permutated with other monosyllables, 'night', 'book', 'lean', 'page' and so on, to create a rhythmical pattern that is flat and steady, and to reflect a safe, enclosed, inviolable experience. Stevens explains the sense of 'becoming the book' in terms of a transformation: the summer night around the reader is 'like the conscious being of the book'. Primary and secondary worlds coalesce. The physical nature of the book recedes and the atmosphere of quiet enveloping the reader is so pervasive as to become 'part of the meaning, part of the mind' that is recreating a story.

All of which is a long way from the plastic chairs, formica tables and steaming anoraks of Portakabin 13 last thing on a dank Wednesday, crowded with the thirty-odd minds, bodies and separate concerns of the second years. Nevertheless, it may be useful to glance now and again at the figure of Wallace Stevens's solitary reader, 'leaning late and reading there' as we consider classroom work with literature.

Independent reading

From Jenkinson (1940) (2) to Whitehead (1977) (3), surveys of children's reading interests have recommended that time be given in schools to 'independent reading' among an extensive selection of readily available books. Aidan Chambers (1973) (4) argued that, 'Wide, voracious, *indiscriminate* reading is the base soil from which discrimination and taste eventually grow,' and translated his belief into practice through his editorship of the very successful Macmillan Topliner series of cheaply priced paperbacks, with a list of over a hundred titles. The success of Topliners provoked several imitations the best of which have been the Nelson Getaway series and Longman Knockouts. Literature teachers in junior and comprehensive schools eager to promote reading among *all* their pupils often made extensive use of these series together with the well-established retail paperbacks such as Puffins and Fontana Lions. The cornerstone of their approach was usually a weekly period allotted to individual reading.

The recommendations of the pundits received fresh impetus in the mid-seventies from a North American scheme known as USSR (Uninterrupted, Sustained, Silent Reading). The scheme depends upon the co-operation of all the teachers on a school's staff (or at least the determination of a strong head teacher), and also upon the provision of a wide range of reading material in each classroom. A period of time is set aside each day (tutor group sessions are sometimes used in secondary schools) for silent reading. According to a group of Canadian elementary school teachers we worked with, their schools really did *stop* when it was time for USSR. Their uncorroborated reports claimed that not only did the children, teachers and principal read their books and magazines, but the catering staff, the janitors and the secretaries settled down to their reading also.

British versions of the scheme in a South London boys' secondary school and a Coventry primary school are described by Janet Maybin (5). Forest Hill Comprehensive School devoted a 35 minute period for four days each week immediately after lunch to private reading. Book boxes containing 75 titles appropriate for a wide range of abilities and interests were prepared by the school librarian for each class, to be changed each half-term. Rather to the staff's surprise, there were few problems about discipline or 'the enduring dilemma of how to get the right book to the right child'. In fact, Janet Maybin reports 'a feeling that, of the boys in any group, about 50–60% are making good use of the reading period, 30–40% can be successfully involved with some encouragement and support and about 5% don't seem to be coping'. (Our own experience with book boxes — we use portable LP record cases — is very similar.) The proposed solution to help the 5% unable to make use of USSR at Forest Hill is that 'they can be withdrawn during the reading period for small counselling groups, where they can discuss their own interests and any books they have enjoyed reading, so that they can be given as much help as possible in choosing a book which will have sufficient appeal to engage their interest'. Clearly, the disinclination of some pupils to read is a major stumbling block to the teacher trying to run reading periods without the support of a school policy; it is invaluable to have the backing of the school's finances, a librarian and, in Forest Hill's case, a member of staff given responsibility for the scheme.

Broad Heath Primary Community School, Coventry, also chose the half hour immediately after lunch for its silent reading period. Children selected what they wanted to read — fiction or non-fiction, encyclopaedias or comics (though they were expected to read from 'a range of reading matter over the week, with a limit of one day a week for comics'). Some of the poorer readers, or children with second language difficulties (80% of the school's pupils were Asians) were able to get individual help from support workers funded by Manpower Services.

USSR is derived ultimately from a belief that 'any reading is better than no reading', and the work of pioneers like Daniel Fader, whose *Hooked on Books* (6) remains one of the most heartening and entertaining 'reads' for teachers of literature. Fader's reading programme in the W.J. Maxey Boys' Training School (a penal institution in Michigan) and the Garnett-Patterson Junior High School in Washington, D.C., was based on the dual concepts of 'saturation' and 'diffusion'. With the liberal financial backing of a News Company in Detroit, Fader poured newspapers, magazines and paperbacks into every class in the schools ('saturation') and asked every teacher in every classroom to 'make the home of literacy attractive'. Books were displayed in wire racks rather than placed on shelves, so that classrooms became more like attractive bookshops than libraries ('diffusion'). With his emphais on reading in every subject and writing as a 'means to all ends', Fader was playing John the Baptist to the Language Across the Curriculum movement. His dictum was, 'every teacher becomes a teacher of English, and English is taught in every classroom'. Fader's English programme was taken up and implemented in 37 states. He describes the experience of Sam Sublett, the Director of the Boys' Training School at St. Charles, Illinois, when the new paperbacks arrived one afternoon just before a needle basketball game.

> Friday evening's game was not just another horserace. The teams were evenly matched and hot. He and other staff members were held spellbound by a real contest. Midway through the second quarter,

up on his feet and yelling, Sam suddenly had that lonely feeling. Only then — for the first time since the game began — did he look around him instead of in front of him. 'How,' he asks now, 'do you tell anybody who wasn't there that *half* those kids were reading paperbound books while a red-hot ballgame was burning up the gym they were reading in?'

In the United Kingdom, Jennie Ingham's account (7) of the Bradford Book Flood Experiment in the late seventies documents the effects of saturating two middle schools with 4500 books each (two-thirds fiction to one-third non-fiction). These schools were compared in the experiment to two 'control' middle schools where no such flood was precipitated. Jennie Ingham's account is of particular interest to teachers in schools where minority cultures are strongly represented, since about a quarter of the pupils from the two inner city schools in Bradford used in the Book Flood were from ethnic minorities — usually of Indian or Pakistani origin. The value of the class library is reiterated in her conclusions:

> Something that pupils, teachers and headteachers in all four schools agreed upon, was that they would like to see the continued use of class libraries in some shape or form after the end of the experiment. The headmaster of the outer city experimental school, where there had been virtually no class libraries before the experiment, had been the most antagonistic towards them and in favour of centralizing all but remedial readers and reading schemes in the school library, yet he was prepared to admit the advantages of class libraries — despite the administrative difficulties involved — by the end of the experiment...
>
> Since availability and accessibility in terms of time as well as location are obviously such important factors, it follows that having books on hand, as it were, in the class base or English base increases the likelihood of children reading, since a visit to the school library is usually of necessity a more formal, less flexible arrangement. The class library facilitates spare-moment reading, and more closely approximates the situation in the home of the advantaged child than does the weekly or fortnightly visit to the school library.

The principle of making such time available seems so obviously *right* that it is surprising that a daily session of independent reading is not as regular a practice as might be expected in most secondary schools and many primary schools.

Why is the practice not more widespread? First, inevitably, there is the matter of finance. A book box or 'class library' of about 110 paperbacks and non-net hardback novels for a mixed class of 25–30 pupils costs no more than three sets of all-class readers. Since different book-boxes can be rotated around the classes in the same year, it can be argued that this is a fair investment. The financial issue then involves the priorities of those who hold the school's purse strings. It may be that literature teachers have not argued their case persuasively enough. The earlier chapters of this book, we believe provide the basis of such a case. If our account of the reading process is accurate, the place of story in the growth of the child and the continuing wellbeing of the adult could hardly be more important. If story *is* a means of making bridges between our 'inner' experience and the 'outer' world in which we move, as Ted Hughes (8) suggests, then his claim that the lines of communication between inner and outer worlds in Western culture have become 'disconnected' cannot be shrugged off. This breakdown in communication, Hughes believes, is no less than the atrophy of the imagination, for the patterning of our experience through the interplay of inner and outer worlds is an essential imaginative activity.

> The inner world, separated from the outer world, is a place of
> demons. The outer world, separated from the inner world, is a place
> of meaningless objects and machines.

All who work in schools, including literature teachers, are under increasing pressures; not the least is the suspicion that those who decide the parameters of their professional work are sometimes sceptical of anything that is not self-evidently 'useful'. Without resort to overstatement or sentimentality, we need to have a clear rationale for why we want children to love stories and poems, if we are to protect ourselves from political pressure without and consequent weariness within.

Such a belief in literature indicates, by implication, a further reason why some schools give no time to private reading. If the teacher is not a reader himself, his classes know; and a scheme like USSR stands little chance of success. One of the aspects of USSR stressed by its advocates is that for at least a considerable portion of a reading period teachers themselves must be seen to be reading. They may also be available to change books, and to advise upon selection, but not to roam the desks intrusively. As in so many classroom enterprises, the catalyst is the attitude of the teacher; he *means* this activity to work. In their survey of 'Twenty-five teacher-tested ways to encourage voluntary reading' (9) Roeder and Lee saw as the most important: '*Exude enthusiasm*. Above all, display a positive, enthusiastic attitude towards reading.' Exuding enthusiasm may be less straightforward than it is made to sound, but the point is fairly made.

Even the most avid teacher-reader can be vulnerable to an insidious sense of guilt about surrendering regular class time for private reading: some teachers genuinely feel anxious when children are 'just reading' — if we aren't teaching them, how can they be learning? The fallacy is clear enough from a distance, but it is true that the issue becomes muddied when there is a syllabus to be covered, examinations to be prepared for, administrative papers to be shuffled, and even parental pressures to be considered. Private reading time is always a probable casualty.

There is a last, even more compelling, reason why some schools do not allow time for independent reading. Teachers have tried it and found that it

97

does not work. We noted in relation to the Forest Hill scheme the advantages of an all-school policy; when a teacher is working alone, even a couple of children who do not want to read can make life very difficult for the rest. Some pupils find a period too long, and indeed there is a case for starting the practice with a shorter time. Others find book selection genuinely difficult, and mask their confusion in a variety of ways, some of which can be disruptive.

In a particularly valuable article (*10*), Mike Raleigh, of the English Centre of the Inner London Education Authority, looks at the reasons behind the unwillingness of some young people to read books of any kind on their own — in or out of school. Like all the publications of the English Centre, his discussion is rooted in real schools; his list might serve as a useful starter in any staff seminar about reading policies. His particular concern was with 4th Year secondary children, but he arranges his list of factors which may cause a pupil's refusal to read 'in a rough order which follows a child's career through primary and secondary school'.

☆ You are a boy.
☆ There isn't much book-reading at home or among relatives and friends.
☆ You were initiated into reading by methods which highlighted the techniques rather than the functions of reading and which communicated to you a narrow sense of what reading is and what it's good for.
☆ At your primary school there was a heavy emphasis on reading aloud to the teacher from 'scheme books' (perhaps taking up to a term to finish one book in this way) and little opportunity for extended silent reading from self-chosen material.
☆ You tended to be slow with your other work in class and so missed most of the opportunities that there were for silent reading 'after you've finished'.
☆ You haven't talked much about books in school or elsewhere.
☆ You don't own any books yourself.
☆ You don't belong to a public library.
☆ The secondary school you go to doesn't have a decent library, or, if it has one, doesn't encourage you to use it.
☆ The school doesn't have adequate class library provision.
☆ Subject teaching in your school makes limited use of texts (i.e. limited as to type of text and kind of use); where it happens, reading is closely guided and frequently interrupted; the teaching stresses the demonstration of competence (literary or otherwise) over the development of interest and purpose in reading.
☆ You've been offered a series of inappropriate books by adults who are keen that you should do some reading.
☆ You see a considerable gap between the kinds of books legitimized in school and the kinds of books you might choose to read yourself if you could find them.

☆ You haven't developed your own reliable criteria for choosing a book and so have made a series of bad choices yourself.

☆ You don't think you're much good at reading.

Some of the items on Mike Raleigh's list contain the seeds of solutions to the problems, though others fall outside the teacher's influence. He goes on to propose that there *are* things to be done in school to help dispel the notion that 'reading books on your own is a tedious, unrewarding and, in any case, rather marginal activity'.

He suggests ten ways in which teachers have tried to promote independent reading, acknowledging that his brief account cannot reflect all local complexities. Shortages of money, time and energy are real constraints, but his proposals make up such a useful checklist that they are worth quoting in full.

Ten things schools could do

1 Do **a survey of reading habits** in the school in order to get precise information about what and how much is read and the sources that children get books from; and set up a system for monitoring changes in the nature and extent of independent reading as children go up the school.

2 Hold joint **meetings with primary schools** about provision for independent reading and consider how useful, detailed information about new secondary pupils' reading might be made available by primary schools.

3 Hold **discussions with parents** about voluntary reading, perhaps with a view to setting up a formal (but optional) 'home-reading' scheme.

4 Form **a library committee** (including pupil representatives) to work with the librarian to ensure that the school library is:
   – adequately stocked with books that children want to read;
   – a place where books are displayed to full advantage and in ways children understand;
   – an attractive and comfortable area;
   – open for general use before school, during breaks and after school.
   Harder: ensure that the library is **planned** into the curriculum of a full range of subjects.

5 Devise **lists** of useful and accessible fiction and information books to support and extend curriculum work in a full range of subjects; these books to be made available within subject classrooms as well as in the library, and the reading of them to be given the status of homework.

6 Establish and maintain **a school bookshop** which is:
   – located in its own permanent, central, secure, attractive premises;
   – funded so that a large, regularly changed stock of books is always available for purchase;
   – able to meet the needs of customers (including teachers and

parents) through an efficient ordering system;
- well-publicized, and open at least three times a week;
- managed (with assistance from pupils) by a teacher with a post of responsibility and/or a couple of extra free periods.

7 Organize **visits** by children to a local library and bookshop in school time so that they all know their way into and around these places.

8 Run a regular **book-fair**, during which special timetabling allows for:
- talks and readings by writers;
- exhibitions and book-sales;
- book-related activities and competitions.

9 Provide a **bookbox** for each class so that children have immediate access to a supply of books which is:
- sufficient in quantity and wide enough in range and type for all children to make a reasonable choice from;
- efficiently managed and maintained so that the books remain available and are regularly added to or changed.

10 Make independent **reading time** a fixture on the timetable so that all children get a regular chance in school just to read. This time could be added to the timetable allocation of English/Integrated Studies or established during extended tutor-periods or given a special timetable slot of its own. Provision could be made within this reading time for:
- 'promotional activities' (i.e. introductions to and discussions of books) suggested and supervized by one or two teachers with specific responsibility;
- direct help to pupils who find reading on their own difficult.

Several of Mike Raleigh's suggestions were also features of the Bradford Book Flood, including the use of school bookshops, class libraries and a regular reading time. We would only add that some of the proposals can be less daunting than they seem. In Chapter 8, we include sources of help and information, many of which relate to Mike Raleigh's list.

The suggestions have much in common with Daniel Fader's belief that the school, and in particular the classroom, should be a place where books are very much around; a place where it feels normal to a pupil to see himself as someone who regularly handles reading matter, a member of a community which finds it normal to read.

The enthusiast

We want to move to a discussion of the sharing of literature by way of a plea for the enthusiast — and even the eccentric, a sadly endangered species in the teaching profession. Edward Blishen (*11*) tells how he was taught arithmetic very badly by 'an Irishman appointed to teach mathematics on the grounds that he was an international lawn tennis player'. Although he ascribes his own innumeracy to this misfortune, Blishen writes:

He used to give us free use of his private library at home. He used to bring us books in a perfectly natural way. He talked about books with joy and pleasure, and also when it was necessary — and it turned out to be often necessary.— talked abusively about books. He had a lovely habit as he came ungowned into Assembly — because, as you know, lawn tennis and a profound passion for literature don't earn you gowns — he had a habit, as he passed between the rows of boys, of tossing a book into your lap as he went by with some murmur of: 'Sh — you'll love this,' or 'Sh — you'll hate this,' or best of all, 'Don't let anybody see that! Keep it quiet!' I remember one of the books he told me to keep quiet about was *Tess of the D'Urbervilles*, and I am eternally grateful, though it was already half a century too late to keep quiet about that. But what a sense of conspiracy he knew how to generate! Pedagogically he was an immensely ingenious man, though in fact in pedagogy he might have rated very low indeed. How simple was all that he did, and how good it was to be made part of his life as a reader! How influential to have this utterly natural exhibition by a grown-up, with whom you were constantly in contact, of the quality of a true reader who displayed before us, quite naturally, all the responses to books, rage as well as deep appreciation. How simple!

Primary teachers can be more flexible than their secondary colleagues. Poems especially can be 'fitted in', prompted by something which crops up in the course of the day; they may be a response to the mood of the class, a turn in the weather, an item of news. Later, we shall discuss the need to 'prepare the way' for stories and poems with classes — much of that discussion is more relevant to the fragmented day of the secondary school than to the fluid timetable of those primary teachers whose enthusiasm for literature and sensitivity to a class make for the natural introduction of poems and stories. Such teachers break the routine, produce the unexpected. They take children by surprise in a way that often sticks. What counts is the infectious spontaneity of someone saying, 'Hey, listen to this, I thought you'd enjoy it.'

Some approaches to the shared text

The case for the sharing of stories is literally as old as language. The people of early societies seem to have valued their oral literature as an entertaining, memorable means of making sense of the world they saw about them, of the behaviour of their fellows, and of themselves. In Ted Hughes's terms, such tales linked inner and outer worlds. The coherence of the stories offered the hope of coherence in life itself. The North-West Coastal Indians of North America, for example, accorded a tribal storyteller the status of a chieftain; upon him depended the health of the community — his tales of ravens and salmon, bears and eagles, told how the animals had prepared the world and given it a pattern in readiness for the arrival of mankind. The storyteller's magic, like that of the Anglo-Saxon scop, the medieval minstrel or the

eighteenth-century balladmonger, (or even a rabbit named Dandelion in
Watership Down), lay in bringing dead words to life in the imaginations of his
audience. The value of shared story and poetry today is of no less importance
than it was for the tribal community.

Experienced teachers of literature will recall occasions when a novel, a
poem or a play has brought a strong consciousness of identity to a group;
often to the surprise, and even embarrassment of its members. We recall a
reading of Graham Greene's 'The Destructors' to a very 'hard' class of
Technical High School boys in an American comprehensive school, which
precipitated sixteen page stories and hesitantly related accounts of vandalism
— told without braggadocio — which had been waiting for an audience for
some time; Arthur Miller's *The Crucible* where the hysteria of the courtroom
scene brought sudden recognitions about coercion to some bright thirteen
year olds; the early chapters of *The Iron Man* provoking uneasy shared
laughter among a class of nine year olds, as the little boy lured the Iron Man
into the trap. It is all too easy to miss such opportunities for children to
respect — and indeed to enjoy — each others' similarities and differences if
we emphasize the text at the expense of the readers. For such qualities
inevitably emerge as the characteristics of the openly shared response to
literature. We do not want to seem excessively idealistic; we also remember a
boy pulling a knife — not in role — during a lesson on *Romeo and Juliet;* but
the abrasiveness of many classrooms and schools at present should not cause
us to lose sight of what *can* be, and what sometimes *is*.

For a moment, let us glance back to Wallace Stevens's absorbed reader.
We have noted how the skilled reader grows practised in allowing his
thoughts and feelings to flicker to and fro between the world in which he sits
and that in which he moves through a compelling narrative, watching and
listening unseen from his place in the shadows, until primary and secondary
worlds coalesce. When we read, we take satisfaction in the turn of a phrase,
the shape of an image, the teasing surprise of a short story, or the subtle
organization of a novel. Repeated experiences of our unique meetings with
poems, stories and novels have made us committed readers.

The pleasure in a shared text should complement, and even enhance, the
pleasure to be taken in solitary reading; the opportunity to bring personal
responses to the same text into play with the reactions of others can lead to a
development, a refinement of each reader's unique experience. The sharing of
a poem or a story in class should not lead to the suppression of the personal
response, or to its submersion in the corporate response of the group.

There are problems. For example, how does a reader know that a reaction
to a poem will not be derided , or a personal experience savaged? How then
can we best preserve and enhance each pupil's reading of a text, so that he
increasingly confirms, and takes pleasure in, his sense of himself as someone
who reads? In answering that question, we must look first at some current
approaches to all-class teaching of literature.

a) The 'transmission' approach   Much teaching of literature at degree
level and for public examinations in the General Certificate of Education (at

both 'A' and 'O' levels) is characterized by two assumptions: the expression of personal, idiosyncratic response is inappropriate, even inadmissible, especially in written work; and the educated opinions of the teacher ultimately carry more weight than those of the students. Perhaps because of their own training, many teachers, with an eye already on the public examinations, carry these assumptions into their literature work with their younger classes in secondary schools. Primary school teachers might refute such an influence on their teaching but many 'comprehension passages' based on novels and poems in junior school text books carry the same assumptions about what is an appropriate response. The expression of an opinion or an anecdote is virtually excluded.

We take one example chiefly to suggest an alternative to the 'list of questions' approach and to clarify what might be meant by the term 'comprehension'. One particular book published in the 1980s for juniors is made up of lively passages, often taken from recent children's fiction. *(12)* The first extract describes the caning of the hero by the infamous Captain Lancaster in Roald Dahl's *Danny, the Champion of the World*. Pupils are then required to move on to fifteen questions. The first three will give the flavour of them all: 'Where was the cane kept?'; 'Describe the cane as fully as you can'; 'What part of the person was caned?'

In what sense do such questions test comprehension? By way of an oblique answer, we offer these unedited, and uncorrected, excerpts from some freewheeling notes made by some eleven year olds in a mixed-ability class in Cornwall. The children had listened to the passage and then, much in the style we have described on pp 12–13 jotted down anything that had passed through their minds as they heard the story. We think they demonstrate a strong sense of how literature really works in the minds of young readers and that 'comprehension' is both a wider and a deeper matter than the usual lists of questions imply.

☆ I was thinking when I had the cane in West Africa, Freetown. And what it would feel like to have a red hot poker on the palm of your hand. And was thinking when I opened a window and the glass fell out.

☆ When he reached up to the top shelf I thought he had got a book. But when he got down the cane I dreaded what was going to happen to the boy.

☆ I would not like that done to me. I thought poor boy it must be a horrible teacher that cane must of hurt. I will neaver do somthing to get the cane. I wonder what his hand would look like after that.

☆ While you were telling that part of a story, a thought went through my head, what if I was that boy, the pain it would of caused me as it had the boy. The teacher just about to strike, the pain and fear just about to strike, the thought about the pain it would cause. A thought went through my head, the thought of relief that I was not that boy.

☆ It was a very tense passage because everything was moving so fast and it seemed as though it was happening in this very classroom.

When he held out his left hand and when it was hit, I could, kind of
see the picture in my mind of it and especially when he was in pain
and I could imagine what he felt like trying not to cry out amongst
all his friends and show him up.

☆ I was thinking about the time me and Druker and Volonte put a slug
in an envelope.

(Sensitive investigation revealed that a caning was administered to the
miscreant Stephen and his henchmen for sealing the envelope and posting it
to a luckless probationer teacher. They were punished for cruelty to man and
beast.)

We would argue that the four major elements of response which we
identified in Chapter 2 (picturing, anticipating and retrospecting, interacting,
and evaluating) are all present in this handful of extracts as indeed they have
been in every investigation of this kind which we have conducted. Even these
snippets reflect the characteristic movement of readers (or listeners), flicker-
ing to and fro between their own lives and Danny's experience. Several
children wrote and talked about feeling pain in their own hands. Many
recalled comparable occasions. If we are ultimately interested in helping
pupils to enjoy the richness offered to them through reading — to see
themselves as readers — we do better to start with such responses than by
asking them where the cane was kept. (What *does* the ability to say where the
cane was kept actually demonstrate?) How we develop the kind of idiosyncratic responses such exercises always reveal is the business of Chapters 6
and 7.

From such comprehension tests to the formal university lecture, there is
no doubt where authority lies in the relationship between teacher and learner.
There can be no opportunity for the learner to enjoy the kind of exploratory
talk which leads to an increasing confidence in himself as a maturing reader.
Such talk presupposes a measure of assurance and, even at postgraduate level,
it sometimes proves necessary for a teacher physically to leave a group on its
own — to remove the accustomed figure of authority — if the students' own
responses are to have the chance of expression.

Previous experience stretching back to infant school may have taught
pupils that the last word belongs with the teacher; or if 'discussions' have
usually been in the context of the whole class, moderated by the teacher, the
contributions have usually been those of the more articulate, confident
members of the group. The diffident are offered no space in which to dispel
their uncertainties through tentative expression of their thoughts — to find
out what they think as they talk. The uninvolved may remain uninvolved,
since it is uncomfortable, or impossible, to challenge the conventions;
moreover, active participation costs effort and suggests enthusiasms which
can lead to criticism by one's peers in some classrooms.

Pupils taught in this 'stand-and-deliver' style learn to suspend response to
a text. If they have read the rules of the game accurately, they know that since
they will be told eventually what to think (and what to write in exams),

problems can be avoided if they leave a mental space blank for others' opinions to be written there. Questions asked of them directly (if these are questions which they expect the teacher to answer in due course) do little to excite engagement or indeed to invade their privacy, beyond calling into play some practised survival tactics. It is true that many who teach in this way claim to provoke and welcome 'a good argument'. Do such arguments commonly result in the participants — teacher or taught — changing their minds? Is the function of such an argument really to sharpen up the teacher's own opinions, so that the class will grasp them more clearly?

This approach may be most deficient in the shared reading of poetry, where more facets of meaning should be revealed as the thoughts and feelings of diverse personalities play upon the compressed language of a text. From the pupils' perspective, a poem can seem to be a kind of crossword puzzle which is too difficult for them, but with solutions which the teacher will gradually reveal. Such teaching, with its stress on the analysis rather than the experience of a poem, may be found even in the early years of secondary schools. Some teachers who work in this way do so from the most worthy of reasons: they deeply wish their pupils to share their own passion for the texts they are reading, for example, or there may be a concern to arm the student effectively for impending skirmishes with the examiner. The problem is that the less confident are excluded from seeing themselves as readers, if the first concern of their teachers is the teaching of the text, not the promotion of a skilled habit in their pupils.

In short, those activities which characterize the committed reader, as we described them in Chapter 1, are being offered scant space for exercise or expression. Pupils perceive few signs that their own thoughts and feelings about novels, stories and poems are valued by their teachers. It is a common-place for adults looking back on their schooldays to report that their enthusiasm for reading was dampened through this kind of teaching, culminating in 'O' level literature examinations — an effect precisely the opposite of what many of their teachers sincerely wished for them.

b) The thematic approach Novels are often used as elements in a thematic or 'project-based' approach, sometimes within integrated programmes of work in junior schools and in the early years of secondary schools. Henry Treece's Miklagaard Trilogy might be raided for brief extracts to enliven a study of the Vikings; a study of 'Transport' might pause for a moment over Auden's 'Night Mail'; a cloze passage from *Tarka the Otter* or lines from Seamus Heaney's 'Trout' might be included in a project on 'River Creatures'. When a lively biologist colleague asks for three poems about insects or rubs his hands over his discovery of Kafka's *Metamorphosis*, it is difficult to suppress a twinge of ambivalence.

If we believe readers become better readers by engaging with whole stories and poems, by learning to enjoy the mental and emotional activities we mentioned in our discussion of the reading process in Part One, we must doubt the value of literature 'used' in this way. For example, the experience of anticipating and retrospecting, or an enjoyment of shape and pattern which lie at the heart of literary pleasure, are virtually excluded from texts presented in this fragmented form. From the perspective of young readers, fiction and poetry may seem to be resource material or text books in thin disguise.

c) The 'false centre' approach   Some English Departments, or individual teachers, not attracted by the thematic approach and wishing to avoid the tedium of 'Poetry on Mondays, Language Work on Tuesdays, Writing on Wednesdays ... ' decide to base virtually all their work in English around a class text. The provision of a unified, continuing experience for their classes is attractive at first sight. The drawback to this approach lies in the disjointed experience of the text which a class may receive and in the implicit message about literature itself communicated to the young reader.

A class basing all its work on a single novel is likely to spend a very long time getting through the book; the journey through the narrative, which for many young readers would normally be extremely rapid, is regularly interrupted to make excursions which deflect the reader away from the continuing story and its characters. Pupils might find themselves asked to restore a passage of dialogue from the last chapter they have read together in *Charlotte's Web*, now presented to them innocent of punctuation. ('When you've finished, you can check it against the correct version on page 25.') The prelude to the next story in an anthology could be a requirement to master ten tricky spellings or hunt out the dictionary meanings of eight unfamiliar words about to crop up in the text. Answers to the insistent question, 'What happens next?' are frustratingly deferred until the habit of asking the question may be stifled.

This kind of work does not draw a reader more closely into the text as literature. The absorbed processes of the committed reader are not merely left out of the account, but may be actively hindered. When Wallace Stevens's reader pauses, he does so to mull over the text, to delve more deeply into it, or to set his own experiences more closely alongside those offered by the book. When required to base all their English work around a literary text, pupils once again may be inclined to decide that novels are really text books in masquerade.

d) The 'springboard' approach   One other approach, fairly common in junior and secondary schools, also requires some discriminating consideration.

Much lively teaching in recent years has involved a wide range of talking, writing, music, drama and work in the visual arts arising from novels, stories and poetry. In preparing such work, there is a temptation to be carried away by the attractiveness of the activity itself or by the lure of remotely related issues; and so to lose sight of the text.

Thus, in a worksheet on Theodore Taylor's *The Cay*, the relationship between an old black American marooned in the Pacific with a young, blind white boy becomes a point of departure for work on racial minorities in the United Kingdom and the occasion for the question, 'What can we do to help old people?' Robert C. O'Brien's *Mrs. Frisby and the Rats of NIMH*, in which some highly trained rats from a research laboratory lend assistance to a widowed fieldmouse whose home is to be demolished, serves as a springboard for poems, stories and taped radio programmes about the ethics of using animals for medical experiments.

We firmly believe in devising opportunities for responses to novels, stories and poems through a wide range of activities. It is unfortunate, however, when the work draws readers swiftly *away* from the text, where no provision is made for the reflective meeting between reader and book. The 'springboard' approach does not foster a response to the text; pupils may be engaged in an activity which is lively in itself, but for which the novel or poem is no more than an illustration or a pretext. Preferably, the wider issues which distantly relate to a text should be deferred until the text itself has been well explored.

The essential weakness of this approach is that the class's work is shaped by both the teacher's interpretation of the book and his interest in either the activities themselves or the issues loosely related to the book, thus inhibiting the exploration and development of a young reader's own thoughts and feelings about a text. In short, there is once again the risk that such teaching does nothing for his sense of himself as a reader.

e) Negative responses   This section deals with a matter which is not so much an approach as a retreat. We want our pupils to *enjoy* literature. Yet, if we are talking with our friends, as opposed to our pupils, about a novel or a poem we have read, we make no requirement that our friends should all have *enjoyed* the book.

No matter how battle-hardened he may be, the enthusiastic teacher of literature probably remains vulnerable to the judgement, 'It's crap'; or, even more telling, 'It's boring'. For a start, we have usually brought the novel or the poem to the class in the hope that they will like it. (Most pupils in literature classes assume that what the teacher brings to them is 'supposed to be good'.) Furthermore, we may have painstakingly laid plans for them to live with this novel or this book of poetry for several periods, and the bookroom shelves may be bare of alternatives anyway. Faced with these judgements, even the most egalitarian teacher may suddenly discover a sense of undermined authority. In this situation, he may understandably assume a defensive stance which, since he is usually in a position of authority, can easily become aggressive or dismissive.

Yet if we want pupils to be discriminating, we must expect — even hope — that they will sometimes discriminate *against*. If we want to honour the individual reader's response, there is little consistency in ignoring negative responses. Certainly, we need to use some discrimination ourselves. 'It's crap' or 'It's boring' may mean all kinds of things, as experienced teachers well know. Some meanings fall outside the concerns of this book: bids for attention, expressions of personal hostility, challenges to authority in general, tokens of apathy or private malaise. However, such judgements *may* often mean, 'This is too difficult. I can't understand what he's getting at'. Where the response is one of confusion or genuine dislike of a particular novel or poem, we believe pupils are usually willing to tease out that initial response if they think they are being seriously heard.

Young readers usually need the means to work out negative responses, just as they need the opportunities to develop their positive responses. In Chapter 6, we shall discuss the use of a reading journal, and this is often the place for two or three word condemnations to be expanded before a more sustained written argument or a discussion. If a pupil continues to feel a rooted dislike for a text, we cannot see much point in asking him to go on with it after a reasonable sampling and, ideally, a thoughtful account of his reactions. The best alternative is probably that such readers then continue with alternative texts, usually of their own choosing.

Where there is a widespread lack of enjoyment in a class text, the best single format we know for making a positive experience out of the situation is a semi-formal debate or 'trial', prepared for by individual notes. The book, the characters or the author might be put 'on trial', for example, and pupils allotted particular roles (defendant, hostile or sympathetic witnesses, members of the jury, chief prosecutor and so on). Whatever the strategy, pupils must believe that genuine negative responses will be honoured.

Framework for a methodology

We need some touchstones by which to judge what we plan to do with a story or a poem. We find it useful to ask two basic questions: 'Will this activity enable the reader to look back on the text and to develop the meanings he has already made?' and 'Does what I plan to do bring reader and text closer together, or does it come between them?' Other questions, shaped by the elements of response we discussed in Part One might be asked of particular texts and specific teaching strategies. Will my pupils have the chance to become 'lost' in the narrative by the way we read the story or the poem? Will it be readily possible for them to enjoy, say, the humour of this poem, or to be moved by the sense of loss in that story? Will there be the means for them to set their own experiences alongside the text? Might they find clarification or confirmation of ideas they have come across before in books or in 'real life'? Will they meet new ideas and be enabled to assess, and perhaps assimilate, these ideas? If they dislike a text, can they say so?

There can be no single formula for teaching a text. The 'best' approach may be dictated by the uniqueness of the book itself and the distinctive character of each group of young readers; and of each teacher. And we need to bear in mind that very frequently the most appropriate approach to a novel, story or poem may be to introduce it to our pupils by reading it aloud or in the silence of private reading, and then to let it be, allowing them and the book to find their own way together.

The model we propose provides a framework for planning literature lessons in which there is room for the individual's response and for later collaborative work, intended to enhance appreciation. Certain general premises underpin the proposal:

☆ Often, there is much to be gained by preparing the way for a text, to create as receptive a context as possible. This is especially true of poetry, which must usually make its effects in less time and space than prose where the writer has time to draw the reader in. So, *before* many poems, and some novels, are begun, we could plan activities which increase their chances of being enjoyed.

☆ We need to think about work for individuals and groups to do *during* the reading of texts — of novels particularly — which might develop, in all our pupils, the processes which characterize a skilled reader. For example, what might we do to encourage the habit of anticipating what is going to happen next, of wondering how things will all end, of setting one's own experiences alongside those offered by a novel, of enjoying the shape of a text — all without coming between the reader and the book in a distracting fashion?

☆ *After* a text is read we need to provide sufficient 'space' for the individual to discover, confirm and perhaps relish his own unique response to it, before the ideas of others (his fellow pupils and his teacher) are considered.

☆ *After* the individual has felt and thought his way into a text, we may often wish to provide the means for the class to share their feelings and thoughts, to refine their ideas and perhaps to develop them further together, although this does not preclude an individual's continued personal exploration of a book or a poem.

The diagram on p. 110 is an attempt to represent our methodology for literature teaching in graphic terms. It is presented rather diffidently, since the whole business of good literature teaching demands a spontaneity born of enthusiasm; and the last thing we want to suggest is slavish conformity to a repeated plan. However, many teachers report that they find the framework represented by the diagram to be helpful.

It is necessary to relate the diagram to short stories, poems and novels separately since, as we have indicated in Part One, the activity of the reader differs according to the kind of text he is reading.

Short stories Preliminary or preparatory work (Stage I) may well be less necessary than with poems or even novels — the short story often makes its own swift impact. Thereafter, Stages II, III, and IV might well follow in sequence.

Poems We have compared the movement of the reader coming to possess a poem — particularly a poem inviting a reflective response — to someone viewing a sculpture from different angles (p. 19). In terms of our diagram, the class might be prepared for the poem by some means (I), meet the text (II), jot for a while individually or in some other way (for example, by sketching) to 'hold' a personal response (III). After this, a teacher might want to reread the poem (thus returning to II), before moving on to some work in

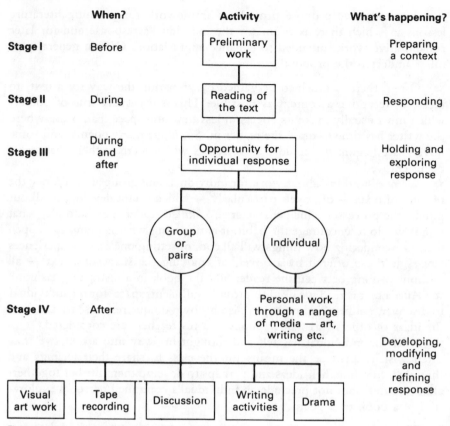

Figure 4   A framework for literature teaching

which responses are compared, or the individual continues a private exploration of the poem (IV). This last stage allows further 'walking around inside the poem' to enable a fuller response to be developed.

Novels   Reading a novel in class obviously takes several days, even weeks. The sequence of activities may well therefore be repeated many times, when it seems helpful to pause in the reading to undertake some work intended to deepen understanding and appreciation of the text. As we have stressed, there may be times when it feels right to allow nothing at all to interrupt a storyline which has a class hungry for more. When this is the case, Stage II properly dominates, I and IV are best forgotten, and III may be kept to the kind of brief activity in a reading journal which we shall describe in detail in the next chapter.

Any uncertainty provoked by this diagram should be dispersed by Chapters 6 and 7, which provide numerous illustrations of practical ways in which the different stages of the diagram can be implemented in the classroom. We move on to such discussion by way of a bridging section which focusses on a fundamental matter reflected in our Stage II — the reading of the text.

The reading of the text

a) The teacher reading aloud A teacher who cannot read aloud well is seriously handicapped. Reading aloud well is not *essentially* a matter of technique — a teacher's reading is an index of the kinds of confidence he has available to him and of his relationship with the class: a willingness to be experimental — playful, even — with his voice, to hold a pause, to characterize anyone from a goose to an archbishop. Ultimately, good reading grows from a sense of personal freedom and security whose discovery, and rediscovery, are at the heart of good teaching.

Technical problems of voice production are beyond our scope, though there are extended discussions of the subject elsewhere (*13*). There are several rules-of-thumb, however, which we have found useful when reading to live audiences in school:

1 The basic pace for reading aloud needs to be slightly slower than that of normal conversational speech. This makes it possible for a voice to carry clearly to distant reaches of the room without words blurring together; and makes variations in tempo much more manageable for dialogue, humour, high excitement or sadness.

2 For audibility, from shouts to whispers, the voice needs to be directed at about the middle of the facing wall.

3 Characters will almost always come alive more vividly, especially for younger listeners, if they are presented as rather larger than life. The more clear distinctions between characters can be made, the better. This applies especially to major characters — too many voices for a large cast of minor characters could be confusing.

4 If planning time and energy permit, passages to be read can be 'marked up' like an acting script. Different coloured fluorescent 'highlighter' pens are useful, especially if some 'editing' to avoid lengthy digressions seems advisable with some classes.

5 Most British speakers tend to drop their voices at the end of sentences. The discriminating use of a raised inflection though it may sound unnatural, carries the listeners' interest on to what may be coming next.

6 On occasions, some *understated* physical movement can both clarify and reinforce the action; standing up may serve this purpose — or to give a specific example, a slowly raised hand, palm upwards as listeners share the anguish of Danny awaiting the stroke of the cane from the savage Captain Lancaster in Roald Dahl's *Danny, the Champion of the World*, (referred to on p. 103) draws a class into closer sympathy with the hero's predicament.

7 It is often helpful to pick up direct eye contact with individual listeners from time to time, to link them to yourself as a reader. This obviously helps to gauge reactions also, and indeed can be a means of control without disturbing the flow of the story. A teacher whose eyes are consistently locked downwards onto the book loses contact with the listeners — an invisible wall divides them.

8 If classrooms are organized with pupils seated around tables, some children will need to turn their seats around before a reading session begins. Although this may seem potentially disruptive, it is in the long run, time very well invested. Some successful teachers of fiction with sufficiently flexible classrooms gather their classes around them for reading sessions — settling them on desks, tables or a carpeted floor, a practice widespread in junior schools. The advantage is not only that it is easier to share the nuances of a story with people close to you; it also signals that, as a group, teacher and class are about to enjoy a story or some poems together. The connotations of pleasure associated with sharing stories are reinforced by this physical regrouping.

There is, of course, no real alternative to practice in this skill. Training institutions can help their students by providing them with plenty of experience of reading to groups of fellow undergraduates, and a taste of the pleasure of being well received by an audience. One pattern is to begin sessions in college with a reading of a page or so from a children's book the group have all been reading that week (sets of paperbacks bought for this purpose and for subsequent use on teaching practice are invaluable in prompting enthusiasm, even addiction). All the students select and practise a page to read, not knowing who will be reading in any particular session since names are ritually drawn from a hat at the start of the class — or students read to each other in clusters of twos or threes. Praise, criticism and occasional demonstration may follow; better to find things out here than on teaching practice, the students quickly agree, and it's rather good fun anyway. Student-teachers may also prepare anthologies for PTA meetings or for lunch-time entertainments in the training institution. The principle becomes self-evident to students — reading aloud well matters, if children are to learn to hear the different rhythms and voices of novels and poems in their own minds' ears as they read silently.

Readers eager to become more effective also benefit from reading in empty classrooms to a supportive but analytical listener (a colleague, perhaps, seated on the back row); and there is much to learn by experimenting with one's own readings into a tape recorder.

b) Alternative ways of reading the text The practice of asking children to read unprepared passages around the class is still the most common variant on the teacher reading the text to the class. A majority of pupils dislike this system; sometimes they say vehemently that they hate it. Good readers scan ahead, impatient with hesitant or stumbling fellow pupils; the poor reader is confirmed publicly in his inadequacy; the drift of the story is easily lost through constant interruptions as readers are changed or poor readers lose the thread and are corrected; consistent characterization is impossible and, if a predictable sequence of readers is used, (up and down the rows, for example) anxious victims silently mouth their paragraphs a couple of turns ahead. Where children feel like this about reading around the class, the system is at best tedious and often humiliating. The implicit message is not only that the teacher does not care about pupils' feelings, but he does not care much about the story either.

It must be admitted, however, that in classes where there is a widespread ability to read aloud well, sharing a novel in this way may be extremely popular — the volunteering hands punch the air at the end of every paragraph. If so, then teacher and class are mutually fortunate — for such enthusiasm usually reflects respect and even affection between children, and an excellent climate for work with literature. Almost anything should be feasible with such groups.

There are more imaginative alternatives to the teacher reading all the text aloud and, for convenience, we set them out as a list:

1 *Reading the highlights* The teacher reads the most demanding, crucial or exciting passages to the class — the 'highlights' as it were — but makes provision for silent reading of the other sections; or, if the conventions of the school reinforce homework, specific readings are assigned to be done in the evenings. (A definite concluding point needs to be fixed, so that the class reading can be picked up together.)

2 *Reading in clusters* Pupils often enjoy reading to each other in the security of a pair or a trio. Surprisingly enough, classroom experience suggests that the noise level rarely becomes intolerable, since the normal reading mode in such groups is at a relatively low pitch.

3 *Taped readings* Sections of the book on tape can be powerful — as though the disembodied voice has a peculiarly liberating effect on the listener's imagination. Some classes like this, others do not — there appears to be no reliable guide except discussion of the technique with a group after trying a taped reading. (Short stories on tape are particularly useful for individual pupils within a group, especially where children can plug in to a recorder at 'listening posts' with individual headphones. They can be of real benefit to the bright, rapid reader and to the child needing a slower pace or an easier story.) The tapes may be prepared by teams from the English Department; although it takes time which is hard to find, the necessary shared inventiveness may do more for departmental morale than meetings devoted to administrative tasks. Students from training institutions could be asked to prepare sections of novels or short stories on cassettes for a class teacher as part of their course work.

4 *Visiting readers* Student teachers on practice in the school (but free that period) might be invited into the class to read. It is an enjoyable, 'safe' experience for students and a welcome chance to work usefully alongside a practising teacher who can provide immediate help and opinion. Idealistic though it may sound, colleagues (not necessarily literature teachers themselves) can be willing to Cox-and-Box free periods to come in and read. Some schools have successfully recruited parents whose commitments allow them to spend time in school. It is not only the variation from their usual teacher that is important to a class. There is a sense of specialness because the teacher and the visiting reader are taking the trouble to set this reading up for the class; this story business must matter to these adults and they, the pupils, evidently matter to them also.

5 Prepared passages or poems If children do read to entire classes as a means of sharing a book, it seems wise if they read only passages they have had opportunity to prepare prior to the lesson (which is cumbersome to arrange) or that 'good readers' take part within the overall narration of the teacher (most obviously by taking roles within dialogue). For the most part, we prefer to reserve this kind of participation to children reading poetry or prose which they have been given class time to prepare in small groups.

None of these techniques can stand over-use. Determining a class's preferences and varying the tactics seem the most likely ways to enhance enjoyment and to avoid tedium.

Chapter 6

Teaching the class novel

Preparing for the journey through the text: Stage I — 'Before'

One of our students was reading Betsy Byars's *The Eighteenth Emergency* with a mixed ability class of eleven year olds. The hero of the book, Bengie (nick-named Mouse) is in the habit of pencilling neat graffiti about his home and person. He labels a cobweb in the living-room UNSAFE FOR PUBLIC SWINGING, the frayed toe of his tennis shoe is marked AIR VENT. What gets him into trouble — and what precipitates the action of the book — is a chart outside the history room at school, showing the ape's progression to Homo Erectus. Mouse neatly inscribes the name of the school bully beneath Neanderthal Man and turns to find himself staring into the anthropoid gaze of Marv Hammerman himself.

Liz decided that before she issued copies of the book, she would have her class write graffiti (on neatly blu-tacked notes). Windows in her second storey classroom were signed EXIT, TEACHERS ONLY, small holes in the skirting board were marked QUIET PLEASE: HILDA AND STAN LIVE HERE and a caption beneath the clock read INSTRUMENT OF TORTURE. The children enjoyed the fun of this — it was an inventive exercise in using concise language and juggling with words. Much more importantly, they became thoroughly intrigued: 'What's Miss up to *now*?' The exercise led them deftly towards the book which, Liz promised, they were to be given the next lesson — 'It'll have something to do with what you've been doing today'. When they read about Mouse's dangerous habit in the first chapter, they were already 'in the know', on the inside of the story.

Similarly, the reading of any of the currently popular novels set during the Second World War (*Carrie's War, The Snow Goose, The Dolphin Crossing, Goodnight, Mister Tom, Fireweed, The Machine-Gunners, The Diary of Anne Frank, Mischling Second Degree*), might be prefaced by providing children with a few questions about the period to ask their parents, grandparents or older friends some days before the story is to be begun in class. (This work could be carried out as taped interviews to be replayed to the class.) Alternatively, someone whose memory goes back to the period — a colleague, the school caretaker, a dinner lady — might be asked to give a 'press conference' style interview which the class has prepared together. Schools could make much more use of local training institutions in this kind of work, inviting students or tutors to come into lessons to role-play characters who could illuminate a text: in this instance, air-raid wardens, evacuees and their 'hosts' or Dunkirk survivors. This kind of experience and the simple research which underpins it are invaluable to student teachers and, again, intriguing for children. Novels about the Second World War need some factual information if pupils are to make sense of the context, and this sort of approach should avoid the arid listing of facts and provide reference points as the class gets further into the novel.

A title may provide a straightforward means of embarking on the journey into the story with heightened anticipation. The question, 'What might a book called *It's My Life/My Mate Shofiq/The Midnight Fox/The Battle of Bubble and Squeak* be about, do you think?', followed by a few moments jotting about possibilities and a pooling of ideas can draw a class into the first chapter curious to check their guesses. A cover to a book (though not the 'blurb' on the back) or a sentence or two from the first couple of pages might be used for similar exercises.

Where some preliminary work does seem likely to be useful, it should be shaped by the novel itself, perhaps arising from the need for background information, some important element in the early chapters or a major theme in the story. It could be useful to foreshadow the conflicting loyalties or the violence beneath the skin of a society (*To the Wild Sky* or *The Wave*); the need to be 'one of the crowd' (*The Chocolate War*); what getting beyond the cliché of 'knowing yourself' means (*A Wizard of Earthsea*); or to provide some facts about the culture and initial difficulties of British Asian families adjusting to the United Kingdom (*Sumitra's Story*).

The decision to undertake such work depends very much on the particular class and the particular novel. Some classes who come to a book with enthusiastic expectations based on previous experience may want little by way of introduction — and might well be irritated by any delay; other groups may need to be 'helped inside' the book. Some books do their own work in drawing readers in, and would indeed lose some of their impact if a class did prefatory work. They may beckon a reader to settle down inside them and become acquainted — even in their opening lines:

> In a hole in the ground there lived a hobbit. Not a nasty, dirty, wet hole, filled with the ends of worms and an oozy smell, nor yet a dry, bare, sandy hole with nothing in it to sit down on or to eat: it was a hobbit-hole, and that means comfort.
>
> It had a perfectly round door like a porthole, painted green, with a shiny yellow brass knob in the exact middle. The door opened on to a tube-shaped hall like a tunnel; a very comfortable tunnel without smoke, with panelled walls, and floors tiled and carpeted, provided with polished chairs, and lots and lots of pegs for hats and coats — the hobbit was fond of visitors.

Tolkien's invitation in *The Hobbit* to drop in at Bag-End, Under-Hill, needs no preliminary.

Other novels so amuse or startle us that we cannot help but read on. A quick jokey epigraph in the idiom beloved of juniors ('What did the cross-eyed teacher say?' 'I can't control my pupils.'), followed by an intriguing opening sentence, ('We'd gone right through the school collecting the teachers' tea money and had got to the canteen door when Danny waved the ten pound note at me.') puts children cheerfully at their ease in Gene Kemp's *The Turbulent Term of Tyke Tiler*. Mary Rodgers demands that you read on into *Freaky Friday* by beginning:

> You are not going to believe me, nobody in their right minds
> could *possibly* believe me, but it's true, really it is!
> *When I woke up this morning, I found I'd turned into my mother.*

Likewise, it would be superfluous to do anything but relish the intrigue and rhythms of the opening lines of Ted Hughes's *The Iron Man*, which almost insist upon vocal participation from their audience:

> The Iron Man came to the top of the cliff.
> How far had he walked? Nobody knows. Where had he come
> from? Nobody knows. How was he made? Nobody knows.
> Taller than a house, the Iron Man stood at the top of the cliff, on
> the very brink, in the darkness.

As the listeners will anticipate, by the end of the page we discover,

> His right foot, his enormous iron right foot, lifted — up, out,
> into space, and the Iron Man stepped forward, off the cliff, into
> nothingness.
> CRRRAAAASSSSSH!

Staying with the story: Stage II — 'During'

There can be few more satisfying experiences for the teacher of literature than those times when an entire class is 'hooked' by a novel. For once in a classroom, we know we are doing absolutely the right thing — sharing the spell of literature. The experience is almost physical, not only in the electricity of the attentiveness, but in postures and facial expressions; often the half smile of the listener who knows an author has him caught in what John Fowles has called a 'teasing relationship' (1).

Doris Lessing's short story 'Through the Tunnel' (2) (a classroom favourite of many teachers) almost always works this kind of magic. In a particularly testing rite of passage, eleven year old Jerry swims through a narrow tunnel beneath a promontory reaching out into the sea. The episode triggers the kind of private questioning characteristic of the engaged reader we described in Chapter 1. Will Jerry get through the tunnel? Will the author 'let' him die? Just what game is she playing when she allows Jerry's hopes — and ours — to soar as he finds a shaft of light only to discover it comes from a crack in the rock above, not the end of the tunnel? What memories of initiation tests and personal challenges are summoned up? What claustrophobic fears? What physical sensations does the reader share — of bursting lungs, of the scraping of rock on the spine? (Some children — and some adults — actually hold their breath and hunch their backs listening to this story.) To return to the question raised on p. 8 — *where* is the reader during the reading? Alongside Jerry, behind him, inside him — or all of those?

When a class virtually insists upon the next episode of a serialized novel, it seems best to read on with as few interruptions as possible, abandoning any other teaching plans until the book is read. To do so is to honour the insistent need to know what happens next. *The Machine-Gunners, The Outsiders,* and *The T.V. Kid* are typical of books that may work in this way; though the fact that *The Machine-Gunners* did the trick with 2C this year is no guarantee at all for next. Teachers who say 'It always works' may be imposing their own enthusiasm for a book upon a class rather than making room to listen to their pupils' responses.

Reading stories with classes where the text provides its own momentum throughout several periods yields an entirely justifiable elation for the literature teacher. In our experience, the occasions when texts and classes fuse in this way are relatively infrequent. Often, activities have to be found to sustain interest and revive involvement on the journey through the book. One quite different problem can arise if pupils take the class reader home. What do you do with those who come in the next morning saying, 'Great. Finished it. What's next?' Our best answers would be to offer them several possibilities: private reading time with books, possibly by the same author, from the class or school libraries; the opportunity to explore the class reader through a prepared sheet of suggested activities or ideas they come up with themselves; or the invitation to 'sit back and enjoy it a second time round with the rest of us'. A class reader should be substantial enough to stand a rereading and in our experiences, for largely worthy reasons, most pupils take the last option.

When a group is well into a novel, there may be a need to refocus their imaginative energies, to draw them into a united concentration upon the story in hand at the start of a lesson. Analogies between teaching and theatrical techniques are usually misleading, but in this case the skills needed by the teacher are very like those used by the performer of a successful one-man show when the audience has reassembled after the distractions of the interval; the invitation is to settle down, to come back into the palm of the hand again, and agree together to continue our imaginative voyage. If we plunge straight into the story, we have to rely upon the power of the narrative itself to refocus the group, and this may be an unreasonable demand, since only the writers of cliffhangers allow for such an episodic rhythm of reading.

We may simply 'recap' the earlier events or recall 'what we were saying yesterday about Miss X and how she was getting on with Mr Y' or 'what happened when Mrs Z decided she would have to ...' Even Wallace Stevens's reader, lost in his quiet house and calm world, might glance back over the last chapter as he settles above the page. If reading is to be consistently associated with pleasure, there is no place here for threat which distances teacher from taught; rapid recapitulation must not be felt as a menacing test of the class's attentiveness and powers of memory. The job may be best done in a gamelike way; for example, the pupils retell recent events by means of a class storytelling routine, in which the teacher points first to one individual, then another, then another. There is a stronger element of gaming if the moving finger stops for irregular periods of time; half a phrase here, but two or three sentences there. And that moving finger must resist the temptation to wag reprovingly. Alternatively, questions might be gathered on the board which the class feels remain unanswered after the last session: for example, 'How will Mouse find a way out of the mess — or will he actually get beaten up by Hammerman?' (*The Eighteenth Emergency*). The class's questions are preferable to the teacher's questions, if we are concerned that young readers become practised in a sustained, interrogatory conversation with the text.

Our final suggestion in this section may seem slightly lunatic — or at least to stem from an 'if-you-can't beat-'em' defeatism. In short, we think it well worth legitimizing doodling. The original notion was suggested by a teacher of juniors who was very excited by the results; and we have seen startling work come from undergraduates as well as children using this approach. If listeners to a story (or a poem) are encouraged, rather than forbidden, to doodle, and given the idea that the doodles must relate to the text, some fascinating consequences ensue. (Indeed, we have found on some occasions that it is useful to *insist* upon doodling.) First, doodling assists concentration for many listeners — the 'slack' of the mind is taken up. Secondly, the listener is recording responses to the text, modifying them and clarifying ideas as the story proceeds. When the story, chapter or poem is completed, the student has a ready-made record of what has passed through his mind — and a way of recalling his responses. We have found that subsequent discussion of the results is not at all flippant or digressive — but usually animated and concentrated. (The illustration on p. 120 is from an admittedly skilled adult doodler, who thus recorded a lecture on the sort of subject matter which is discussed in Chapter 1.) As with all the suggestions throughout this book, we can only urge that teachers test, and develop, the idea for themselves.

Activities along the way: Stage III 'During'

It may be helpful to recall briefly our discussion of the processes of active reading. Skilled readers regularly seem to be engaged in making mental pictures, whose strength may be visual or emotional, or both; in looking forwards, or back, or around 'inside' a story; in allowing their own experiences to interplay with those offered by the book; in bringing their judgement to bear upon the way in which the story is being told — its descriptive power, characterization, humour, liveliness of dialogue, or structure. So, our argument runs, what can we do in our classrooms to encourage the development of such processes for those who do not yet see

Figure 5   Student's lecture doodle

themselves as habitual readers? How can we help them, as well as our already committed readers, to enjoy their journeys through a story?

The suggestions which follow have all been 'tested' by classroom teachers. Clearly, any single technique can be overworked. Some techniques are more appropriate for particular texts than others, and individual teachers may feel some are more suitable for different age groups than others. Our hope is that such a list might be of use to students and teachers coming into

English teaching; and serve as an *aide memoire* for the experienced when inspiration in lesson-planning is proving elusive.

1 Reading journals or logs   The reading journal is perhaps the most flexible and useful proposal in this list — many of the suggestions which follow could be entered or begun in the kind of journal we envisage. Readers are provided with notebooks in which they respond in any way they choose to a novel including speculations about how the story will develop, judgements, comparisons with their own experience, illustrations of characters, reflections on moments or themes from the book, comments on how the author is telling the story and notes about their own experiences prompted by the book. Most pupils need help to get started on this kind of subjective, exploratory writing: for some it will be refreshingly new, others need to 'unlearn' the more objective mode of the book report. It is helpful to suggest that although journals are often the place to record random thoughts or make stray jottings, it is best to keep them in an orderly fashion, dating each entry.

It is very useful to discuss the format of such a journal with the pupils. One middle school class talked together about what to call their notebooks and voted to describe them as 'logs' rather than 'journals', preferring the notion of the adventures of an explorer to the reflections of a scholar. The debate allowed the teacher to clarify (to herself as well as the children) the purpose of the notebook and the nature of the entries whilst engaging the pupils in a decision about their own work. It is significant that when a class has entered into such decisions, they often make their logs or journals more individually their own through appropriate decoration.

Initially, class time probably needs to be set aside for journal writing, but as the practice becomes familiar, some pupils may make entries as and when they think appropriate and the writing, which will vary in length, can best be done out of class. Comments by the teacher, made at regular intervals, are necessarily conversational rather than evaluative, and this seems a clear case for not correcting mechanical errors. 'Marking' journals is very time-consuming; our advice is that teachers should not attempt to have more than one of their classes committed to journals in any one term, though individual pupils may well decide to keep them going long after the assigned period is completed.

A clear rationale is needed for introducing this kind of work, since the freest possible explorations, no matter how tentative, are to be encouraged. Personal writing in journals is sometimes revelatory in the extreme. The confidentiality of the confessional ought to be observed, since many class novels provoke writing about personal hopes and anxieties and, inevitably, tensions within the school and the family. Such work could become the target for criticism by parents and even other colleagues — hence the need for clear thinking about why it is undertaken and, preferably, the support of an agreed departmental belief.

These four uncorrected extracts from the journals of a small group of middle school children reading *Tuck Everlasting* by Natalie Babbitt give something of the flavour of their notes as they moved through the book. We make no comment beyond noting how each could be a point of departure for further discussion or writing:

☆ When someone says kidnap I think of coming back from scouts at night and round the corner is some kidnappers so I run and jump past the corner in case of a trip wire. But I always look to see if anyone is there. But there never is.

☆ I learnt quite a lot about how a writer writes a story with a slow bit first and then a short build up to the climax of the story.

☆ I was like a gardian angle I was looking over, telling them to do different things and weather what they did was right.

☆ No thoughts just sadness.

2 An extended journal   Bob Zeeb, the English Co-Ordinator to the City of Newton, Massachusetts, prepared notes for teachers using 'literary journals' with their pupils and provides a valuable model which teachers might adapt to their own concerns. (3) He suggests that the journal should be a loose-leaf file, subdivided — perhaps by coloured leaves — into five sections. We summarize his guidelines here:

☆ Notes: brief, fragmentary, scattered preparations for longer work.

☆ Formal Assignments: responses, usually literary or academic in nature, to assignments or clusters of assignments made by the teacher or selected from a list.

☆ Reflections: self-initiated, often personal, related to the literature but not necessarily academic or literary in nature.

☆ Comparisons: comparisons between two different stories or poems — usually literary, but sometimes personal in emphasis. Some may be responses to assignments, some self-initiated.

☆ Passages: extracts copied from literature.

3 Short term anticipation   The shared reading of the novel is briefly interrupted at appropriate points with the questions 'What do you think will happen when . . .?' or simply 'What do you think will happen next?' Pupils might jot privately for three or four minutes (on loose paper or in journals), share ideas with neighbours, speculate as a class — or any combination of these. Too frequent a use of this strategy becomes irritating, diminishing the group's involvement in the forward movement of the story. The intention is exactly the opposite — to heighten the sense of anticipation.

4 Long term anticipation   The basic question here is, 'How do you think it will all end?' but this can be modified in relation to the futures of individual characters or strands in the plot. The same techniques as for 3 above are appropriate. As we saw in Chapter 1, we are continually speculating, consciously or not, about eventual outcomes as we move through a novel; we need to encourage readers to become practised in exercising their sense of an ending.

5 'Genuine' questions   Individuals or groups are asked to devise genuine questions (that is, questions to which they do not know the answers) based on the text so far. In the process of preparing such questions, idiosyncratic perceptions and plain misunderstandings frequently become evident. Pupils become more practised in making connections — in looking back in a text to make sense of the present and the future. Groups might exchange questions in the class.

6 Character or theme wallcharts Individuals or groups of three or four make wall charts of short quotations from the text-to-date which capture the *essence* of a character or theme. These can be begun after a few chapters. Groups might 'adopt' a character or theme and, in class time set aside for the purpose, keep track of developments by adding to their chart, reporting from time to time to the rest of the class. The teacher serves as the pupils' scribe not only to ensure clarity of writing, but to promote discussion about why a choice has been made before it is written into the chart.

7 Supposing ... Pairs or small groups improvize around *possible* ways in which events might develop. ('Acting out' what has already happened tends to diminish rather than enhance a text.) It is useful here *not* to have the text in hand since the improviser becomes inhibited by a notion of 'correctness'. Pupils need a clear starting point: they need to know *who* they are, *where* they are at this moment, and *what* the issue at stake is. This kind of work needs practice, since children inexperienced in improvization may fall back upon the safety of cliché or be fairly wooden at first.

8 Cartoon Groups or individuals encapsulate specific episodes or moments in cartoon form, using captions or ballons for 'says' and 'thinks'. Readers are thus encouraged to reflect on what is important to them in the story.

9 Family tree Since students often 'tune out' from stories when they confuse (or never establish) the relationships between characters, a family tree, gradually completed as a wall poster, is a useful reference point throughout the reading of a novel. (To avoid confusion in lay-out, the teacher may need to have worked out a feasible shape for the tree in advance, even though he may incorporate class suggestions as the tree grows.)

10 Time lines Chronological charts of events, brought up to date as the story progresses, are particularly useful when the narrative viewpoint shifts in a novel or when complex events take place over a long period. (See the time line for Natalie Babbitt's *Tuck Everlasting* on p. 124.) This strategy is also helpful in avoiding confusion and in pointing up contrasts or comparisons when plots divide and two or more parallel time lines can be maintained. The consequences of an author saying, in effect, 'Meanwhile, ...' are graphically emphasized and understanding re-inforced. Time lines also distinguish between chronological sequence and the order in which an author reveals events.

11 Maps For the many journey or quest novels which make good class readers (for example, *The Silver Sword, The Hobbit, I Am David*), or where a neighbourhood is important (*Terry on the Fence* or *My Mate Shofiq*), it is often clarifying to be able to refer to a developing wall map showing the territory and to plot the movements of characters within it.

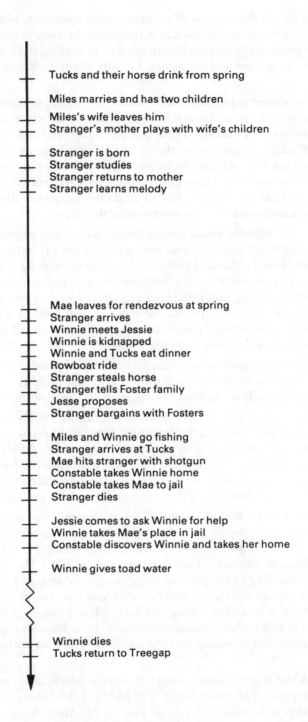

Tucks and their horse drink from spring

Miles marries and has two children
Miles's wife leaves him
Stranger's mother plays with wife's children

Stranger is born
Stranger studies
Stranger returns to mother
Stranger learns melody

Mae leaves for rendezvous at spring
Stranger arrives
Winnie meets Jessie
Winnie is kidnapped
Winnie and Tucks eat dinner
Rowboat ride
Stranger steals horse
Stranger tells Foster family
Jesse proposes
Stranger bargains with Fosters

Miles and Winnie go fishing
Stranger arrives at Tucks
Mae hits stranger with shotgun
Constable takes Winnie home
Constable takes Mae to jail
Stranger dies

Jessie comes to ask Winnie for help
Winnie takes Mae's place in jail
Constable discovers Winnie and takes her home

Winnie gives toad water

Winnie dies
Tucks return to Treegap

Figure 6   Time line for Natalie Babbitt's *Tuck Everlasting* (4)

12 Thumb-nail sketches Children make lightning sketches of characters, settings or incidents, to sharpen the 'pictures in the head' and to compare them with other pupils' mental images. Careful drawings at this point are counter-productive, inhibiting those who are poor artists ('Can't draw, Miss') and also tending to delay the reading of the novel. The meticulous child artist may be troubled by this activity initially, but he can be urged to see the sketch as a way of 'holding' an idea for more considered work later.

13 'I'd like to ask ...' What comments or suggestions would pupils like to make to particular characters in the book about their past or future actions? Jottings, letters, talk with partners, teacher-led discussion could be used. This activity can be used as a preface to **14**.

14 Television or radio interviews Characters in the book are asked about events or for their opinions (it seems best to move gradually from factual to more evaluative questions). Depending on the ability of the class, characters may be role-played by individual class members, by two or three pupils making a composite character whom they have studied together, by the teacher or by visitors (for example, colleagues or student teachers).

15 Diaries Pupils write extracts from different characters' diaries which might include their guesses about what might happen, their plans, their opinions of other characters, as well as accounts and appraisals of things past. Any one character within the plot, other than a narrator, clearly has a different perspective from that initially offered to the reader. (It is important that the character is one who might well keep a diary.)

16 Impression notes Pupils write impressions of another character or event recently encountered, perhaps in a form suggested by the novel (for example, the evacuee Carrie's first letter home in *Carrie's War*).

17 Striking thoughts What's caught the imagination so far? Place, character, event, object, idea? Pupils jot notes or lists and share ideas or, perhaps, store them in notebooks or journals for later writing.

18 The author speaks ... The teacher role-plays the author. The class asks questions (possibly prepared for a few moments beforehand) for clarification and makes comments about the book so far. (The 'author' does not tell them what's going to happen, obviously!)

19 Literary consequences The teacher makes a series of factual statements stemming from the events of a chapter and asks, after each, 'And the consequence was ... ?' An alternative game is to ask (in encouraging a class's speculative powers in reading) 'And the consequence might be ...?'

20 Letters Two important incidents are chosen, each involving two characters. The class is divided into pairs; A writes to B about the first incident in role as one of the characters whilst B writes to A, also in role, about the second incident. The writers should explain why they behaved as they did, what their thoughts and feelings were during the episode. A and B exchange letters and reply, still in role. (As in **15**, it is necessary to keep within the limits of credibility. Characters such as Clogger and Boddser in *The Machine-Gunners* would be improbable correspondents.)

21 Reports   Since many texts involve schools, (*The Otterbury Incident, The Chocolate War, The Wave,* the School on Roke in *A Wizard of Earthsea*) blank report forms, suitably designed, can often provide a very firm structure for pupils of all abilities to write succinctly about particular characters.

Retracing steps: Stage IV 'After'

There is a danger of diminishing a reader's pleasure if we organize too lengthy a period of work on the text once the book has been completed. There *is* room however for reactions to be developed and refined. It may be valuable for a strong personal response to a novel to be sustained and explored more fully — if thoughts and reactions are to achieve some kind of synthesis. We may then need to give a pupil individual space — it is surely necessary to avoid being seduced by a doctrinaire, even fashionable, belief in group work. On other occasions, individual reactions may be honed and modified by contact with different opinions.

Given the subjective nature of a reader's response, the method of working on a novel at this stage will probably be most satisfyingly determined in those classrooms where negotiation rather than rigid direction is the means by which work is set in hand. It would clearly be impracticable to engage in thirty or more simultaneous negotiations; however, a choice of activities may well be offered by means of written suggestions, if possible enlivened with humour and illustration, phrased as a series of invitations rather than commands. Teachers have sometimes found it helpful to group suggestions in two or more stages, asking pupils to complete some work from the first stage before moving on to the second. A first range of choices might largely consist of talking and writing; the second series of choices might involve work requiring a wider range of resources and perhaps work spaces if a school's facilities make this feasible; art materials, tape-recorders, spaces for small groups in drama, for example. A final 'choice' might be, 'Any suggestions you'd like to propose ...?'

This kind of work, in which pupils are engaged in differing activities, can be chaotic and unproductive, inviting (and usually receiving) the hostile criticism of more traditional colleagues whose classes, and even personal security, are menaced by potentially noisy gaggles of unsupervized children. It is certainly easier to teach well in this way if colleagues share a belief in its value. The lone operator can manage well enough, however, if he is irreproachably well-organized; for much the most demanding aspect of this kind of teaching is the out-of-class preparation to enable the lesson itself to run crisply. The rationale for such teaching is rooted, as we have emphasized, in an underlying belief that we must make space for the response of the individual. The rightness of the approach is reassuringly confirmed by the commitment pupils usually bring to it.

Much of the best work will grow uniquely from a particular story; but the activities listed in the following pages have proved valuable to experienced classroom teachers. (Many of the suggestions listed on pp. 121–126 can also be used *after* a novel has been read.) We have suggested in Chapter 5 that the touchstones by which possible work can be tested are: 'Will this enable a young reader to look back on the text and to develop the meanings he has already made?' and 'Does what I plan to do bring reader and text closer together, or does it come between them?'

a) Chiefly for individuals

1 Portrait gallery   One or two — or possibly a series of — written 'cameos' of characters, perhaps accompanied by sketches, either in 'some setting in the novel', in 'some place where you'd expect to find them' or 'as if he or she were coming through that door *now*'. Suggested lay-out and word limits may liberate rather than restrict writers — inventiveness is often freed by constraints. They may be helped also if they are urged to concentrate on those physical details which reflect personality, mannerisms, or a phrase or two which would be characteristic of the individual. Particular plots may suggest variations on the format here: 'Wanted' or 'Missing' posters, obituaries, even file index cards such as school records.

2 The film of the book   A poster for the 'film of the book', giving not only the title but also the stars (imaginary or real) playing specific characters ('Featuring Dustin Hoffman as . . .'), a phrase to catch the attention of passers-by, perhaps 'What the Critics Say'. Including the name of the cinema, show times and so on makes for a more committed piece of work.

3 New book covers   A cover for a new edition, with a design (abstract or concrete) which captures some essential quality of the novel — a mood, a key moment, contrasting elements. Children find it useful first to compile a list of what normally appears on a paperback — title, author, spine-wording, publisher's logo, blurb, ISBN number, international price details — and to work to a 'flat' cover, with the back, spine and front laid out as a template.

4 Letter exchange   A letter to a friend about a book which has been especially enjoyed. This activity is most successful if there is a real recipient of the letter, perhaps in another school. The work might best be managed therefore by two teachers in different schools, perhaps as part of a wider exchange (of letters, information and tapes, for example).

5 'Dear author'   A letter to the author of a book (via the publisher) containing questions, expressions of enjoyment or reservations. The general (but not quite universal) experience of this activity is that children's writers are not merely long-suffering, but actively welcome the contact with their rather elusive audience. (It is, we suggest, unfair to an author to assign this activity to an entire class, as is sometimes the practice. It should be a positive choice for an interested reader only.)

b) Chiefly for pairs, groups or the whole class

1 A phrase collage   Looking back through a novel, children select perhaps twelve to twenty phrases which seem memorable to them. These can be arranged on card as a wall-display, perhaps within an appropriate graphic design; or (a task best suited to older or more able groups) set into a speech-collage, in which the group might use the phrases (or parts of them), repeat words as a refrain, juxtapose contrasting ideas and so on. Thorough preparation takes much time (and it is very frustrating to committed pupils if they are hurried through this task); but the process of discussion, selection and preparation affords a rigorous review of the text. Tape is useful here both in self-criticism in preparation and sometimes in presentation, though much can be done in a live performance through the physical relationships of the speakers.

2 Wall frieze For novels involving changing locales, (perhaps when characters embark on quests or journeys), a long frieze with people, forests or factories, cottages or castles, mounted upon it can be an enjoyable way of reworking the experience of a novel and making a final 'statement' about it. (This activity can be begun *during* the reading of the novel also, making a pleasant complement to writing tasks.)

3 Strip cartoon Not merely a story in separate pictures, but a story on a long roll of paper — possibly wallpaper or lining paper — to be fixed at each end around a pair of 'rollers' (e.g. long rulers, cricket stumps) for display. Cartoons can also be effectively drawn onto a roll of transparency for use on an overhead projector.

4 Front page The front page of a national or local newspaper reporting on incidents and characters from the plot, with interviews, artists' sketches or photographs ('adapted' from other papers or actually posed, if this is feasible); complete with title banner, price, date, advertisements, weather forecasts, sports announcements, Stop Press — all of which should be consistent with the novel, and if possible based on information within the text.

5 The book programme A taped or 'live' programme about the book (with a definite time limit — say, seven minutes). It is as well to determine the purpose of the programme (for example, to introduce the book to potential readers *or* to discuss the novel on the assumption that your listeners have also read it).

6 Radio playlets A *short* extract from the novel is reworked as a play for radio, including perhaps a context-setting introduction, sound effects (home-made rather than prerecorded) and mood music. A specific audience is a very effective spur — the rest of the class or other, younger classes.

7 Sound track The 'sound track' of a very short extract from a novel. Action-packed pieces are most appropriate for this work, which promotes very close reading of the text. (As with *1* this activity may seem to take a disproportionate amount of time, but it is possible to gauge its value by the attentiveness with which a group is rereading the text and by the commitment to the task.)

8 Hype   Pupils become a 'team' whose brief is to promote a book as it is launched on a highly competitive paperback market. It may be best to specify tasks the first time a group undertakes this project. They might include, for example, a three minute interview with the (role-played) author for television or radio; a promotional leaflet of not more than 100 words including pupils' illustrations of the book (could be a dust-wrapper); four or five comments by reviewers of the book when it was in hardback; a list of 'selling-points' for publishers' representatives to use when trying to sell copies to bookshops or schools. Groups might compete in promoting the same novel or, if small groups have been reading different novels, each 'promotions team' works on its own book. The teacher or a V.I.P. judges the effectiveness of the promotions and packages.

9 'Readers ask ...'   A simulated 'Phone-In' on tape with calls either to characters in a book, asking about their motives, attitudes or actions, or to the author. The teacher can judge how heavily he needs to become involved in this, depending on the abilities of his class and how accustomed they are to this sort of task. Time constraints produce sharper work.

10 Open questions   A set of questions which invite opinions rather than demand the checking of facts. The notional or real users are individuals or groups in younger classes.

11 'Would it make a movie?'   The group is employed by a movie tycoon to 'vet' the novel as a possible film. Would the book make a good film? Has it box office appeal, and for what kind of audience? Is it likely to be interesting *to look at?* Will the dialogue as it stands in the book sound like 'real speech' or will it have to be rewritten? Do any stars immediately seem appropriate for any of the roles? The group might present its findings on a report form devised by the teacher if some firm structure is likely to be helpful.

12 Puppet play   A retelling of a *short* extract from the story with puppets. (Short, because it seems better to become immersed in a close and thorough reading rather than spreading energies too thinly. Teachers who work with puppets often comment on the increased fluency pupils find when speaking through a different physical persona.)

13 'Worth borrowing?'   Pupils work in pairs — 'A' is a librarian, 'B' is a borrower who likes to know what a book is about before taking it home. B cross-questions A about plot, characters, setting and 'the way it's written'; and decides.

14 Truth telling   Individual members of a group are assigned characters from the novel with contrasting views of either the main events or the main characters. The 'time' is fixed — perhaps at a point part way through the novel, perhaps at the end. Standing in a circle, characters make statements about their thoughts and feelings about a topic set by the teacher — an incident or a character from the novel. This activity can be developed (often without a teacher's bidding): for example, characters may begin to respond to

129

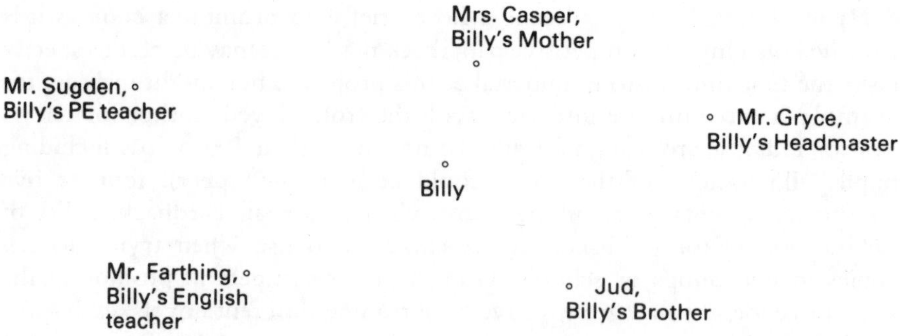

Mrs. Casper,
Billy's Mother
∘

Mr. Sugden, ∘
Billy's PE teacher

∘ Mr. Gryce,
Billy's Headmaster

∘
Billy

Mr. Farthing, ∘
Billy's English
teacher

∘ Jud,
Billy's Brother

Figure 7   Diagram based on *Kes*

each other in their statements; a 'victim' character (see diagram based on *Kes* above) can be placed seated but silent on the floor in the centre of the circle whilst other characters make statements above him; after some time, at a signal from the teacher, he is allowed to respond, in a way he never could in the world of the book, saying what he really thinks.

15 Between the lines   Fictional encounters often take place which are not directly reported by an author — or which would be inevitable after the book has ended. These often make firm starting places for writing or improvizational work in pairs or threes.

16 Chapter titles I   Chapters in many books are numbered but not titled. On small file cards, groups decide on titles for chapters, then shuffle them and pass the cards on to other groups who try to sequence them with appropriate chapter numbers. The preparation of these cards is also a very useful means of understanding the structure of a novel. Questions arise such as, how is the novel *planned?* Cards can also be arranged in patterns (for example, reflecting the ascent to a climax, and the subsequent decline) as ways of examining the structure.

17 Chapter titles II   Where a book *does* have chapter titles, these can be written onto file cards, shuffled and distributed to groups who are asked to sequence them correctly without looking back at the book. In this way, children are provided with a means of talking their way back through a book, recreating — and often discussing and evaluating — the narrative. As in 16 the structure of a book is made clear.

18 Liaisons   The story is represented in diagrammatic form. For example, with 'Good'/'Bad' characters balancing each other in two columns; or a cluster around a central character whose connections with other characters are indicated; links may be drawn between characters in different colours. Groups often need help with a suggested shape when first tackling this work — it may be best to do a diagram on the board as a first model.

19 Close readings   Transparencies for overhead projectors of important passages are typed out on a jumbo typewriter or reproduced so that the whole class can focus on these together. Ideas can be connected by underlining, circling and linking, highlighting in different colours etc.

20 Characters and their goals Each group is given a page headed by the name of a particular character; below is a series of sentences to be completed, designed with that character in mind. From the viewpoint of that character, pupils complete such sentences as 'What I most want to happen is ...', 'What I really like is ...' or 'I can't understand why ...' Alternatively, an 'all-purpose' sheet of unfinished sentences is issued, one per group. Each group is assigned a different character and completes the sheet for that character. This second method points up contrasts sharply.

21 Catalogue blurb In their annual catalogues (examples readily available in most schools), publishers often introduce a novel in four or five lines of blurb. Groups concoct such introductions for the novel they have been reading.

22 'Thinks and says' Where two characters have been in close interaction, a 'summarizing statement' of their relationship at the end of the book can sometimes be made by using this format, (though this basic pattern can be usefully varied):

A said to B	'I ...'
B said to A	'I ...'
A thought about B	'You ...'
B thought about A	'You ...'
Together, they were meaning	'We ...'

23 Who said it? In groups, pupils prepare a 'Character Quiz' consisting of a list of brief extracts of dialogue which are very characteristic of perhaps half-a-dozen speakers. Often, a single sentence or phrase is enough. After the teacher has checked that the chosen examples are sufficiently characteristic, the quiz is either taken by the rest of the class or groups swap quizzes. (This is an interesting activity to conduct in the forum of the whole class, in fact, since much useful comment about characters and characterization occurs along the way.)

In practice

It might be helpful to suggest how the principles and techniques we have discussed might be applied to a well-known class reader, C.S. Lewis's, *The Lion, The Witch and the Wardrobe*. The marginal initials 'B', 'D' and 'A' indicate whether an activity might be used 'Before starting the book', 'During the reading of the book', or 'After the book has been read': These notes are for the teacher, not the class, since teachers need to make local changes to suit their own circumstances and preferences (5).

B   1   **Doorways** Some fairly rapid work might be done on unusual 'doorways': readings and talk about entries to 'other worlds' (Alice's rabbit-hole, the ruined church in Garner's *Elidor*); a pooling of literary memories from the class (e.g. Max's bedroom in *Where The Wild Things Are*); personal recollections of places they knew when younger which they, their families or friends fantasized as strange 'doorways'. Drama work could be based on inventing doorways and exploring what lies beyond them.

B   2   **Pictures**   Xerox or (preferably) make overhead transparencies of several of the Pauline Baynes illustrations (e.g. pages 12, 18, 34, 71, 86, 109). Without confirming the 'rightness' of the guesses, ask for suggestions about what these pictures might be illustrating — the intention being obviously to arouse curiosity in the story they are about to read.

B   3   **Title**   What *might* a book called *The Lion, The Witch and the Wardrobe* be about? Five minutes of individual jotting or discussion in pairs, followed by a sharing of ideas in groups or as a class.

D/A   4   **Maps**   Create a wall-map of Narnia which 'fits' the text. Certain features must be included (lamp-post, Beavers' Home, The Stone Table, Cair Paravel etc.). The map could be begun after several chapters, but modified definitively on completion of the novel.

D/A   5   **Food**   Food seems to be used by Lewis as an indicator of mood or character. Pupils could draw up lists of what they *know* to be in the larders of Mr Tumnus, Mr and Mrs Beaver and the White Witch and subsequently add what else they might *expect* to be there. Illustrations of shelves or tables. And a suitably regal menu for the celebratory feast at Cair Paravel mentioned on p. 165.

D/A   6   **The unfreezing**   An all-class or group collage based on the description of the unfreezing of the Witch's victims on p. 153. Drama work in which children find appropriate sounds and movements for the creatures; then into frozen postures; then a slow unfreezing; and then gradually rediscovered sound and movement. Possible percussion or other musical accompaniment.

D/A   7   **Viewpoints**   A group is given *one* of the four children to concentrate upon. Each group is also given a copy of a duplicated sheet of half-sentences to complete in the voice of their allocated character. For example: 'I am afraid that . . .', 'I believe the witch . . .', 'When Aslan was killed at the Stone Table, I . . .', 'When we were having dinner at the Beavers, I . . .'. Such sheets will obviously achieve different results depending on the point of the story at which they are used. Comparisons of attitudes can subsequently be made.

D/A   8   **'Missing' posters**   When some of the animals whom the witch froze mysteriously disappeared, their friends might have put up 'Missing' posters. Pupils select a minor character (e.g. Rumblebuffin, Mr Tumnus) and design the poster to make up a wall-display. Children may find it helpful to have a 'model' framework.

A   9   *An interview with Aslan*   Aslan is 'corporately' role-played by a group of four or five pupils. They spend time agreeing on Aslan's character and his part in the story, while the rest of the class work out questions they would like to ask him. A kind of 'press conference' follows.

A   10   *Quiz*   Groups prepare for other groups a 'Who said this?' quiz — maybe ten questions. The teacher has to vet questions for fairness — they must be characteristic or made at crucial moments. For example: 'Locks and bolts make no difference to me' (Father Christmas); 'Yah, Silly Old Aslan! How do you like being a stone?' (Edmund); 'Let him first be shaved!' (The Witch). The questions could be extended to ask 'When?' or 'Where?'.

Titles referred to in this chapter (in order of mention)

Betsy Byars   *The Eighteenth Emergency*   (Puffin, Macmillan M Books)
Nina Bawden   *Carrie's War*   (Puffin, Heinemann New Windmill)
Paul Gallico   *The Snow Goose*   (Penguin)
Jill Paton Walsh   *The Dolphin Crossing*   (Puffin)
Michelle Magorian   *Goodnight, Mister Tom*   (Puffin)
Jill Paton Walsh   *Fireweed*   (Puffin, Macmillan M Books)
Robert Westall   *The Machine-Gunners*   (Puffin, Macmillan M Books)
Anne Frank   *The Diary of Anne Frank*   (Pan)
Ilse Koehn   *Mischling Second Degree*   (Puffin Plus, Collins Cascades)
Robert Leeson   *It's My Life*   (Fontana Lions, Collins Cascades)
Jan Needle   *My Mate Shofiq*   (Fontana Lions, Collins Cascades)
Betsy Byars   *The Midnight Fox*   (Fontana Lions,
         Heinemann New Windmill)
Philippa Pearce   *The Battle of Bubble and Squeak*   (Puffin,
         Macmillan M Books)
Ivan Southall   *To The Wild Sky*   (Puffin)
Moreton Rhue   *The Wave*   (Puffin Plus)
William Golding   *The Lord of the Flies*   (Faber)
Robert Cormier   *The Chocolate War*   (Fontana Lions,
         Macmillan M Books)
Ursula Le Guin   *A Wizard of Earthsea*   (Puffin,
         Heinemann New Windmill)
Rukshana Smith   *Sumitra's Story*   (Bodley Head)
J.R.R. Tolkien   *The Hobbit*   (Unwin Books)
Gene Kemp   *The Turbulent Term of Tyke Tiler*
         (Puffin, Collins Cascades)
Ted Hughes   *The Iron Man*   (Faber)
Roald Dahl   *Danny, the Champion of the World*   (Puffin,
         Heinemann New Windmill)
S.E. Hinton   *The Outsiders*   (Fontana Lions, Macmillan M Books)

Betsy Byars   *The T.V. Kid*   (Puffin, Macmillan M Books)
Natalie Babbitt   *Tuck Everlasting*   (Fontana Lions, Collins Cascades)
Ann Holm   *I Am David*   (Magnet, Macmillan M Books)
Robert Leeson   *The Third Class Genie*   (Fontana Lions, Collins Cascades)
Ian Serraillier   *The Silver Sword*   (Puffin, Heinemann New Windmill)
C. Day Lewis   *The Otterbury Incident*   (Puffin, Heinemann New Windmill)
C.S. Lewis   *The Lion, The Witch and The Wardrobe*   (Fontana Lions,
          Collins Cascades)

Chapter 7

Teaching poems

Preparing the way

So much depends on the expectations of the class; there is little hope for a poem in classrooms where it is read once, points of difficulty are identified by teacher or textbook and, through questioning or explication, are 'resolved'. The implicit assumption is that the poem cannot be readily understood; by the class, that is. In our view, it should be possible for a poem — its excitement, its fun, its mystery or its sadness — to be 'felt on the pulse' of its audience at first meeting.

It may be that as enjoyment of poetry becomes the norm for a class — when a group *expects* to have a good time in poetry lessons — some few moments of imposed stillness or a request to erase the events which have preceded the lesson are all that is needed; and, of course, there are charismatic teachers whose skilful reading could make the school rules compel instant attentiveness.

For most of us, the planning of poetry lessons needs to be as much concerned with the audience as with the text. It is useful to try to sit where they are sitting, to feel what they are feeling — just in from the playground, agog with last period's Maths test, flushed with P.E. or moving on from another activity in our own English lesson. If it is helpful to focus the attentiveness of a group before reading a story, as we suggested in the last chapter, the need is often much greater in introducing certain poems. For where our task with prose is primarily to reinforce the narrative's power to draw a reader into itself, most poems must make a more immediate impact and their compressed language demands greater concentration. Poems tend to assume the responsiveness of their readers to bring them alive. The teacher planning a poetry lesson must ask:

Where would I like my pupils to be — emotionally, mentally, and even physically — when they first meet this poem?
What can I do to prepare a receptive mood for this particular poem?

Three further questions provoked by the 'three dimensional' or sculptural qualities of a poem we mentioned in Chapter 2 (p. 19) which invite us to move around, shifting our vantage point to appreciate different aspects of the text are:

When and how will the poem first be heard? seen? and read?

The most straightforward preparation is to lead pupils towards a poem through a period of concentration, which serves to draw the class into a corporate mood, to focus thoughts and perhaps to provide any information essential to understanding the poem. Time spent here is well invested; preparation cannot be hurried.

The creation of an appropriate context for hearing a poem is best prompted by the ideas or form of that particular poem. As with some prose texts, there are poems which grab the reader's attention and demand to be heard — comic poems, and nonsense poems, for example, would suffer from an extensive, 'top-heavy' introduction. They make their points, amuse or intrigue, and that's that. Those poems which ask us to walk around inside them more reflectively, looking from this angle or that, are the ones which may gain from a carefully considered preparation of their audience.

As an illustration, it seems best to take a well-known poem — Wilfred Owen's 'Dulce et Decorum Est'; no doubt, many readers of this book will have taught it themselves. It is a poem which might well be read with the upper end of our age group and it suggests a variety of preparatory approaches.

1 A class might be asked to pool as rapidly as possible whatever items of factual information they have about life at the front in the First World War; these are collected on the board to develop a scenario and to support later work. (When we recently introduced the poem to a class in this way, a boy offered, 'Napoleon lost it'. Apart from any other benefits, this approach often provides opportunities to clear up confusions which it is impossible to foresee and which may block any kind of meeting between reader and text.)

The impact of the Latin tag in the last lines has to be prepared for by telling the class what the aphorism means, ideally in such a way that their curiosity is aroused. Then, perhaps with eyes closed, pupils are 'talked into' the situation of the poem; they might answer in the silence of their imaginations a sequence of questions to draw them all towards a feeling for what it was like to be in the front line — patterned by the teacher upon a mental checklist of the senses. 'You're a soldier in the trenches in the First World War ... ' (it seems best to plunge pupils straight in, as with dramatic improvization, rather than to use the tentative 'Try to imagine ...'). 'You're exhausted; strained to the last nerve end; aching in every muscle; drained right out. You've been in action again today ... fought off another attack.' (Pause.) 'Things are fairly quiet at the moment. Look around ... along the trench to your mates. How do they look?' (From this point on, pauses are left between questions to allow each individual to explore his silent reply.) 'How do you feel about them? What can you hear? Look down at the walls and the bottom of the trench ... what do you see? What can you smell? When you think of your family ... of people you know ... what sort of picture have they got of what it's like for you here?' (Then, more crisply, almost as a military order.) 'Right, your group has the order to withdraw ... you're all trudging slowly back through the maze of trenches ... turning one way, then the other, keeping your heads down ... until it's safe to clamber out onto a muddy track. You're all lining up, you among them, a couple of mates alongside you. Ready to move back behind the lines for a bit of a rest, some

hot food, a decent dry bed perhaps. You're given the order to march ...'
After a short silence comes the poem itself:

> Bent double, like old beggars under sacks,
>
> Knock-kneed, coughing like hags, we cursed through sludge....

either read 'live' by the teacher, or on tape by another voice, or by two or
three members of the class who have spent time preparing a good reading in a
previous lesson.

2   The poem might be prefaced by some of the songs from *Oh, What a
Lovely War* ('Hush, Here Comes a Whizzbang' and 'Gassed Last Night, And
Gassed the Night Before', for example, available on Decca PA/SPA 27). The
themes of the songs are clear enough to require no comment, and the music
usually commands the attention of classes.

3   Many schools make diverse use of a stock of post cards and full-size
replicas of posters from the First World War obtainable from the Imperial
War Museum (for example, 'What did you do in the war, Daddy?', 'Women
of Britian Say "Go!"', 'V.A.D. Nursing Members, Cooks, Kitchen Maids,
Ward Maids, Clerks, House-Maids, Laundresses, Motor Drivers etc. are
Urgently Needed'). Clearly, it is little use simply urging pupils to 'look at
these'. They need some 'way-in'; perhaps a listing of suggestions about what
the poster designer intended his audience to feel, and how he tried to achieve
his aims. Alternatively, a part or all of the caption to the poster could be
concealed whilst the class suggests what the hidden words might be.

Elements of such approaches could clearly be used to supplement each
other. The aim is, in short, to enable pupils to be already *there*, tuned in the
same key as Owen's poem, so that they have as good a chance as we can
provide of hearing the language of the poem responsively — of seeing its
images and tasting its bitterness.

Anticipation can also be focused by giving a class the titles of certain
poems. Pupils jot individually, speculate in pairs, or brainstorm as a class on
what the title leads them to expect of the poem. Specific titles like 'The Stag'
(see p. 20) or 'The Loch Ness Monster's Song' (see p. 27) work well; general
ones like 'Preludes' and 'Alone' do not. When the poem is read, there is a far
greater possibility that the listeners will be able to hear the poem, even if the
route towards it has been indirect.

As we suggested in 3 above, pictures, photographs or slides which
themselves pose questions related to the theme of the poem also work well.
The teacher's role is that of a fairly silent chairperson, holding up or
projecting the pictures and inviting pupils to ask questions of one another to
explain what is going on in the illustration, or to make up stories together
about them. In selecting pictures, it is crucial to avoid those which 'close
down' discussion — to which the reaction can only be, 'What more is there to
be said?'

Dramatic exercises have a particular potency in creating a receptive
physical and psychological context for some poems. For example, one
teacher prepared the way for Stephen Spender's 'The Express' by pushing the
desks back before the lesson, greeting his eleven year olds as a rather authori-

tarian railway official dealing with confused passengers arriving at a terminal, directing them to wait on different 'platforms' and then broadcasting a prerecorded reading of the poem over the classroom tannoy. He might well, with such preparations, have begun with Mike Rosen's mangled station announcement ('The train now standing at Flatworm's Heaven', see p. 81) and ended with T.S. Eliot's 'Skimbleshanks', perhaps sung in the splendidly rhythmic version from *Cats* (Polydor 2478 150), to make up a small railway anthology. A possible danger, in our view, in using drama in this way is that a class becomes so caught up in the dramatic work that the poem, when it arrives, is experienced more as an afterthought than a climax. If the exercise is sustained too long, or is too intrinsically absorbing, it may be that the language of the poem, which we want pupils to hear with greater awareness through our preparations, is drowned.

The poems by Owen and Spender which we have used as illustrations often find responsive audiences among young readers normally attracted by action and movement. Other poems, given the contexts a teacher can devise, may demand a more reflective mood. Consider Richard Church's poem. 'Quiet':

> The night was so quiet
> That the hum of the candle burning
> Came to my ear,
> A sound of breath drawn through a reed
> Far off.
>
> The night was so quiet
> That the air in the room
> Poised, waiting to crack
> Like a straining
> Stick.
>
> The night was so quiet
> That the blood and the flesh,
> My visible self sunk in the chair,
> Was a power-house giant, pulsing
> Through the night.

The need here may be to open up a way between the text and each reader's solitary moments. Children might be asked to write, in silence, for a few moments about 'a time you can remember — or can imagine — being indoors alone late at night. Try to jot down what sounds are to be heard.' Again, the class might be asked to suggest things they usually think of as making no noise, unless they are able to listen really hard. Pupils can be required to be so quiet that they can hear, and then try to describe, the sound of an actual candle burning in the classroom. A standard drama exercise is useful here also; pupils are asked to isolate different sounds progressively — 'outside the school grounds', 'inside the school but outside this room', 'inside this room' and 'inside yourself' (best not attempted immediately before or after lunch). With verse three in mind, pupils could be asked to listen to their own blood through their bone structure, or to describe the sounds they hear when they cup their hands over their ears.

These approaches may not be easily used until there is a strong bond between teacher and taught; yet without the establishment of a mood of calm and even some retrospection, poems like 'Quiet' have no hope of being heard; and an invaluable dimension of poetic experience is ignored. Where else in school will pupils have the opportunity to acknowledge together their reflective, and often vulnerable, selves?

Making a poem your own

As we saw in Chapter 1, the reader of a novel constantly glances forward and, less frequently, back; the essential movement is linear. If we tried to represent in graphic form the way we come to possess a poem, we would surely have to sketch something of an opening spiral as we move around and around the poem, gathering (and discarding) meanings as we go. (In Chapter 2, we compared this process with viewing a piece of sculpture.) Transcripts suggest that such a spiralling movement is also to be discerned in the discussions of small groups of children accustomed to sharing poems together, especially when no teacher is present (1). Children left to themselves spend time rereading a few lines or a single phrase of a poem out loud. In doing so, they are in effect saying to each other, 'This bit sounds good' or 'Listen to this again'; or, sometimes, 'I don't get this bit'. What seems difficult for us (intent upon *teaching* children something) is to make space for this gradual taking possession of a poem. It may be that poems are too often taught as if they were prose (we move steadily through them from first line to last, perhaps disentangling meanings through questions as we go, and that's the poem read.) Sometimes poetry fails to interest children through our poor choice of material, as we have suggested in Chapter 4; but some of the dislike they express may stem from the inappropriate mode of reading imposed upon them. It is inevitable that many children will mistrust poetry if it is implicitly presented as being beyond them.

Most poems, including even long narrative poems and ballads, therefore need to be read and heard more than once, if readers and listeners are to catch a sense of their rhythms and shapes. It would be rare for us as individual readers to put aside a poem which interested us after a single reading. We come to like it more, obviously, through successive readings. And we usually read a poem several times in preparing a poetry lesson. (Limericks and haiku, with their immediate impacts, are perhaps exceptions.) Class readings need not be — and with longer poems are probably better not — on the same day. A class might be best introduced to 'The Lady of Shalott', for example, by listening to the poem two or three times (and by trying it out on their own tongues) at intervals during the two weeks prior to a closer reading of the poem. The intricacies of W.S. Gilbert's 'Nightmare Song' from *Iolanthe*, the mysteries of Charles Causley's 'Green Man in the Garden' or the bitter images of John Cooper Clarke's 'Beasley Street' make their effects differently each time they are heard.

If we acknowledge the need for most poems to be encountered more than once, we need to give some thought to the *first* reading. It may be that our decision is implicit in the way we have chosen to prepare the way for the poem — as in some of the examples in the last section. Where this is not so, it is worth thinking the matter through. Will the class have the printed poem in front of them — and if so, will it be best to see it on the page of a book, perhaps in an anthology which takes pains to link the text to an illustration? If we want them at some stage to be able to jot notes, to highlight themes or underline recurring words in different colours, to pick out a technical effect, then clearly we need to prepare a duplicated copy. Will a silent reading be useful before they hear the poem? If they are to hear the poem, should the reading be 'live' or on tape? By the teacher? By pupils who have prepared the poem beforehand? By a visitor to the classroom? By one or more voices?

Some poems can gain considerably by being presented on the overhead projector, drawing the response of the class physically together. (This may be true even of short comic poems. Consider Gareth Owen's 'Unemployable':

'I usth thu workth in the thircusth,'
He said,
Between the intermittent showers that emerged from his mouth.
'Oh,' I said, 'what did you do?'
'I usth thu catcth bulleth in my theeth.'

The last line can make a heightened impact if the poem is written onto a transparency, the unfortunate ex-performer's dialogue written in a different colour, and the lines revealed one at a time.)

Dramatic presentations of poems prepared by groups or pairs of children can also be very effective. The habit of bringing poems to life in this way may not be quickly or easily acquired. Structure, advice and practice are needed at first. By 'dramatic', we do not mean 'acting out', for this usually serves to limit rather than release the impact of the language upon the imagination. We are thinking rather of the use of different voices to lend strength to an interpretation by readers in significant physical relationships to each other, or by groups deciding how to prepare their listeners to hear a poem. A four-voice reading of 'Macavity' in a darkened room with conspiratorial voices coming from different quarters can bring the criminal feline elusively alive; a reading of Robert Frost's 'Out, Out', in which two voices pick up and sustain as a menacing undercurrent the buzz-saw's 'snarl and rattle' beneath the narration of a third voice, intensifies the loss of the boy's hand and the empty silence after the accident. (One trio of teachers we worked with began with their backs to us; as the central figure turned towards us, she mutely held up her huge, long-fingered red hand, shaped from paper. The powerful visual image lingered throughout the reading, until 'they, since they were not the one dead, turned to their affairs,' leaving us staring at three silent backs.)

For younger classes, orchestrated full class readings (with sound effects) of such narrative poems as Masefield's 'Reynard the Fox' (with wind, hounds, horses, cries of the huntsmen) or Roger McGough's 'P.C. Plod and the Dale Street Dog Strangler' (police whistles, the last gasps of a stifled pekinese) or 'The Lesson' (hand grenades, shot guns, garrottings) mean that children taste the language of the poems on their tongues several times as they move towards presentation. Although the teacher receives suggestions from the class, it is best in these all-class readings if he exercises the control of a conductor in rehearsal, dictating the tempo and bringing in different sections of the 'orchestra' on cue.

Tape can be useful in presenting poems, as we suggested in proposing the compilation of a *Poetry Please* programme in Chapter 2 (p. 31). The recorder is also invaluable in helping groups to judge how they are getting on in preparation; it is a stimulus in itself and, to be realistic, a control in classes for whom partially supervized group work leads to aimlessness. Demanding time deadlines and impending performances also release inventive commitment from children — and provide a secure framework.

The audience may initially be other members of the class. Beyond that lie possibilities of preparing 'Poetry Shows' for other classes, for assemblies, for parent-teacher meetings, for visits to younger classes, possibly in other schools. Local radio stations may be glad of the offer of well-prepared readings from schools. Elderly people in residential homes make welcoming, if peculiarly demanding, audiences for a short programme. Such preparation, in fact, is not separable from the experience of the poem. In working on good presentations, pupils need to talk through the appropriateness of their selection for their listeners, as well as the interpretation of words, lines and verses; a far richer mode of response than a 'guess what's in the teacher's head' question and answer session.

We conclude this section by outlining three rather different approaches which offer ways of helping pupils to hear the poem more keenly on subsequent meetings.

1 Pairs or groups are presented with the poem with particular words omitted and asked to speculate about what might best fit in. If carefully chosen words are left out rather than, say, every seventh word as in standard cloze procedure, attention can be focussed on specific aspects of the poem — imagery, rhyme, or rhythm, for example, as well as diction.

2 Pairs or groups are presented with a poem cut into segments to be placed in what they judge to be the 'right' order. Experience will quickly demonstrate the need for some cunning work with the scissors to prevent this exercise turning into a simple jig-saw. The difficulty of the exercise can easily be adjusted to the level of the pupils both by choice of poem and the length of each segment.

3 Some 'wrong' words — perhaps a declared specific number — are included in a version of the poem. In pairs or groups, pupils decide which they are and propose alternatives.

In all three exercises, much of the value of the work develops during a final 'checking' stage when the whole class or the groups compare their versions with the original poem and discuss their relative merits. These exercises can be preliminary to one or more readings of the poem in its entirety — the exercises would be self-defeating if the poems were left in fragments. Alternatively, an exercise might be prefaced by a single reading of the poem. At first glance these exercises — for that is what they are — may appear mechanical and even destructive. In practice, this has not been the case: children have much enjoyed the challenge to memory and inventiveness — the game-like qualities inherent in these tasks. They have been enabled to find their ways around inside a poem in a fashion which seems to us to reflect the 'spiralling' movement characteristic of the response of the mature reader of poetry.

Finding — and holding — an individual response

With juniors and the youngest secondary children, it may sometimes be best to enjoy a variety of poems — and, after a couple of readings, leave things there. Certainly, we want to avoid any suggestion of murder by dissection; but we do believe that by increasing a sense of engagement with a poem which has been initially enjoyed, we enhance that pleasure.

Even after two or three readings (silent or spoken) in class, it may well be that a pupil does not feel at all caught up in a poem. It is often helpful if a teacher engineers something of a 'space' for the reader in which he has the chance to make and confirm a personal response (much as we suggested in the diagram on p. 110).

What this space should *not* invite is an early evaluation of the poem. The question 'Do you like it?' in relation to the whole poem, or to its language, rhyme, rhythm or imagery is best deferred as long as possible, or even not asked at all. The response to the question is, almost always, characterized by indifference or brevity, seemingly reflecting an unreadiness for the question at this stage. Once teachers find themselves caught up in the cross-examination of 'Yes, but *why* do/don't you like . . .?', the interrogator has supplanted the fellow-reader, genuinely interested in another's reactions.

We list below several ways of providing the kind of space which allows the reader of a poem time and the means to discover more fully what he thinks and feels before opening that response to the ideas of the teacher or the class.

1 Personal jotting A mode of response parallel to the kind of exploratory writing we have suggested in relation to novels (see p. 121). It may well be that the same reading journal is the appropriate place for such writing.

Pupils are encouraged to write freely about a poem in an almost headlong fashion ('Let your hand follow your pen — see where it takes you') once they have read or heard the poem two or three times. It may be that pupils puzzle away at lines they do not yet fully understand; record a liking for an idea — an image perhaps; make connections with other poems or with their own experiences; express irritation, antipathy or indifference. Pupils will often find greater freedom in writing of this kind if they are initially asked to work within brief time limits. The principle is similar to the 'hundred yards' dash' exercises advocated by Ted Hughes in helping children to write poetry:

> These artificial limits create a crisis, which rouses the brain's resources: the compulsion towards haste overthrows the ordinary precautions, flings everything into top gear, and many things that are usually hidden find themselves rushed into the open. Barriers break down, prisoners come out of their cells. (2)

If closer reading of the poems is subsequently undertaken by a group or the class, these initial jottings invariably lead to a high proportion of pupils feeling they have something worth saying: a case of 'How do I know what I think until I see what I've written?' It may also be that a teacher decides that the best way to draw out a particular pupil is through a direct question. From the pupil's perspective, his few lines of jotting make a secure platform from which to reply; whilst the teacher need not fear that he is making an unreasonable or even aggressive demand upon a quiet or uncertain pupil. We have found this basic technique invaluable, whether working with junior school children or postgraduates; there are the same needs for each person to feel involvement in a poem and the same anxieties about exposing tentative, sometimes revealing, thoughts before apparently more confident or unsympathetic classmates.

2 Questions Since framing questions often involves identifying difficulties and glimpsing answers, it can be helpful to ask pupils to list their own questions about a poem as a preliminary to sharing these with a group or the class. It is often useful to collect some of these questions on the board, as reference points throughout a discussion. The focus of the questions may be left undefined or pupils may specifically be asked to concentrate upon 'the ideas' or 'the techniques' of the poem. The rationale which underpins this activity is, once again, that a reader should develop the habit of engaging in a questioning conversation with a text.

3 Picturing Since we believe one of the reasons that readers find poetry difficult is a failure to 'make pictures in the head', we often ask pupils to make literal pictures. It is necessary to stress that the question of being unable to draw well is irrelevant to this exercise, though many pupils require some persuasion since we may seem to be contradicting what they have been taught elsewhere. Short time limits reinforce the suggestion that a sketch rather than a carefully crafted picture is what is wanted. Having met a poem, pupils might be asked to select 'any word pictures which strike you — say three or four at the most — and make very quick sketches of what they make you think about. (A poem as difficult but potentially rich as Yeats's 'Second Coming' can be opened up for thirteen or fourteen year olds in this way.) Pupils are then invited to select one sketch to work on further on a fresh piece of paper until they feel as satisfied as possible with it. Finally, they integrate the appropriate words from the poem in their sketch in some way. If reprographic resources permit, it is fascinating to make overhead transparencies from pupils' sketches and to compare how different imaginations work on the same text. One of the useful features of working with an overhead projector is that the teacher can be quietly busy operating the machine, so making more evident room for the class to talk in response to each transparency as it comes up. The semi-darkness and the focus of the class upon the screen (rather than each other) encourages a more personal kind of comment.

4 Collages   Pupils select several ideas from a poem and using either pictures from supplements or their own art-work, organize a collage which makes a statement about the poem as they see it. A development of this idea is to give pupils three or four poems which share a theme (possibly, but not necessarily, by the same poet) and ask them to compose a collage which draws out the elements they find common to the poems, arranging them (and perhaps some lines from the poems) as they think appropriate. This kind of work takes a long time; but since a pupil is becoming increasingly absorbed into a poem, or even a few lines from a poem, the work is likely to prove memorable. Such work is usually thoroughly enjoyed, helping to develop positive associations with poetry itself. Making collages *can* have all the aimless busy-ness of bad project work: scissors, glue, magic markers, scraps of material, abandoned offcuts of card, ankle-deep balls of colour supplements — and a shapeless product. Our job is to promote careful selection of materials and thoughtful composition which regularly returns to the text as its controlling influence.

5 First impressions   Two pupils write brief 'instant reaction' notes and swap them, commenting on the other's thoughts before contributing to a larger group. (Although there is some risk of losing the unique response of each pupil, an enjoyable variation of this approach is to organise immediate discussions of a poem in pairs around the classroom before more public work is begun.)

6 Missing titles   The title of a poem is witheld. After the poem itself has been read two or three times, individuals or pairs decide upon a possible title, a task demanding a kind of concentrated comprehension. These titles may later be justified, argued over or voted upon, until perhaps consensus is reached. Lastly, the poet's title is disclosed, compared and evaluated alongside the proposals of the class.

7 Commonplace books   Well-liked poems are copied out (and perhaps 'decorated') in a personal commonplace book. As with journals, it may be best to provide a strong structure for this work at first: for example, by asking pupils to look back on several weeks' work on poetry and to select two or three poems to record in their commonplace books. The very act of copying the poem can be a way of reworking the experience, and selecting favourites emphasizes the idea of rereading poems. A department with a strong belief in commonplace books might arrange for them to be continued from one year to the next.

Refining response

Having encouraged pupils to find personal readings of a poem, we need now to help them develop that reading, without losing their sense of themselves as unique readers of that poem. As we indicated in our diagram (p. 110) an automatic, even fashionable transition to group work after the initial readings of a poem is misguided. A single example of some work will demonstrate how a young reader can work his way into a poem finding a way of making a statement about it. (*3*)

The class of fifteen year olds had been asked first to read silently Roger McGough's poem, 'The Hippopotamusman'.

THE HIPPOPOTAMUSMAN

Into a world of the red glass bus
came a man with a face like a hippopotamus

Grotesqueeruptions made horrific
an otherwise normal ugly face
Wartsscrambled over his head
peeping between thin twigs of dry hair
like pink shiny sunsets
hanging below the neckline
like grapes festering on a vine
And when he blinked
you could glimpse the drunken dance
in the whites of his eyes
like the flash of underpants
through unbuttoned trouserflies

Had the passengers been in groups
there might have been laughter
But they were all singles
and turning their faces to the windows
did not see the view
but behind the privacy of eyelids
had a mental spew

Limpinggropingly looking for a place
went the substandard man
with the hunchbacked face
and finding one sat
and beholding his mudstudded boots
the hippopotamusman
wondered whether it was wednesday

As an assignment, the class was required to 'Write about a day in the life of the Hippopotamusman'. Matthew's teacher had expected his pupils to develop an understanding of the poem by putting themselves in the position of the disfigured man as he goes through the day, trying to lead some kind of normal life. Matthew's response did not fulfil such expectations:

A Day in the Life of the Hippopotamusman

Who are you? Why am I here? How do you dare to make me write this? Am I a poem? Do you really want to 'understand' me? You make me write my name — you make me write — HIPPOPOTAMUS. Clever, clever. Your little poem is so clever. I am a man. That is my introduction to you. I am the man who horrifies and moves you so that you write that clever poem with its ingenious use of words. Indeed. You call me that substandard man. I am therefore below you, as the normal poet. May I tell you that my poetry, although never published is far above yours and that my body —

You have caused me to remember my body. For ten years, using techniques developed by myself, I have caused the mental image of myself to fade into nothing. There are no mirrors in my house, no reminders. Ten years, I have been successful; then one day along with many other books a book of poetry comes into my dark world and there I read about myself and know it is myself.

Do you really want to know what I am like? Surely you would prefer to keep me just 'Hippopotamusman' who has ordinary thoughts. (I do not have ordinary thoughts and have never, never wondered whether it was Wednesday — why I should think such thoughts escapes me entirely.) I am like you; but you are too ashamed to admit what you feel.

Had the passengers been in groups, there might well have been laughter. Had I been in a group I might have laughed at you, sitting alone, turning to your window, having a 'mental spew' or were you conceiving your clever poem? I might have laughed at your inability to see beyond anyone's body, except your own.

When I get on a bus I see people who believe that they are normal, yet their minds are as deformed as my body. My festering face may horrify you, why not then your vomiting minds? I do not want to die, I have so much to live for, and only a very small reason for dying. I pity you for your emptiness; your perfect body cannot change your mind. My mind can change my body, my body need not exist in my mind.

People treat me lazily. They laugh and continue to laugh, or worse, laugh and then excuse themselves, analyse themselves. They say.
    'I don't know how to treat them.'
    'Them.' They say: 'Them.'

They say that they pity me when really they pity themselves because they can't place me in their schemes.

I don't want people to treat me in any way because I am one of them although they are too ashamed to admit it. They cannot believe that someone as ugly as me can be one of them and so they turn me into a problem.

This piece gives the lie to those who argue that an imaginative response to literature cannot also be a piece of criticism — and that such responses are therefore 'not examinable'. Matthew has surely fused a powerful emotional response with a close evaluative reading. In the course of his piece, he provides a critique of the poem's tone, of its language, and of the quality of the poet's thought.

Our immediate purpose in offering the poem and the response, however, is to suggest that it can be best to make opportunity for an *individual* way forward for some readers as they become more deeply engaged by a poem. It is very difficult to legislate for the unique response. A catch-all title, such as Matthew's teacher provided, may help. Beyond this, the freedom to propose their own further work may be better exercised by pupils than we often imagine. Pupils need to know they are free to negotiate work with us; this is time consuming, even messy. The gain is that people are working on what they believe is valuable to them.

Having made a plea for encouraging individual work to be pursued, we turn to the sharing, modifying and development of individual responses in small groups or as a class. The activities which the teacher plans can again be tested by the same touchstones we proposed in the case of prose (Chapter 5, p. 108). 'Will this activity enable the reader to look back on the text and to develop the meanings he has already made?' and 'Does what I plan to do bring reader and text closer together, or does it come between them?'

1 Discussion Group discussion has perhaps been too easily advocated by theorists. In schools where it is a little known practice, such discussions can be barren or a source of chaos. Where there is no tradition of group work, it seems best to proceed slowly through strongly structured tasks involving activities or end-products (making a tape, for example) so that pupils are in fact engaged in discussions about practical concerns along the way. As one of our students put it, 'Kids have the best discussions when they don't know they're having a discussion'. An open brief 'to discuss a poem' may be a task appropriate only for pupils experienced in group work. Some teachers find it helpful to foster the skill of discussing in groups by providing a framework of open-ended questions. We would however resist the notion that group discussions are exclusively for older pupils: such a view perhaps grows from a belief that discussions should reflect an exchange of value judgements about texts, in the style of university seminars. As we have suggested earlier (p. 139), younger children often share their feelings and thoughts about the text by rereading sections of the poem without protracted comment, by asking each other for explanations and by telling anecdotes which — in ways often not immediately perceptible — relate to the text.

2 Poster poems   Pairs plan and make posters with appropriate art work to set off the poem. Posters are then left for three weeks or so in classrooms or 'safe areas' around the school, or gathered into an exhibition.

3 Serial poems   Illustrations made by a group for episodic poems (ballads, for example) are presented:

>   in a frieze to be displayed on the wall;
>   as pages in a large loose-leaf 'book';
>   as separate transparencies for an overhead projector.

These are then shown during a rehearsed reading of the poem by the group.

4 Illustrated readings   Groups choose photographs (from colour supplements) or slides (from a resources centre) to accompany their prepared reading of a poem.

5 Changing the form   Pupils rework a poem in a different form (as a newspaper item, an anecdote or a dramatised dialogue, for example). What has been gained and what lost?

6 Matters of opinion   Groups prepare open-ended questions (possibly a prescribed number) on matters of *opinion* for other groups to discuss. It can greatly increase the confidence of a group in themselves as poetry readers to work on poems and questions appropriate for younger classes.

7 'But what we still don't get is ...'   A list of unresolved questions on matters of fact or interpretation in readiness for discussion with the teacher when he visits the group.

8 Desert island poems   A group or a pair prepare and present an anthology of the favourite poems they would take for sustenance and pleasure during a sojourn on a Desert Island, with brief reasons supporting their selection. This can be developed on tape into a full 'Roy Plomley production' modelled on the BBC format, or presented 'live'.

9 Alternative versions   Pupils are provided with a tape of several contrasting readings of a poem and asked to determine an order of preference, supported by reasons for their choice. (These tapes may be prepared by members of the English Department, but able pupil readers might themselves be invited to devise a tape of alternative readings of a poem.)

10 Mime or movement   Pupils prepare mime or movement work to accompany a reading of a poem. The integration of music in such presentations adds much to their effectiveness. There is little point in undertaking this kind of work unless it is done very thoroughly. Hurried work is a superficial and unsatisfying charade. Much depends on the skills of the teacher and the experience of the class.

11 Taped anthologies   Groups make taped versions of poems, with sound effects and music perhaps, for their own class, year, or other classes. Secondary pupils could make tapes for primary children and possibly vice versa. Some teachers have very profitably developed exchanges with 'pen-friend' classes in another part of the country — one tape might be a poetry presentation. This is particularly suitable as an activity for a group of enthusiasts — perhaps a Poetry Club, meeting outside class hours. Since groups doing this kind of work might gain from considerable adult support, making such a tape is a good opportunity for a student-teacher on practice in the school.

12 Parody Pupils attempt parody or imitation of a whole poem, or of specific techniques (for example, the ballad rhythm) or of a poetic form (for example, shape poems).

We would add a final suggestion, which at first sight may seem at odds with the emphasis on enjoyment of literature which, we hope, informs this book.

13 Learning by heart The practice of committing poems to memory has become unfashionable — mercifully so where learning homeworks involved tears of frustration followed by the tedium and tension of thirty or more faltering versions the next day before an apoplectic inquisitor. Memorizing 'Ozymandias' at the age of ten can damage your health. But where a desire to know a poem by heart arises naturally out of genuine enthusiasm (for the poem itself or for a task in hand) as it sometimes does, it needs to be encouraged, and even seen as a potentially sustaining investment for later life. A group preparing a live 'poetry show' of the kind we mentioned on p. 141, like a group preparing a play, will very probably reach a point where holding a copy of the book hinders any further development.

It is easy for hard-pressed teachers to dwell only on the reluctance of some pupils to show a flicker of enthusiasm for what we offer them. Understandably we protect ourselves through scepticism, unable to believe that what we have grown to value can ever become as important to our pupils. In their massed ranks, that often seems to be so — it was probably ever thus. (Ursula, in Lawrence's *The Rainbow*, felt much the same, it will be recalled; 'She had come to them full of kindness and love, and they would have torn her to pieces'.) In the personal writings of a reading journal, for example, or the kind of response Matthew wrote to 'The Hippopotamusman', we often find a sensitivity which it is difficult for young people to risk in the arena of the classroom, unless we make room for it in our planning.

Chapter 8

In touch

An article of faith which has been implicit throughout this book is that a literature teacher must love and know stories and poems. Such tenets are easy to assert, but difficult to practise, especially for Primary School teachers who may attend one in-service course after another where specialists exhort them to love and know not only their literature, but everything from country dancing to computers.

In this chapter, we have tried to offer the most helpful means we know by which a busy classroom teacher can fuel a commitment to literature. The aim is not to urge yet more work upon those who have little time to spare already; but to help save time without losing the confidence that the job is being thoroughly carried out. Our list is deliberately brief, for to go into further detail would have defeated our intentions. However, we have tried to indicate where fuller information on some topics can be found. One difficulty is that no sooner are lists published than they are obsolescent. We have, accordingly, included suggestions about how to keep up to date, so that teachers may feel they are adequately 'in touch'.

For ease of reference, and because our list does not fall into any natural sequence, we offer our survival kit alphabetically.

All-class readers   Everyone has favourites, so that the two lists of 'Top Tens' which we offer are likely to surprise experienced teachers in their neglect of one title or their inclusion of another. There may be one or two new possibilities to consider here however; and for the less experienced, this may be a place to begin. We have limited our choice to paperbacks but also mention, where available, the educational hardback publisher.

For 9–11
Betsy Byars   *The Eighteenth Emergency*   (Puffin, Macmillan M Books)
Roald Dahl   *Fantastic Mr Fox*   (Puffin)
Andrew Davies   *Conrad's War*   (Hippo, Heinemann New Windmill)
Florence Heide   *The Shrinking of Treehorn*   (Young Puffin)
Ted Hughes   *The Iron Man*   (Faber)
Gene Kemp   *The Turbulent Term of Tyke Tiler*   (Puffin, Collins Cascades)
Robert Leeson   *The Third Class Genie*   (Fontana Lions, Collins Cascades)
Philippa Pearce   *The Battle of Bubble and Squeak*   (Puffin,
            Macmillan M Books)
George Selden   *The Cricket in Times Square*   (Puffin)
E.B. White   *Charlotte's Web*   (Puffin, Macmillan M Books)

For 12–14

Natalie Babbitt   *Tuck Everlasting*   (Fontana Lions, Collins Cascades)

Nina Bawden   *Carrie's War*   (Puffin, Heinemann New Windmill)

John Christopher   *The Guardians*   (Puffin, Heinemann New Windmill)

C. Day Lewis   *The Otterbury Incident*   (Puffin, Heinemann New Windmill)

Alan Garner   *Elidor*   (Puffin, Macmillan M Books)

Ursula Le Guin   *A Wizard of Earthsea*   (Puffin,
　　　　　Heinemann New Windmill)

Jan Needle   *My Mate Shofiq*   (Fontana Lions, Collins Cascades)

Robert C. O'Brien   *Mrs Frisby and the Rats of NIMH*   (Puffin,
　　　　　Heinemann New Windmill)

Ian Serraillier   *The Silver Sword*   (Puffin, Heinemann New Windmill)

Robert Westall   *The Machine-Gunners*   (Puffin, Macmillan M Books)

Book boxes   The lists of 'Recommended reading' given in Chapters 3 and 4 provide a possible basis for teachers wishing to establish book boxes and class libraries. Two commercially produced book boxes, designed to promote 'individualized reading', are well worth consideration for those who, through lack of time or confidence, prefer to follow the advice of experts. Heinemann Educational offer Reading Resource Sets made up from their 'New Windmill' series, which are reasonably priced and durable. Set A offers 50 titles for ten year olds and over, Set B 40 titles for twelve year olds and over and Set C 50 titles for thirteen years olds and over. The Kaleidoscope boxes, selected by Cliff Moon and Michael Jones, are organized according to readers' ages from infants to fifteen year olds, containing about 40 paperbacks in each box. These kits come in portable display boxes and include plastic jackets to preserve the books and record sheets to enable a teacher to log and monitor an individual pupil's reading activity. Details of Kaleidoscope boxes from: Books for Students Ltd., 58–64, Berrington Road, Sydenham Industrial Estate, Leamington Spa, Warwickshire CV31 1BR.

Card files   As a way of keeping a check on your own reading so that you can bring the 'right book to the right child', we recommend maintaining a very simple filing system of A7 74 × 105mm cards. Excessively lengthy entries reduce the usefulness of the system; we suggest that author, title and brief indication of the plot would be a helpful minimum. More refinements will no doubt suggest themselves: for example, potential age range, ability of appropriate reader, grouping by genre, 'star ratings'.

Classics   One of the few disadvantages of the proliferation of good children's books in the last twenty years has been the fact that there is now no 'body of literature' which large numbers of children have in common. Without wishing to wave a banner of reaction, we feel it is a pity if children have not met a fair number of the following titles — even though the attitudes expressed in some of them may now seem illiberal; children are not incapable of recognizing how values change.

Louisa M. Alcott	*Little Women*
R.M. Ballantyne	*Coral Island*
L. Frank Baum	*The Wizard of Oz*
R.D. Blackmore	*Lorna Doone*
F. Hodgson Burnett	*The Secret Garden*
Lewis Carroll	*Alice's Adventures in Wonderland*
J. Meade Falkner	*Moonfleet*
Kenneth Grahame	*The Wind in the Willows*
H. Rider Haggard	*King Solomon's Mines*
Thomas Hughes	*Tom Brown's Schooldays*
Rudyard Kipling	*Just So Stories, The Jungle Books*
E. Nesbit	*The Railway Children*
Arthur Ransome	*Swallows and Amazons* (and series)
Felix Salten	*Bambi*
Anna Sewell	*Black Beauty*
Johanna Spyri	*Heidi*
R.L. Stevenson	*Treasure Island, Kidnapped*
Mark Twain	*Tom Sawyer*
T.H. White	*The Sword in the Stone*
J.D. Wyss	*The Swiss Family Robinson*

Collections of articles There are numerous specialized books about aspects of children's literature, but perhaps the 'best buys' or 'borrows' are collections of articles. We recommend four particularly:

Nancy Chambers	*The Signal Approach to Children's Books* (Kestrel)
Sheila Egoff *et al*	*Only Connect* (O.U.P.)
Geoff Fox *et al*	*Writers, Critics, and Children* (Heinemann Educational Books)
Margaret Meek *et al*	*The Cool Web* (Bodley Head)

Films, filmstrips and tapes The experts in the visual field are Weston Woods Ltd., 14, Friday Street, Henley-on-Thames, Oxon. RG9 1PZ. Their catalogue includes over 200 titles of filmstrips of picture books with accompanying tape cassettes, as well as animated films of picture books and films about illustrators. We have used these materials not only with children, but also for local teachers' meetings, PTA evenings and bookfairs. Most of the films and sound filmstrips are available free of charge for teachers' and librarians' meetings or courses. There is also an increasing supply of stories produced commercially on tape, which are especially useful in classrooms equipped with headphone sets for cassette players or a 'group listening unit' able to accommodate up to six sets of headphones at once. Argo (The Decca Record Co., Decca House, Albert Embankment, London SE1 7SW) and Caedmon (Teakfield Ltd., 1, Westmead, Farnborough, Hants.) are well worth attention. *The Spoken Word Catalogue* produced by *Gramophone* magazine is invaluable (from 177–179, Kenton Road, Harrow, Middx. HA3 OHA).

Groups The practice of local teachers' groups meeting to discuss children's books and to listen to authors and assorted pundits is widespread and increasing. This seems one of the best ways to keep a healthy addiction going, through sharing books we have recently discovered and talking, laughing, and disagreeing together. There is simply not time to keep up with the flow of new fiction and poetry, even in the present economic retrenchment, and a supportive group makes a good arena for sharing new titles and classroom ideas. (See also 'Reviewing' and 'Self-help' below.)

Hardbacks Initial publication patterns are changing, so that some children's books now make their first appearance in 'flexiback'. The old-style hardback is appropriate for a school library, but there are series of non-net educational hardbacks including many of the best children's novels which cost very little more than the paperbacks. The aim of their designers is to give the volumes the appeal of a paperback but the durability of a hardback. It is worth checking the catalogues of the following series before purchasing class library books or all-class readers:

   Collins Cascades
   Heinemann Educational Books New Windmill series
   Macmillan M Books
   Oxford Archway Novels

Historical surveys Teachers who wish to have a sense of the historical development of children's books could consult Brian Alderson's attractive and scholarly Third Edition of F.J. Harvey Darton's *Children's Books in England* (Cambridge University Press). A survey which is available in paperback form is John Rowe Townsend's *Written For Children* (Kestrel and Pelican), which comes up to the 1980s. Though this field of knowledge is rarely of direct value in the classroom, it is fascinating in itself for the enthusiast.

Journals Two journals publish lengthy articles about children's books. *Signal* (three issues per year) is edited by Nancy Chambers. Subscription details from: The Thimble Press, Lockwood, Station Road, South Woodchester, Stroud, Glos. GL5 5EQ. *Signal* also produces useful lists and booklets, such as Jill Bennett's *Learning to Read with Picture Books* and *Poetry for Children*, edited by Jill Bennett and Aidan Chambers.

   Children's literature in education began as a British journal but is now published in New York as an international quarterly. It has retained its UK editorial committee, who now work alongside an American counterpart. British subscription details from: Mrs B. Collinge, 2 Sunwine Place, Exmouth, Devon. Correspondence concerning articles etc., to: Geoff Fox, School of Education, Exeter University, St. Luke's, Heavitree Road, Exeter EX1 2LU.

Multi-cultural books Judith Elkin's list, *Multi-Racial Books for the Classroom* has been regularly revised since it first appeared. It is available from the Youth Libraries Group (for address, see 'Queries'). *Signal* (see 'Journals') offers *We All Live Here* — a multi-cultural list provided by the National Book League. *The English Magazine*, published by the ILEA English Centre, is a reliable guide to new stories in the field (for address, see 'Reviewing'). Fuller information is available in the Open University pack (see 'Self-Help') and could also be obtained from the Educational Publishers' Council, The Publishers' Association, 19 Bedford Square, London WC1B 3HJ. See also the magazine *Dragons Teeth* from the Centre for Multi-cultural Education, University of London, 20 Bedford Way, London WC1.

Queries If you have access to the Open University pack *Children, Language and Literature* (see 'Self-Help' below), you may well find an answer to any queries there. Otherwise, 'When in doubt, try the National Book League' seems a sound axiom. The League is a liberal source of information through its Children's Books Officer and produces series of booklists on particular subjects and themes for specific age groups. The NBL's address is: National Book League, Book House, 45 East Hill, Wandsworth, London SW18 2QZ; Scottish Office: 15a Lynedoch Street, Glasgow G3 6EF. Useful lists are also available from The School Library Association, (SLA), Victoria House, 29–31 George Street, Oxford OX1 2AY; and The Youth Libraries Group of the Libraries Association (YLG), 7 Ridgmount Street, London WC1E 7AE.

Reviewing One of the offshoots of the teachers' groups we mentioned above is frequently a booklet or xeroxed broadsheet of book reviews by members. Some of these are produced by an LEA at the initiative of a committee including an Adviser (*The Essex Review*, published three times a year, is a good example; it is available from: The South East Essex Teachers' Centre, Benfleet Road, Hadleigh, Essex, SS7 1QN). More modest productions by teachers from a very local area may be of less help to their readers, but are invaluable for the group itself.

There are several commercially produced magazines which review new books and books recently published in paperback. Of these, we especially recommend *Books For Keeps* (6 issues per year) which is attractively produced, refreshing in tone and ranges over the whole field from Infant to Secondary. Its reviewers know about real children in real schools, as well as about books. It is the magazine of the School Bookshop Association (see 'School Bookshops' for address). We also recommend *The School Librarian*, the journal of The School Library Association, which is produced quarterly (address see 'Queries'). *Teaching English* (3 issues per annum, from Moray House College of Education, Holyrood Road, Edinburgh) and *The English Magazine* (3 issues per annum, from The English Centre, Sutherland Street, London SW1) include reliable reviews, usually by practising teachers.

The weekly reviews and the Children's Book Numbers (3 per year) of *The Times Educational Supplement* are also very useful guides.

School bookshops   Teachers wishing to make books readily available to pupils who find it difficult to get into bookshops (and who might be offered no informed assistance when they get there) have started bookshops in their own schools. The following are guides which give practical advice and preclude financial disaster: Peter Kennerley's *Running a School Bookshop; theory and practice* (Ward Lock Educational) and the School Bookshop Association pamphlet, *How to Set Up and Run a School Bookshop* by Richard Hill and Pat Triggs. The SBA's address is: 1 Effingham Road, Lee, London SE12 8NZ.

Self-help   If an individual or a group feels ready for a thorough-going approach to children's books, we very strongly recommend the Open University's Inset Pack, *Children, Language and Literature*, available from Learning Materials Service, Centre for Continuing Education, P.O. Box 188, Milton Keynes, MK3 6HW. The pack is designed to assist either the isolated teacher or the group working regularly together and covers such matters as social values in children's books, poetry, myths and legends, oral literature and practical suggestions for classroom teaching. It also includes the fullest convenient guide to sources, resources, bibliographies and organisations.

Every school should have one.

Surveys   The most recent survey of children's reading interests is that carried out by Frank Whitehead and his team at the Sheffield University School of Education. It is entitled *Children's Reading Interests* (Macmillan Educational).

Who's who   Macmillan's *Twentieth Century Children's Writers* contains short critical articles about more than 600 children's authors and poets, as well as lists of their publications and brief biographical notes. A more idiosyncratic kind of reference book is Margery Fisher's *Who's Who in Children's Literature* (Weidenfeld and Nicolson) which makes for enjoyable browsing, since she covers fictional characters rather than their authors and the book is attractively illustrated. O.U.P. has produced *The Oxford Companion to Children's Literature*, an exhaustive reference volume compiled by Humphrey Carpenter and Mari Prichard.

References

Chapter 1

1   E.M. Forster, *Aspects of the Novel*, Edward Arnold, 1949 Pocket Edition, p. 105
2   Laurence Sterne, *Tristram Shandy*, Pocket Library Edition, 1957, pp. 369–371 (Book 6, Chapters 37–38)
3   Henry Fielding, *The History of Tom Jones*, Modern Library Edition, p. 75 (Book 3, Chapter 1)
4   Henry James, 'The Atlantic Monthly', October, 1866, p. 485. (Quoted in Wayne C. Booth, *The Rhetoric of Fiction*, University of Chicago Press, 1961, p. 302)
5   Virginia Woolf, 'Jane Austen' in *The Common Reader*, The Hogarth Press, 1925, p. 74
6   Alan Garner, 'Coming to Terms' in 'Children's literature in education,' Ward Lock Educational, 1970
7   Maurice Sendak, quoted in Reinbert Tabbert, 'The impact of Children's Books — Cases and Concepts' in Geoff Fox and Graham Hammond (eds.), *Responses to Children's Literature*, K.G. Saur, 1980, p. 40
8   J.R.R. Tolkien, 'On Fairy-Stories' in *Tree and Leaf*, Allen and Unwin, 1964 edition, p. 36
9   We are grateful to David Horner, Head of English at Great Sankey High School, Warrington, for bringing to our notice the comments by Lesley Anne, Colin and, on p. 9, Catherine.
10 D.W. Winnicott, *Playing and Reality*, Penguin, 1974 p. 121
11 Quoted in Geoffrey Sully, *A Heuristic Study of the Stated Responses of Eight Children to a Variety of Fictional Texts with Particular Reference to Ideation*, MA (Ed) dissertation, University of Southampton, 1982, p. 154
12 James Britton, 'Reading the Game', 'The English Magazine', No. 1, Spring, 1979, p. 20
13 Kenneth Grahame, *The Wind in the Willows*, Methuen, 1961 edition, pp. 122–123
14 D.W. Harding, 'Considered Experience: The Invitation to the Novel', in 'English in Education', Vol. 1, No. 2, Summer, 1967. p. 12
15 Geoff Fox, 'Dark Watchers: Young Readers and Their Fiction', in 'English in Education', Vol. 13, No. 1, Spring, 1979. p. 32
16 Norman Holland, *The Dynamics of Literary Response*, Norton edition, 1975, p. 65
17 See 9 above

18   Wayne C. Booth, op. cit., p. 155
19   S.T. Coleridge, *Biographia Literaria*, Everyman edition, Dent, 1906, p. 150
20   Henry Fielding, op. cit., p. 819
21   Thomas Hughes, *Tom Brown's Schooldays*, Penguin edition, 1971, p. 14
22   G. Josipovici (ed), *The Modern English Novel: the reader, the writer and the work*, Open Books, 1976, p. 258
23   D.W. Harding, 'Psychological Processes in the Reading of Fiction', in Margaret Meek et al (eds.), *The Cool Web*, The Bodley Head, 1977, p. 66
24   See Fred Inglis in 'Four Critics' in 'The English Magazine', No. 4, Summer, 1980, p. 11. Also his *The Promise of Happiness*, C.U.P., 1981, pp. 4, 15–16
25   Norman Holland, *Five Readers Reading*, Yale University Press, 1975, p. 131

Chapter 2

1   Ted Hughes, 'The Stag' from *Season Songs*, Faber, 1976, pp. 56–57
2   Ted Hughes, *Poetry in the Making*, Faber, 1967, p. 18
3   D.H. Lawrence, 'Preface' to *Chariot of the Sun* by Harry Crosby in E.D. Macdonald (ed), *Phoenix*, Heinemann, 1961, p. 255
4   Robert Witkin, *The Intelligence of Feeling*, Heinemann Educational Books, 1974
5   The term Wayne Booth uses to distinguish the real author of everyday life from the implied one as revealed in the text. See his *The Rhetoric of Fiction*, University of Chicago Press, 1961, pp. 71–6
6   Archibald MacLeish, *Collected Poems*, Houghton Mifflin, 1963, pp. 50–51
7   Edwin Morgan, 'The Loch Ness Monster's Song' from *From Glasgow to Saturn*, Carcanet Press, 1973, p. 35
8   T.S. Eliot, 'Matthew Arnold' in *The Use of Poetry and The Use of Criticism* Harvard University Press, 1933, p. 111
9   See especially: Douglas Barnes, *Language, the Learner and The School*, Penguin, 1969; Douglas Barnes, *From Communication to Curriculum*, Penguin, 1976; Douglas Barnes and Frankie Todd, *Communication and Learning in Small Groups*, Routledge and Kegan Paul, 1977
10   L.A.G. Strong, 'Poetry in School', in *The Teaching of English in Schools: A Symposium*, edited by V. da Sola Pinto, Macmillan, 1946, p. 1

Chapter 3

1   Broadly speaking, those who have discussed development in the reading of literature have done so in one of four ways:
     a)   personal reminiscence of bookish childhoods, e.g. George Sampson, 'A Boy and His Books' in *Seven Essays*, C.U.P., 1947; Fred Inglis, 'Looking Back into the Blank of my Infancy', in *The Promise of Happiness*, C.U.P., 1981

b)   the growth of the child's sense of story in relation to the Piagetian stages of development, e.g., Arthur Applebee, *The Child's Concept of Story: Ages Two to Seventeen*, Chicago University Press, 1978; Nicholas Tucker, *The Child and the Book*, C.U.P., 1981

c)   consideration of children as readers, with the idea of matching individual and age-group needs to appropriate books, e.g. Margery Fisher, *Intent Upon Reading*, Brockhampton Press, 1964; Margaret Meek *Learning to Read*, The Bodley Head, 1982

d)   deductions about development drawn from surveys of children's reading interests and habits, e.g. A.J. Jenkinson, *What do Boys and Girls Read?*, Methuen, 1940; Frank Whitehead et al, *Children and their Books*, Macmillan, 1977

Of course, these are emphases, not discrete categories; and there is the danger, when giving pairs of examples, of implying a marriage of two minds when individual approaches to the study of children and their books may contain marked differences within a broadly similar approach. Nevertheless, no serious violence is done by this arrangement and it does offer teachers a clear way-in to the study of reading development. Interested readers are advised to begin with Meek and move on to Tucker and Applebee.

2   C.S. Lewis, 'On Three Ways of Writing for Children', 1952, in Sheila Egoff et al, *Only Connect: Readings on Children's Literature*, Toronto, Oxford University Press, 1969

3   John Rowe Townsend, *Written for Children*, Penguin, 1976, p. 14

4   Frank Whitehead et al, op. cit., pp. 111–112

5   See, for example: Aidan Chambers, 'The Reader in the Book' in 'Signal', No. 23, May, 1977; C.S. Lewis, 'A Letter to James E. Higgins' in Margaret Meek et al, (eds.) *The Cool Web*, The Bodley Head, 1977; Myles McDowell, 'Fiction for Children and Adults: Some Essential Differences' in 'Children's literature in education', No. 10, March, 1973

6   Peter Dickinson, 'A Defence of Rubbish', in 'Children's literature in education', No. 3, November, 1970

7   Terry Eagleton, seminar given at Nottingham University, 1982. See also 'Four Critics' in 'The English Magazine', No. 4, Summer, 1980

8   Peter Benton, 'The Oxfordshire Poetry Project'; unpublished research, 1982

9   Peter Hollindale, *Choosing Books for Children*, Paul Elek Ltd., 1974, p. 109

Fairy tales, myths and legends

1   The Brothers Grimm, 'The Juniper Tree' in *Grimms' Fairy Tales*, Puffin, 1948 pp. 260–261

2   Kevin Crossley-Holland, *Beowulf*, illus. Charles Keeping, O.U.P., 1983, pp. 2–3

3   Elizabeth Cook, *The Ordinary and the Fabulous*, C.U.P., 1969, p. 1

4   Ted Hughes, 'Myth and Education' in *Writers, Critics, and Children*, ed. Geoff Fox et al, Heinemann Educational Books, 1976, p. 92

5   J.R.R. Tolkien, 'On Fairy-Stories' in *Tree and Leaf*, Unwin Books, 1964, p. 19

6   Andrew Lang, *Tales of Troy and Greece*, Faber, 1968, p. 15

7   Elizabeth Cook, op. cit., p. 4

8   Further specific suggestions will be found in the following: Tony Aylwin, 'Using Myths and Legends in School' in 'Children's literature in education', Vol. 12, No. 2, Summer, 1981, pp. 82–89; David Marigold, 'The ILEA's myths and legends project' and Anne Reyersbach, 'Working with the ILEA's myths and legends pilot project', both in *Children, Language and Literature*, ed. Mary Hoffman et al, Open University Press, 1982, pp. 80–83

Science fiction and fantasy

1   Dougles Hill, *Galactic Warlord*, Gollancz, 1979

2   J.R.R. Tolkien, *The Hobbit*, Allen and Unwin, 1937 and *The Lord of the Rings* Allen and Unwin, trilogy published 1954–1956

3   Ursula Le Guin, *A Wizard of Earthsea*, Gollancz, 1971; *The Tombs of Atuan*, Gollancz, 1972; *The Farthest Shore*, Gollancz 1973

4   Rosemary Jackson, *Fantasy*, Methuen, 1981

5   C.S. Lewis, *The Lion, The Witch, and The Wardrobe*, Bles, 1950

6   Alan Garner, *Elidor*, Collins, 1965

7   Philippa Pearce, *Tom's Midnight Garden*, O.U.P., 1958

8   Alison Uttley, *A Traveller In Time*, Faber, 1939

9   William Mayne, *A Game of Dark*, Hamish Hamilton, 1971

10 Catherine Storr, *Marianne Dreams*, Faber, 1958

11 Natalie Babbitt, *Tuck Everlasting*, Chatto and Windus, 1977

12 Penelope Farmer, *Charlotte Sometimes*, Chatto and Windus, 1969

13 Mary Rodgers, *Freaky Friday*, Hamish Hamilton, 1973

14 Kenneth Grahame, *The Wind in the Willows*, Methuen, 1908

15 E.B. White, *Charlotte's Web*, Hamish Hamilton, 1952

16 R.C. O'Brien, *Mrs Frisby and the Rats of NIMH*, Gollancz, 1972

17 Russell Hoban, *The Mouse and His Child*, Faber, 1969

18 Nicholas Fisk, *Grinny*, Heinemann, 1973

19 John Christopher, *The Prince In Waiting*, Hamish Hamilton, 1970

20 John Christopher, *Empty World*, Hamish Hamilton, 1977

21 Chris Powling, *The Mustang Machine*, Abelard, 1981

22 Robert Leeson, *The Third Class Genie*, Fontana Lions, 1975

23 Andrew Davies, *Marmalade and Rufus*, Abelard, 1979

24 Philip Curtis, *Mr Browser and the Brain Sharpeners*, Andersen, 1979

Short stories

1   Kaye Webb, (ed), *Author's Choice*, Puffin, 1973

2   V.S. Pritchett, 'The Short Story — three comments' in *London Magazine Stories* No. 15, London Magazine Editions, 1967, p. 216

3   Isaac Bashevis Singer, *Naftali the Storyteller and His Horse Sus and Other Stories*, O.U.P., 1977, pp. 5–6 and 11

4   Alan Garner, *The Stone Book*, Collins, 1976

5   Roald Dahl, 'The Hitch-hiker' in *The Wonderful Story of Henry Sugar and*

Other Stories, Heinemann New Windmill, 1979

6   Frank O'Connor, 'First Confession' in *My Oedipus Complex and Other Stories*, Penguin, 1963, pp. 43–51

7   David Holbrook, (ed), *People and Diamonds, Book 3*, C.U.P., 1965, pp. 80–88

8   Ian Reid, *The Short Story*, Methuen, 1977, p. 54

Growing up through stories

1   Paul Zindel, *The Pigman*, Bodley Head, 1968

2   J.D. Salinger, *The Catcher in the Rye*, Hamish Hamilton, 1951

3   Judy Blume, *Forever*, Gollancz, 1976

4   Robert Cormier, *The Chocolate War*, Gollancz, 1976

5   Alice Childress, *A Hero Ain't Nothing but a Sandwich*, Avon Books, 1974

6   John Rowe Townsend, *Gumble's Yard*, Hutchinson, 1961

7   John Rowe Townsend, *Goodnight, Prof., Love*, 1970, *The Summer People*, 1972, and *Noah's Castle*, 1975, all published by O.U.P.

8   Peter Carter, *Under Goliath*, O.U.P., 1977

9   Rukshana Smith, *Sumitra's Story*, Bodley Head, 1982

10   Robert Leeson, *It's My Life*, Collins, 1980

11   Larry Bograd, *Bad Apple*, Bodley Head, 1983

12   Olivier Beer, *Pas De Deux*, Gollancz, 1980

Chapter 4

Picture books

1   Elaine Moss, *Picture Books for Young People, 9–13*, A 'Signal' Bookguide, The Thimble Press, 1981

2   Raymond Briggs, *The Snowman*, Hamish Hamilton, 1978 and Picture Puffin, 1980

3   Shirley Hughes, *Up and Up*, Bodley Head, 1979 and Picture Lions, 1981

4   Janet and Allan Ahlberg, *Each Peach Pear Plum*, Kestrel, 1978 and Picture Lions, 1980

5   Pat Hutchins, *Rosie's Walk*, Bodley Head, 1968 and Picture Puffin, 1970

6   John Burningham, *Come Away From The Water, Shirley*, Cape, 1977 and Picture Lions, 1983

7   Arnold Lobel, *Frog and Toad All Year*, World's Work paperbacks, 1972

Poetry 9–11

1   Isaac Watts, from 'Against Quarrelling and Fighting' in *Divine Songs*, 1715, O.U.P. edition, ed. J.H.P. Pafford, 1971, p. 171

2   Michael Rosen, 'I'm the youngest in our house', in *Wouldn't You Like to Know*, Deutsch, 1977, 1981.

3   Michael Rosen, 'My dad's thumb' in *Mind Your Own Business*, Deutsch, 1974

4   Heinrich Hoffman, 'The Story of Little Suck-a-Thumb' in *Struwwelpeter*, Piccolo Picture Books, 1972

5   Roy Fuller, from 'Advice to Children' in *Seen Grandpa Lately?*, Deutsch, 1972

6   Roy Fuller, 'The National Union of Children' and 'The National Association of Parents', ibid.
7   James Reeves, *Prefabulous Animiles*, Heinemann, 1957
8   Spike Milligan, 'Ye Tortures' in *A Dustbin Full of Milligan*, Dobson Books, 1961
9   Roger McGough, *In the Glassroom*, Cape, 1976
10 Michael Rosen, from 'The train now standing' in op. cit., 1977
11 Lewis Carroll, 'In stature the manlet was dwarfish', from *Sylvie and Bruno*, in *Complete Works of Lewis Carroll*, Nonesuch edition, p. 605
12 Charles Causley, *Figgie Hobbin*, Puffin, 1979, pp. 24 and 20
13 Edward Lear, 'Nonsense Botany' in *A Book of Bosh* ed. Brian Alderson, Puffin, 1975, pp. 132–133
14 Roger McGough, op. cit., p. 14
15 Walter de la Mare, 'The Magnifying Glass', in *Collected Rhymes and Verses*, Faber, 1944, p. 245
16 James Reeves, 'Cows' in *Complete Poems for Children*, Heinemann, 1973, p. 79
17 Ted Hughes, *Season Songs*, Faber, 1976; *Moon-Bells and Other Poems*, Chatto and Windus, 1976; *Under The North Star*, Faber, 1981
18 Charles Causley, op. cit.
19 Kaye Webb, *I Like This Poem*, Puffin, 1979
20 Helen Morris, *Where's That Poem?*, Blackwell, 1974

Poetry 12–14
1   Ted Hughes, *Season Songs*, Faber, 1976
2   See the LP record, *Coleridge*, read by Yvonne Bonnamy, Richard Burton, William Devlin and John Neville in the English Poets Series, recorded in association with the British Council and O.U.P. and directed by George Rylands. PLP 1039, Argo/Decca
3   Seamus Heaney and Ted Hughes, *The Rattlebag*, Faber, 1982

Chapter 5

1   Wallace Stevens, 'The House Was Quiet', in *Selected Poems*, Faber, 1965, p. 90
2   A.J. Jenkinson, *What Do Boys and Girls Read?*, Methuen, 1940
3   Frank Whitehead et al, *Children and Their Books*, Macmillan Educational, 1977
4   Aidan Chambers, *Introducing Books to Children*, Heinemann Educational Books, 1983, p. 103
5   Janet Maybin, 'Whole-school reading periods', in *Children, Language, and Literature*, Open University Press, 1982 pp. 119–121
6   Daniel N. Fader, *Hooked on Books*, Pergamon, 1969, p. 51
7   Jennie Ingham, *Books and Reading Development*, (Second Edition), Heinemann Educational Books, 1982, p. 232
8   Ted Hughes in 'Myth and Education' in *Writers, Critics, and Children*, ed. Geoff Fox et al, Heinemann Educational Books, 1976 p. 92

9   Harold H. Roeder and Nancy Lee, 'Twenty-five teacher-tested ways to encourage voluntary reading' in *Children, Language and Literature*, Open University Press, 1982, pp. 100–101

10   Mike Raleigh, *The English Magazine*, No. 10, Autumn, 1982

11   Edward Blishen in 'That's All', in *Writers, Critics, and Children* ed. Geoff Fox et al, Heinemann Educational Books, 1976, pp. 242–243

12   Betty Kerr, *Check-Up Tests in English Comprehension*, Macmillan Educational, 1980

13   Eileen Colwell, *Storytelling*, Bodley Head, 1980; and Cicely Berry, *Your Voice: How to Use it Successfully*, Harrap, 1975

Chapter 6

1   John Fowles, in a talk to an English Teachers' Meeting at Exeter University, November, 1979

2   Doris Lessing, 'Through the Tunnel', in *The Habit of Loving*, MacGibbon and Kee, 1957

3   Another way of organizing the reading journal has been helpfully described by David Jackson in 'Children's literature in education', Vol. 11, No. 4, Winter, 1980

4   This example of a time-line was prepared at a Teachers' Workshop organized and led by Bob Zeeb, (see p. 122), who notes, 'The time line is a particularly interesting project for the child who is not an able writer ... (who) enjoys ordering things and trying to make visual representations'.

5   These notes are extracted from the 'Teaching Ideas' prepared by Geoff Fox which teachers using the Collins Cascades edition of the book may request.

Chapter 7

1   Peter Benton, 'The Oxfordshire Poetry Project', unpublished research; and Barrie Wade, 'Assessing Pupils' Contributions in Appreciating a Poem', in 'Journal of Education for Teaching', Vol. 7, No. 1, Jan, 1981

2   Ted Hughes, *Poetry in the Making*, Faber, 1967, p. 23

3   We are most grateful to the writer of this piece, Matthew Bradbury, for permission to print it here; and to Mr Tim Newton, of the staff of Crown Woods School, whose M.A. thesis brought it to our attention. Matthew was 15 when he wrote the essay.

Index

Acknowledgements

The publishers would like to thank the following for permission to reprint copyright material:

John Burningham: Figure 1 from *Come Away from the Water, Shirley*. Published in UK by Jonathan Cape Ltd. and in USA by Thomas Crowell.
Kevin Crossley-Holland: extract from *Beowulf*. © Kevin Crossley-Holland 1982. Reprinted from *Beowulf* by Charles Keeping and Kevin Crossley-Holland (1982) by permission of Oxford University Press.
Roy Fuller: from 'Advice to Children' from *Seen Grandpa Lately?*. Reprinted by permission of Andre Deutsch.
Ted Hughes: 'The Stag' from *Season Songs*. Copyright © 1968, 1973, 1975 by Ted Hughes. Reprinted by permission of Faber and Faber Ltd. and Viking Penguin Inc. Extract from *The Iron Man*, reprinted by permission of Faber and Faber Ltd.
Extract from 'The Juniper Tree'. Reprinted from *Grimms' Fairy Tales* (Puffin Books 1948) pp 260–261. By permission of Penguin Books Ltd.
Arnold Lobel: Figure 2 from *Frog and Toad All Year* (pp 60–61). Published in UK by World's Work Ltd. and in USA by Harper and Row.
Roger McGough: 'The Hippopotamusman' from *Watchwords*. Reprinted by permission of Jonathan Cape Ltd.
Archibald MacLeish: 'Ars Poetica' from *New and Collected Poems 1917–1976*. Copyright © 1976 by Archibald MacLeish. Reprinted by permission of Houghton Mifflin Company.
Walter de la Mare: 'The Magnifying Glass' from *Collected Rhyme and Verses* (1944). Reprinted by permission of The Literary Trustees of Walter de la Mare and The Society of Authors as their representative.
Edwin Morgan: 'The Loch Ness Monster's Song'. © Edwin Morgan: *Poems of Thirty Years*, Carcanet, Manchester, 1982. Reprinted by permission of Carcanet Press Ltd.
James Reeves: extract from 'Cows'. Reprinted from *The Blackbird in the Lilac* (1952) by permission of Oxford University Press.
Theodore Roethke: 'Child on Top of a Greenhouse'. Copyright © 1946 by Editorial Publications, Inc. from the book *The Collected Poems of Theodore Roethke*. Reprinted by permission of Doubleday & Company, Inc.
Michael Rosen: 'I'm the Youngest in our House' and extract from 'The train now standing' both from *Wouldn't You Like to Know* (1977). Reprinted by permission of Andre Deutsch.
Wallace Stevens: 'The House was Quiet'. Copyright © 1947 by Wallace Stevens. Reprinted from *The Collected Poems of Wallace Stevens* by permission of Alfred A. Knopf Inc. and Faber and Faber Ltd.
J.R.R. Tolkein: extract from 'On Fairy-Stories' from *Tree and Leaf*. Reprinted by kind permission of George Allen & Unwin.

'The Ancient Mariner' illustration is by Peter Joyce.
Cover illustration by Sue Heap.